An Index to Profiles in The New Yorker

by

Robert Owen Johnson

The Scarecrow Press, Inc.
Metuchen, N.J. 1972

ISBN 0-8108-0473-5

Library of Congress Catalog Card Number 71-186947

I wish to dedicate this volume to those who have helped me with its preparation: Monica Bell, Nancy Carlson, Judy Haswell, Barbara Johnson, Susan Johnson.

R. O. J.

Table of Contents

Introduction	v
Part One	
TITLE INDEX	1
Part Two	
NAME INDEX	
A. Profiles of Individuals	95
B. Profiles Not of Individuals	130
Part Three	
SUBJECT CATEGORY INDEX	
Subject Categories	134
Index	135
Part Four	
AUTHOR INDEX	183

INTRODUCTION

While my three-volume Index to Literature in The New Yorker was in preparation, it occurred to me that a separate index to Profiles would be of use to persons in other fields of study, particularly biographers. The main index lists all Profiles by title, and contains cross-references to literary figures (as liberally defined), but one will not find figures in other fields listed by name or occupation.

The present volume indexes Volumes I through XLVI (February 21, 1925 through February 13, 1971) of The New Yorker, and is divided into four sections. Section one is alphabetized by title and contains the complete citation; each entry has been given an identifying number which is used in the other sections. Section two is an alphabetical listing by person, place, or thing profiled; section three is divided into some 50 occupational categories; and section four is the author index.

Use of the asterisk in the volume, page and date designator has been discussed in detail in the first volume of the main index, but it should be repeated here. From October 5, 1929 through April 2, 1960, The New Yorker published both a New York edition and an Out-of-town edition, and libraries around the country were sent magazines from both. In many cases page numbers vary widely because different advertisements were used and material was reshuffled.

An asterisk indicates that the citation is from the Out-of-town edition (which may be identified by a small five-pointed star on the cover of the magazine just before the date), and a user who has the New York edition may have to look a few pages away. Because Profiles appear in the same relative position in all issues, the matter will not cause a great deal of difficulty for users of this volume, but I wanted to be accurate.

A Profile appeared in the very first issue of The New Yorker, and a different one appeared each week until 1927, when a five-part study of William Randolph Hearst, and several weeks without Profiles, broke the pattern. By 1971 only fourteen or fifteen were appearing each year. Early Profiles were only two or three pages long; contemporary Profiles are much more complete.

The user will find riches: Wolcott Gibbs's parody of Time magazine in his Profile of Henry Luce in 1936; Janet Flanner's three-part study of Adolf Hitler in 1938; St. Clair McKelway's six-part Profile of Walter Winchell (which resulted in Harold Ross's permanent exclusion from the Stork Club) in 1940; Rachel Carson's "The Sea" and "The Edge of the Sea" in 1951 and 1955; Mollie Panter-Downes' portrait of Swinburne and Watts-Dunton in early 1971. The list is over 1100 entries long.

Pullman, Washington
February 1972

Part I

TITLE INDEX

TITLE INDEX

The absolute frontier, by Angelica Gibbs. (MARTHA GRAHAM: Dancer) 23:28-37 D 27 '47. 1

An abstract art, by Joseph Wechsberg. (RAFFAELE MATTIOLI: Publisher; historian; translator; economist) 42:52-76 Ap 30 '66. 2

Abstraction-flowers, by Robert M. Coates. (GEORGIA O'KEEFFE: Artist) 5:21-4 Jy 6 '29. 3

An accepting house, by Joseph Wechsberg. (HAMBROS BANK LTD.: Merchant bank) 41:42-83 F 5 '66. 4

An accident of casting, by William Whitworth. (CHET HUNTLEY AND DAVID BRINKLEY: Television news commentators) 44:34-60 Ag 3 '68. 5

Accoucheur, by S. N. Behrman. (MAX DREYFUS: Music publisher) 7:20-4 F 6 '32. 6

Action of West Fifty-third Street, by Dwight Macdonald. (ALFRED H. BARR, JR.: Director of Collections, Museum of Modern Art) 29:49-82 D 12 '53; 29: 35-72 D 19 '53. 7

Active sparker, by Geoffrey T. Hellman. (NATALIE WALES LATHAM: Founder, Bundles for Britain) 17:21-6 *Ap 19 '41. 8

Actress-manager, by Gilbert Seldes. (KATHARINE CORNELL: Actress) 6:23-5 F 14 '31. 9

Acts of witness, by Francine du Plessix Gray. (DANIEL BERRIGAN AND PHILIP BERRIGAN: Roman Catholic priests; militant pacifist leaders; authors) 46: 44-121 Mr 14 '70. 10

The adventure of the behaviorist, by Kenneth Macgowan. (JOHN BROADUS WATSON: Professor of Experimental and Comparative Psychology, Johns Hopkins University; author) 4:30-2 O 6 '28. 11

Adventuress with a difference, by Waldo Frank. (HELEN WESTLEY: Actress; director of Theatre Guild) 2:15-16 Mr 27 '26. 12

After enough years have passed, by Robert M. Coates. (JOHN SLOAN: Historical artist) 25:36-51 My 7 '49. 13

After June 30, the deluge, by Alexander Woollcott. (E. HALDEMAN-JULIUS: Publisher) 1:7-8 Je 20 '25. 14

Agriculture's acrobatic friend, by A. J. Liebling. (GEORGE A. HAMID: President, amusement park booking agency) 12:18-21 *S 26 '36. 15

Ah boy! by Winthrop Sargeant. (BIRGIT NILSSON: Singer, Metropolitan Opera Company) 42:66-92 O 29 '66. 16

Ah, packages! by Philip Hamburger. (JAMES E. CASEY: President, United Parcel Service) 23:34-49 My 10 '47. 17

Ahoy, Listerine! by Jack Alexander. (GERARD B. LAMBERT: Yachtsman; President, Lambert Company) 14:20-6 *Jy 16 '38. 18

Aider and abettor, by Alva Johnston. (JO MIELZINER: Theatre set designer) 24:37-51 O 23 '48; 24:28-39 O 30 '48. 19

Airman-about-town, by Geoffrey T. Hellman. (SHERMAN MILLS FAIRCHILD: Airplane manufacturer; authority on aerial photography) 17:22-31 D 27 '41. 20

Alias Nero Wolfe, by Alva Johnston. (REX STOUT: Mystery story writer) 25:26-38 *Jy 16 '49; 25:30-43 Jy 23 '49. 21

All for art, by Henry F. Pringle. (JOSEF VON STERNBERG: Motion picture director) 7:26-9 Mr 28 '31. 22

All in fun, by G. F. T. Ryall. (ALFRED GWYNNE VANDERBILT: Race track operator) 16:26-33 *S 28 '40. 23

All the king's horses, by Niven Busch, Jr. (SAMUEL

HILDRETH: Racehorse trainer) 5:20-3 Ag 24 '29. 24

All-American, by John R. Tunis. (HAROLD E. [Red] GRANGE: Football player) 1:11-12 O 31 '25. 25

Alligators' idol, by Henry Anton Steig. (BENNY GOODMAN: Orchestra leader; clarinetist) 13:27-34 *Ap 17 '37. 26

The alluring roadway, by Stanley Edgar Hyman. (BROOKLYN BRIDGE) 28:39-84 My 17 '52. 27

The almighty buck, by Lillian Ross. (ABRAHAM ELLIS: Hat check concessionaire) 27:30-47 My 26 '51. 28

Also ran, by Henry F. Pringle. (NORMAN THOMAS: Presidential candidate, Socialist Party) 5:28-31 N 9 '29. 29

Alt wein, by Hollister Noble. (ARTUR BODANZKY: Conductor, Metropolitan Opera Company) 6:23-6 Mr 15 '30. 30

Amateur, by Robert Shaplen. (AVERY BRUNDAGE: President, International Olympic Committee) 36:28-71 Jy 23 '60. 31

Amateur at work, by Noel F. Busch. (WILLIAM TURNESA: Golfer) 15:21-6 *S 9 '39. 32

Ambassador, by Robert Shaplen. (JOHN MOORS CABOT: U.S. Ambassador to Brazil) 37:39-90 Mr 4 '61. 33

The ambassador in the sanctuary, by Joseph Wechsberg. (HENRI SOULE: Maître d'hôtel) 29:37-64 Mr 28 '53. 34

American boy, by John Bainbridge. (ALFRED CARLTON GILBERT: Founder, A.C. Gilbert Co. [toys]) 28:36-55 D 20 '52. 35

American classic, by Louise Bogan. (WILLA CATHER: Novelist) 7:19-22 *Ag 8 '31. 36

American maestro, by Alva Johnston. (WERNER JANSSEN: Conductor, New York Philharmonic Orchestra) 10:22-6 *O 20 '34; 10:23-6 O 27 '34. 37

The American Museum, by Geoffrey T. Hellman. (THE

AMERICAN MUSEUM OF NATURAL HISTORY) 44:68-150 N 30 '68; 44:65-136 D 7 '68. 38

American pro tem, by Virgilia Peterson Ross. (GRETA GARBO: Motion picture actress) 7:28-31 Mr 7 '31 39

American town, by Jean Stafford. (NEWPORT, RHODE ISLAND) 24:26-34 Ag 28 '48. 40

The amiable innkeeper, by William Weimar. (JOHN McENTEE BOWMAN: Director, Bowman Biltmore Hotels Corporation) 3:25-7 N 12 '27. 41

Among the wild things, by Nat Hentoff. (MAURICE SENDAK: Author; illustrator of children's books) 41:39-73 Ja 22 '66. 42

The analytical engine, by Jeremy Bernstein. (ELECTRONIC COMPUTERS) 39:58-96 O 19 '63; 39:54-108 O 26 '63. 43

Anatomy of a commercial interruption, by Lillian Ross. (OTTO PREMINGER: Motion picture producer and director) 41:42-129 F 19 '66. 44

Anesthesiologist, by Mark Murphy. (EMERY ANDREW ROVENSTINE: Director, Department of Anesthesia, Bellevue Hospital) 23:36-45 O 25 '47; 23:33-43 N 1 '47; 23:38-51 N 8 '47. 45

The angel in May, by Alan Moorehead. (ANGELO POLIZIANO: Poet) 27:34-65 F 24 '51. 46

The anonymous man, by Alva Johnston. (CARR VATELL VAN ANDA: Managing Editor, New York Times) 11:26-32 *S 7 '35. 47

Another glorified girl, by Helena Huntington Smith. (HELEN WILLS: Tennis player) 3:16-18 Ag 27 '27. 48

Another opening, another show, by Herbert Warren Wind. (ROBERT RUSSELL BENNETT: Orchestrator for musical comedies) 27:46-71 *N 17 '51. 49

Another true story, by Oliver H. P. Garrett. (BERNARR MacFADDEN: Publisher; physical fitness advocate) 1:9-10 S 19 '25. 50

An answer to everything, by Hubbard Hoover. (HARRY

OTIS: Life insurance salesman) 20:28-38 F 3 '45. 51

Any bonds today? by Geoffrey T. Hellman. (HENRY MORGENTHAU, JR.: U.S. Secretary of the Treasury) 19:24-32 Ja 22 '44; 19:26-36 Ja 29 '44. 52

Apollonian, by Joseph Roddy. (GLENN GOULD: Concert pianist) 36:51-93 My 14 '60. 53

Apostle of perfection, by Robert A. Simon. (WILLEM MENGELBERG: Director, New York Philharmonic Orchestra) 1:9-10 D 5 '25. 54

An appetite for motion, by Calvin Tomkins. (MERCE CUNNINGHAM: Choreographer) 44:52-126 My 4 '68. 55

Arachnologist, by Eugene Kinkead. (ALEXANDER I. PETRUNKEVITCH: Expert on spiders) 26:38-59 Ap 22 '50; 26:37-55 Ap 29 '50. 56

Architect, by Herbert Warren Wind. (WALLACE KIRKMAN HARRISON: Director of planning, U.N. headquarters) 30:51-79 N 20 '54; 30:51-85 N 27 '54; 30:55-85 D 4 '54. 57

An aristocrat, by Esther Carples. (SERGEI VASSILIEVITCH RACHMANINOFF: Composer) 1:15-16 Ja 9 '26. 58

Army man at work, by L.D. Dunbar. (BREHON BURKE SOMERVELL: Works Progress Administrator for New York City; Colonel, U.S. Army) 15:22-7 F 10 '40; 16:27-30 *F 17 '40. 59

Artie, by Robert M. Coates. (ARTIE McGOVERN: Head, McGovern's Gymnasium; prizefighter) 13:23-7 *My 22 '37. 60

Artist, by Richard O. Boyer. (GEORGE GROSZ: Artist) 19:32-43 N 27 '43; 19:39-48 D 4 '43; 19:37-44 D 11 '43. 61

Artist in a factory, by Gilbert Seldes. (HENRY DREYFUSS: Theatrical designer) 7:22-4 Ag 29 '31. 62

"Artist of the people," by Salamith Ish-Kishor. (FEODOR C. CHALIAPIN: Singer, Metropolitan Opera Company) 4:29-31 Ap 7 '28. 63

The artist's reward, by Dorothy Parker. (ERNEST HEMINGWAY: Novelist) 5:28-31 N 30 '29. 64

At home with the Durands, by John Bainbridge. (MAX SHEROVER: President, Linguaphone Institute of America [language teaching]) 23:30-43 Je 28 '47. 65

At the heart of UNICEF, by Joseph Wechsberg. (MAURICE PATE: Executive director, United Nations International Children's Emergency Fund) 37:69-112 D 2 '61. 66

At the Pines, by Mollie Panter-Downes. (ALGERNON CHARLES SWINBURNE AND WALTER THEODORE WATTS-DUNTON: Poet. Poet; novelist; critic) 46:40-65 Ja 23 '71; 46:31-43 Ja 30 '71; 46:40-71 F 6 '71. 67

The atheist pope, by Alva Johnston. (JOSEPH LEWIS: Publisher) 8:22-5 O 8 '32. 68

Atlas with ideas, by John McCarten. (ADOLF AUGUSTUS BERLE, JR.: U.S. Assistant Secretary of State) 18:22-30 Ja 16 '43; 18:20-9 *Ja 23 '43. 69

Auction sale this day, by Carlton Brown. (PETER DUFF, pseud.: Auctioneer) 13:19-23 *Ag 7 '37. 70

Autobiographical notes, by Jorge Luis Borges and Norman Thomas di Giovanni. (JORGE LUIS BORGES: Novelist; poet; short story writer) 46:40-99 S 19 '70. 71

Autocrat of the card table, by Helena Huntington Smith. (MILTON C. WORK: Auction bridge authority) 3:18-19 Ja 14 '28. 72

Average cop, by St. Clair McKelway. (ALBERT MORAN WILLIAMS: Patrolman, New York City) 9:23-7 F 10 '34. 73

The Babe, by Arthur Robinson. (GEORGE HERMAN [Babe] RUTH: Baseball player) 2:15-17 Jy 31 '26. 74

Bail-bond baron, by Meyer Berger. (SAM ROTHBERG [Stitch McCarthy]: Bondsman) 9:18-21 Mr 25 '33. 75

Banker, old style, by Geoffrey T. Hellman. (JAMES SPEYER: Banker; patron of arts) 8:20-3 *F 27 '32. 76

Barber's progress, by Richard O. Boyer. (CHARLES DeZEMBLER: Barber shop owner) 22:37-56 N 16 '46. 77

The bard in the delicatessen, by Philip Hamburger. (LOUIS G. SCHWARTZ: Waiter; war bond salesman) 20:32-45 Mr 18 '44. 78

Bearded Cupid, by Meyer Berger. (LOUIS RUBIN: Marriage broker) 14:16-21 *Je 11 '38. 79

Beau Belmont, by G. F. T. Ryall. (JOSEPH E. WIDENER: Horse breeder; owner, Belmont Park) 3:17-19 S 3 '27. 80

Beautiful, by Whitney Balliett. (BUDDY RICH: Jazz drummer) 42:35-66 Ja 21 '67. 81

Beautiful but not dumb, by Helena Huntington Smith. (ADOLPHE MENJOU: Motion picture actor) 2:18-21 Ja 15 '27. 82

The beautiful flower, by Joseph Mitchell. (DANIEL J. CAMPION: New York City Police detective) 31:39-89 Je 4 '55. 83

Beauty in jars and vials, by Jo Swerling. (HELENA RUBINSTEIN: Cosmetics manufacturer) 4:20-3 Je 30 '28. 84

Beer and baseball, by Alva Johnston. (JACOB RUPPERT: Brewer; owner, New York Yankees; U. S. Congressman) 8:20-4 S 24 '32. 85

Behind the tanks, by A. J. Liebling. (CHARLES M. BREDER, JR.: Director, New York Aquarium) 13:18-23 *F 5 '38. 86

Behind the throne, by Marya Mannes. (THERESA HELBURN: Director, The Theatre Guild) 6:31 D 6 '30. 87

Benign heretic, by Charles W. Wood. (WILLIAM MONTGOMERY BROWN: Bishop of Arkansas) 1:17-18 Ja 23 '26. 88

The best I know how, by Winthrop Sargeant. (WILLIAM FRANCIS GIBBS: Naval architect) 40:49-84 Je 6 '64. 89

Best in show, by E. J. Kahn, Jr. (NORNAY SADDLER: Smooth haired fox terrier) 16:24-32 *N 2 '40. 90

Best neighbor, by Geoffrey T. Hellman. (NELSON ALDRICH ROCKEFELLER: Governor, New York State; Latin American expert) 18:23-30 Ap 11 '42; 18:22-32 Ap 18 '42. 91

The best of the best, by Geoffrey T. Hellman. (JOSEPH DONON: Private chef) 38:47-78 Mr 10 '62. 92

Beyond the machine, by Calvin Tomkins. (JEAN TINGUELY: Motion sculptor) 37:44-93 F 10 '62. 93

Big geographer, by E.J. Kahn, Jr. (JOHN KIRTLAND WRIGHT: Director, American Geographical Society) 17:20-8 *Jy 26 '41. 94

The big hello, by Richard H. Rovere. (PETER J. McGUINNESS: Democratic leader, Greenpoint, Brooklyn) 21:29-38 *Ja 12 '46; 21:26-38 *Ja 19 '46. 95

Big Jim, by Alva Johnston. (JAMES A. FARLEY: Politician; U.S. Postmaster General) 7:23-7 N 28 '31. 96

Big Nemo, by Wolcott Gibbs. (ALEXANDER WOOLLCOTT: Critic; author; columnist; radio personality) 15:24-9 *Mr 18 '39; 15:24-9 *Mr 25 '39; 15:22-7 *Ap 1 '39. 97

Big operator, by E.J. Kahn, Jr. (WILLIAM ZECKENDORF: Realtor) 27:46-61 D 8 '51; 27:41-68 D 15 '51. 98

Big Red, by Arthur Bartlett. (MAN O' WAR: Racehorse) 13:24-31 *D 18 '37. 99

Big shot-at, by Joel Sayre. (JACK [Legs] DIAMOND: Gambler; racketeer) 7:24-7 *Je 13 '31. 100

The big stone, by Lillian Ross. (HARRY WINSTON: Jewelry dealer) 30:36-69 My 8 '54; 30:45-73 My 15 '54. 101

Big-time urchin, by Margaret Case Harriman. (LARRY ADLER: Harmonica player) 18:19-28 Jy 18 '42. 102

A billion-dollar banker, by John K. Winkler. (CLARENCE DILLON: Banker) 4:29-36 O 20 '28. 103

Birds in the hand, by Geoffrey T. Hellman. (VICTOR BORGE: Comedian; pianist; poultry breeder) 31:51-87 My 7 '55. 104

Black beans and white beans, by J.J. O'Malley. (GEORGE HORACE GALLUP: Public opinion poll taker) 16:20-4 Mr 2 '40. 105

Black duck - 40, by Geoffrey T. Hellman. (ORSON D. MUNN: Publisher, Scientific American; patent attorney) 15:20-5 *Ja 27 '40. 106

The Black Eagle, by Morris Markey. (HUBERT JULIAN: Aviator; parachute jumper; Minister of Air, Abyssinia) 7:22-5 *Jy 11 '31; 7:20-3 *Jy 18 '31. 107

The black hat, by Gilbert W. Gabriel. (MORRIS GEST: Theatrical producer) 1:7-8 Je 27 '25. 108

Black tie and cyanide jar, by Geoffrey T. Hellman. (ANDREY AVINOFF: Lepidopterist; painter) 24:32-47 Ag 21 '48. 109

Blind ... deaf ... dumb, by Robert M. Coates. (HELEN KELLER: Author, lecturer) 5:24-6 Ja 25 '30. 110

The blues is a slow story, by Whitney Balliett. (HENRY [Red] ALLEN: Jazz trumpet player) 42:33-52 Je 25 '66. 111

Blumey, by Alva Johnston. (ALFRED CLEVELAND BLUMENTHAL: Real estate, theatrical promoter) 8:19-23 F 4 '33; 8:21-4 F 11 '33. 112

Bojangles, by St. Clair McKelway. (BILL ROBINSON: Dancer; philanthropist) 10:26-8 O 6 '34; 10:26-30 *O 13 '34. 113

Bolshevik businessman, by William C. White. (PETER ALEXYEVITCH BOGDANOV: Chairman, Amtorg Corporation) 9:16-20 Jy 15 '33. 114

Book scout, by Stanley Edgar Hyman. (LOUIS SCHER: Book scout) 28:39-84 N 8 '52. 115

Bop, by Richard O. Boyer. (JOHN BIRKS [Dizzy] GILLESPIE: Orchestra leader; trumpet player) 24:28-37 Jy 3 '48. 116

Borough defender, by Robert Lewis Taylor. (LARRY Mac PHAIL: President, Brooklyn Dodgers) 17:20-8 *Jy

12 '41; 17:20-8 *Jy 19 '41. 117

The boss, by Helena Huntington Smith. (EDWIN GOODMAN: Owner, Bergdorf Goodman) 10:24-8 N 3 '34. 118

Boss of the circus/big top, by Alva Johnston. (SAMUEL W. GUMPERTZ: Director, Ringling Brothers and Barnum & Bailey Circus) 9:27-30 *My 6 '33; 9:21-3 My 13 '33. 119

Boss of the kinkers, by Robert Lewis Taylor. (PATRICK FRANCIS VALDO: Personnel director, Ringling Brothers and Barnum & Bailey Circus) 28:39-57 Ap 19 '52; 28:43-64 Ap 26 '52. 120

Boss without cigar, by Noel F. Busch. (KENNETH F. SIMPSON: Chairman, New York County Republican Party) 15:21-7 *O 28 '39. 121

Bostonian through the looking-glass, by Niven Busch, Jr. (WINTHROP AMES: Theatrical producer) 5:30-3 O 19 '29. 122

The bottom of the harbor, by Joseph Mitchell. (NEW YORK HARBOR) 26:36-52 Ja 6 '51. 123

Bowery bum, by Russel Crouse. (JOHN McGOORTY: Tramp) 7:23-6 O 31 '31. 124

Boxing taught without punishment, by A. J. Liebling. ([Philadelphia] JACK O'BRIEN, pseud.: Head, health gymnasium) 13:20-6 *Ja 8 '38. 125

A boy in a barn, by Marc Connelly. (JOE COOK: Vaudeville performer) 4:29-31 Mr 31 '28. 126

Boy meets bullfinch, by Geoffrey T. Hellman. (FRANK M. CHAPMAN: Curator of Ornithology, American Museum of Natural History) 15:22-7 *Mr 4 '39. 127

Boy orator grows older, by Richard O. Boyer. (WILLIAM I. SIROVICH: U.S. Congressman, Fourteenth District, New York; orator; physician) 14:24-30 *N 5 '38. 128

Boy wanted, by Anthony Gibbs. (THOMAS LIPTON: Importer; merchant) 6:30-3 S 13 '30. 129

The boys, by John Bainbridge. (SMITH BROTHERS, INC. - William W. Smith, II and Robert Lansing Smith: Cough drop manufacturers) 23:32-45 S 6 '47. 130

The boys, by Margaret Case Harriman. (JOHN-FREDERICS, INC. - John Harburger and Frederic Hurst: Milliners) 11:21-4 *D 28 '35. 131

The boys from Syracuse, by A.J. Liebling. (LEE SHUBERT AND J.J. SHUBERT: Theatre operators) 15:26-30 *N 18 '39; 15:23-7 *N 25 '39; 15:33-7 *D 2 '39. 132

Bread, love, and neo-realismo, by Winthrop Sargeant. (VITTORIO De SICA: Motion picture director; actor) 33:35-58 Je 29 '57; 33:35-53 Jy 6 '57. 133

The brilliant jughead, by John Hersey. (JOHN DANIEL RAMEY: American soldier) 21:25-39 Jy 28 '45. 134

Bringing up the city fathers, by Henry F. Pringle. (JOSEPH VINCENT McKEE: President, New York City Board of Aldermen) 3:19-22 S 10 '27. 135

Britain's best, by Henry F. Pringle. (BEATRICE LILLIE: Comedienne; actress) 7:22-5 S 19 '31. 136

Broadway chiseller, by Meyer Berger. (MARTY FRANKLIN, pseud.: Confidence man) 11:22-6 *Ap 20 '35. 137

Broadway storekeeper, by A.J. Liebling. (IZZY YERESHERSKY: Cigar store owner) 14:24-7 *O 15 '38. 138

The brown derby and the bee, by Arthur Krock. (ALFRED E. SMITH: Governor of New York) 2:16-18 My 29 '26. 139

The Budapest, by Joseph Wechsberg. (BUDAPEST STRING QUARTET:- Alexander Schneider; Mischa Schneider; Joseph Roisman; Boris Kroyt) 35:59-112 N 14 '59 140

A bugler's progress, by Alva Johnston. (JESSE L. LASKY: Motion picture executive) 13:18-24 *Jy 10 '37. 141

Business and show business, by Robert Rice. (LAWRENCE LANGNER: Co-director of Theatre Guild; lawyer; author) 25:34-48 O 1 '49; 25:34-51 O 8 '49. 142

Business behind the lines, by John Bainbridge. (GEORGE

FIELDING ELIOT: Military analyst; author) 18:20-8 S 5 '42; 18:22-9 S 12 '42. 143

Business is business, by Henry F. Pringle. (NICHOLAS M. SCHENCK: President, Loew's Incorporated, and Metro-Goldwin-Meyer) 8:22-5 *Ap 30 '32. 144

A businessman, sir, by St. Clair McKelway. (DONALD M. NELSON: Industrialist; Chairman, War Production Board) 18:25-34 Mr 28 '42. 145

C.P.O., by John Kirkpatrick. (PAUL HODGE: Chief Petty Officer, U.S. Navy) 18:22-8 *Ja 30 '43. 146

Camera shy, by Terry Ramsaye. (GEORGE EASTMAN: Inventor; industrialist) 4:27-30 N 3 '28. 147

The candor kid, by Margaret Case Harriman. (CLARE BOOTHE: Playwright; U.S. Ambassador to Italy) 16: 21-9 *Ja 4 '41; 16:22-30 *Ja 11 '41. 148

Caprice viennois, by Kenneth Macgowan. (JOSEPH URBAN: Theatrical stage designer; architect) 3:21-3 Je 25 '27. 149

Captain among the synthetics, by Robert Lewis Taylor. (LUIS de FLOREZ: Captain, U.S. Naval Reserve; mechanical engineer; inventor of synthetic training devices) 20:34-43 N 11 '44; 20:32-43 N 18 '44. 150

Captains courageous, by A.J. Liebling. (JOHN W. TIEBOR I, JOHN W. TIEBOR II, AND ROLAND TIEBOR: Seal trainers) 13:22-7 *Ap 24 '37. 151

Cardinal shepherd, by Thomas Sugrue. (PATRICK JOSEPH HAYES: Cardinal, Archdiocese of New York) 10:22-7 F 17 '34. 152

Cash and carry, by Alva Johnston. (C.C. PYLE: Sports promoter) 4:31-4 D 8 '28. 153

Cassandra, Inc., by George R. Leighton. (LEO M. CHERNE: Executive Secretary, Research Institute of America) 16:23-32 *O 5 '40. 154

A caste, a culture, a market, by Dwight Macdonald. (EUGENE GILBERT: Advertising researcher for teen culture; author) 34:57-94 N 22 '58; 34:57-107 N 29 '58. 155

Cauliflower king, by Alva Johnston. (LOU [Lou Ingber] STILLMAN: Owner, Stillman's Gymnasium) 9:24-6 Ap 8 '33; 9:18-20 Ap 15 '33. 156

Cauliflowers and pachyderms, by Alva Johnston. (JACK CURLEY: Sports promoter) 10:21-5 Jy 14 '34; 10:20-5 Jy 21 '34; 10:20-4 Jy 28 '34. 157

The cave, by Joseph Mitchell. (SLOPPY LOUIE'S AND LOUIS MORINO: Restaurant; proprietor) 28:32-55 Je 28 '52. 158

A cellist in exile, by Bernard Taper. (PABLO CASALS: Concert cellist) 38:38-98 F 24 '62. 159

The celluloid prince, by Carl Brandt. (SAMUEL GOLDWIN: Motion picture producer) 1:13-14 Ap 25 '25. 160

Centenarian, by Alva Johnston. (JOHN R. VOORHIS: New York State Superintendent of Elections) 5:23-6 Je 22 '29. 161

Center of a new world, by Christopher Rand. (CAMBRIDGE, MASSACHUSETTS) 40:43-90 Ap 11 '64; 40:57-107 Ap 18 '64; 40:55-129 Ap 25 '64. 162

Central Park, by Eugene Kinkead and Russell Maloney. (CENTRAL PARK) 17:24-32 *S 13 '41; 17:34-41 *S 20 '41; 17:23-31 *S 27 '41. 163

A certain attitude toward change, by Calvin Tomkins. (SAMUEL B. GOULD: Chancellor, State University of New York) 43:67-128 N 18 '67. 164

A certain person, by Oliver H. P. Garrett. (MRS. HENRY MOSKOWITZ: Director of publicity, New York State Democratic Committee) 2:26-8 O 9 '26. 165

C'est la guerre and laissez faire, by Philip Hamburger. (JOSEPH PLATZKER: Director, New York City Vacancy Listing Bureau) 21:28-39 Mr 31 '45. 166

Challenge and delight, by Berton Roueché. (FRANK EMERSON DENISON: Tea grader and blender) 24:33-47 Ja 15 '49. 167

The Chief, by Robert Lewis Taylor. (PATRICK WALSH: Fire Chief, New York City) 18:21-9 Ap 25 '42. 168

Chief Justice, by Henry F. Pringle. (CHARLES EVANS HUGHES: U.S. Supreme Court Chief Justice) 11:20-4 *Je 29 '35; 11:18-22 *Jy 6 '35; 11:18-23 *Jy 13 '35. 169

Chief of staff, by A.J. Liebling. (GEORGE CATLETT MARSHALL: U.S. Secretary of State; Chief of Staff, U.S. Army) 16:26-35 *O 26 '40. 170

Chief operator, by Jack Alexander. (WALTER SHERMAN GIFFORD: President, American Telephone & Telegraph Company) 13:22-7 *Je 5 '37; 13:22-7 *Je 12 '37; 13:22-8 *Je 19 '37. 171

The child who was mother to a woman, by R. Hale. (MARGARET SANGER: Author; birth control advocate) 1:11-12 Ap 11 '25. 172

The child wonder, by Edward E. Paramore, Jr. (ANITA LOOS: Author; playwright) 2:25-8 N 6 '26. 173

Children's friend, by E.J. Kahn, Jr. (THEODOR SEUSS GEISEL [Dr. Seuss]: Author; illustrator of children's books) 36:47-93 D 17 '60. 174

Choreographer, by Angelica Gibbs. (AGNES de MILLE: Theatrical choreographer) 22:32-45 S 14 '46. 175

Choreographer, by Bernard Taper. (GEORGE BALANCHINE: Chief choreographer, New York City Ballet) 36:49-131 Ap 16 '60; 36:51-115 Ap 23 '60. 176

Church, by Robert Rice. (CHURCH OF ST. MATTHEW AND ST. TIMOTHY [and] JAMES A. GUSWELLER: Episcopal church; Episcopal minister) 40:41-60 Ag 1 '64; 40:37-73 Ag 8 '64. 177

"Chutspo," by S.N. Behrman. (EDDIE CANTOR: Comedian; actor) 8:23-7 D 10 '32. 178

The cinema cherub, by Elsie McCormick. (EMIL JANNINGS: Motion picture actor) 3:20-3 Ja 28 '28. 179

Circuit rider, by Herbert Warren Wind. (JOHN MASON BROWN: Drama critic; editor; author; lecturer) 28:44-71 *O 18 '52; 28:39-73 O 25 '52. 180

Cit, by Dwight Macdonald. (GEORGE HERVEY HALLETT, JR.: Executive Secretary, Citizens Union; reformer) 29:31-49 Ag 22 '53. 181

City of dreadful night, by Ved Mehta. (CALCUTTA) 46:47-112 Mr 21 '70. 182

A city of stone, by Mary McCarthy. (FLORENCE) 35:36-75 Ag 8 '59; 35:32-79 *Ag 15 '59; 35:38-94 Ag 22 '59. 183

City of the baroque, by Joseph Wechsberg. (VIENNA) 44:50-87 S 28 '68; 44:58-90 O 5 '68; 44:60-100 O 12 '68. 184

The cleanup man, by Robert Rice. (DAVID BRUBECK: Jazz pianist; orchestra leader) 37:41-89 Je 3 '61. 185

The cloister and the bench, by Babette Deutsch. (BENJAMIN NATHAN CARDOZO: Chief Justice, New York Supreme Court) 6:25-8 Mr 22 '30. 186

Closings and openings, by E.J. Kahn, Jr. (ROGER LACEY STEVENS: Theatrical producer; real estate tycoon) 29:37-56 F 13 '54; 30:41-61 F 20 '54. 187

A cocky mick, by Henry F. Pringle. (JOHN KENLON: Chief, New York City Fire Department) 2:15-16 Je 12 '26. 188

Coiffeur pour dames, by Bessie Breuer. (ANTOINE CIERPLIKOWSKI: Coiffeur) 7:23-6 N 21 '31. 189

Colonel of the 7th, by Victor Weybright. (RALPH C. TOBIN: Colonel, 7th Regiment, New York City; socialite) 11:20-4 *Ja 11 '36. 190

Color nut, by Richard O. Boyer. (RAYMOND G. TWYEFFORT: Custom tailor) 15:22-7 *S 23 '39. 191

Coloratura salesmanship, by Alva Johnston. (JAMES W. ELLIOT: Sales promoter) 8:21-5 S 17 '32. 192

The colossus of children, by Waldo Frank. (THEODORE DREISER: Novelist) 1:6-7 Ag 15 '25. 193

Come as someone else, by Janet Flanner. (ELSA MAXWELL: Party giver) 9:24-7 N 25 '33. 194

Come, let me clutch thee, by E.J. Kahn, Jr. (THOMAS LAMB: Designer of handles) 30:33-51 My 29 '54. 195

Come, ye disconsolate, by Charles MacArthur. (FRANK E. CAMPBELL: Mortician) 2:25-8 N 20 '26. 196

Comedian, by Robert Lewis Taylor. (BOBBY CLARK: Comedian) 23:35-43 S 13 '47; 23:32-41 S 20 '47; 23:36-46 S 27 '47. 197

Comedy, by Alva Johnston. (JOE E. BROWN: Comedian; actor) 21:26-34 Jy 7 '45. 198

Comet, by Janet Flanner. (ELSA SCHIAPARELLI: Couturière) 8:19-23 Je 18 '32. 199

The commander, by Virgilia Peterson Ross. (EVANGELINE BOOTH: Commander, Salvation Army) 6:22-5 Je 21 '30. 200

Commander with a camera, by Matthew Josephson. (EDWARD STEICHEN: Photographer; Commander, U.S. Navy) 20:30-6 Je 3 '44; 20:29-41 Je 10 '44. 201

The Common Market, by John Brooks. (COMMON MARKET) 38:47-85 S 22 '58; 38:47-97 S 29 '58. 202

The communicator, by Thomas Whiteside. (SYLVESTER L. [Pat] WEAVER, JR.: President, National Broadcasting Company) 30:37-64 O 16 '54; 30:43-76 O 23 '54. 203

Compleat angler, by Geoffrey T. Hellman. (EDWARD RINGWOOD HEWITT: Director, International Motor Company; fisherman; inventor) 10:23-6 F 24 '34. 204

Compleat angler, by Joel Sayre. (JAMES JAY JOHNSTON: Boxing promoter; Assistant to President, Madison Square Garden) 7:21-4 Ja 23 '32. 205

The compleat sculptor, by Cameron Rogers. (PAUL MANSHIP: Sculptor) 4:21-3 S 1 '28. 206

The comptroller, by Edward Angly. (MORRIS SAWYER TREMAINE: Comptroller, New York State) 12:18-23 *Ag 29 '36. 207

Con lenezza, by Marcia Davenport. (EFREM ZIMBALIST: Concert violinist) 7:24-7 D 5 '31. 208

A condition of enormous improbability, by Joseph Alsop. (KONRAD Z. LORENZ: Zoologist; authority on aggression; author) 45:39-93 Mr 8 '69. 209

Conducted by the spirits, by Samuel Chotzinoff. (ARTURO TOSCANINI: Conductor, New York Philharmonic) 5:23-6 F 23 '29. 210

Contented crusader, by Alva Johnston. (JOHN S. SUMNER: Censor; Secretary, New York Society for the Suppression of Vice) 13:22-7 *F 20 '37. 211

Conversations with Max, by S. N. Behrman. (HENRY MAXIMILIAN [Max] BEERBOHM: Caricaturist; author; critic) 35:45-88 F 6 '60; 35:40-86 F 13 '60; 36:50-98 F 20 '60; 36:43-99 F 27 '60; 36:47-119 Mr 5 '60; 36:59-108 Mr 12 '60; 36:50-112 Mr 19 '60. 212

The cop in the silk shirt, by Niven Busch, Jr. and A. Barr Gray. (JOHN D. COUGHLIN: Police inspector) 2:22-4 S 25 '26. 213

Cop's cop, by Milton MacKaye. (EDWARD PIERCE MULROONEY: Police Commissioner, New York City) 7:22-6 O 24 '31. 214

"Cosmos," by Alva Johnston. (NICHOLAS MURRAY BUTLER: President, Columbia University; author) 6:28-32 N 8 '30; 6:33-41 N 15 '30. 215

Cotton-dress girl, by Janet Flanner. (BETTE DAVIS: Motion picture actress) 19:19-29 F 20 '43. 216

Counsel for the defense, by Helena Huntington Smith. (LEWIS E. LAWES: Warden, New York State Prison) 2:15-17 Jy 10 '26. 217

Courtesy of Coca-Cola, by Geoffrey T. Hellman. (GRAHAM McNAMEE: Radio announcer) 6:20-2 Ag 9 '30. 218

Courtroom warrior, by Alva Johnston. (EMERY R. BUCKNER: Lawyer) 8:21-3 *Mr 12 '32; 8:24-7 *Mr 19 '32. 219

The crackin', shakin', breakin' sounds, by Nat Hentoff. (BOB DYLAN: Popular music composer; singer) 40:64-90 O 24 '64. 220

Crazy over horses, by Helena Huntington Smith. (MR. AND MRS. JOHN D. HERTZ: Horse breeders) 6:22-5 Je 7 '30. 221

Creating an atmosphere, by Joseph Wechsberg. (ROBERT BELLET: Chief purser, S.S. Liberté) 33:35-78 Ag 17 '57. 222

The creative situation, by Calvin Tomkins. (ERIC HOFFER: Philosopher; author; longshoreman) 42:34-77 Ja 7 '67. 223

The crier, by Philip Hamburger. (GABRIEL HEATTER: Radio commentator) 20:23-33 Ja 20 '45. 224

Croesus in politics, by Homer Joseph Dodge. (ANDREW W. MELLON: Financier; U.S. Secretary of the Treasury) 4:18-21 Ag 4 '28. 225

Cubit-adder, by Russell Lord. (NEWMAN LEANDER HOOPINGARNER: Professor of Business Psychology, New York University) 8:21-4 *Ap 16 '32. 226

The culture business, by Milton MacKaye. (JAMES BURTON POND: Owner, lecture agency) 8:18-22 Ag 27 '32; 8:22-5 S 3 '32. 227

Curator getting around, Geoffrey T. Hellman. (SIDNEY DILLON RIPLEY, II: Associate Curator of Zoology, Peabody Museum; authority on birds of Far East) 26:31-49 Ag 26 '50. 228

Custodian, by Geoffrey T. Hellman. (CHESTER DALE: President, National Gallery of Art; investment banker) 34:49-87 O 25 '58. 229

The customer is always wrong, by Wolcott Gibbs. (RICHARD SYLVESTER MANEY: Broadway press agent) 17:27-39 *O 11 '41. 230

Czar and elder, by Alva Johnston. (WILL H. HAYS: Director, Motion Picture Producers and Distributors' Association of America; censor) 9:18-21 Je 10 '33; 9:16-19 Je 17 '33. 231

Czar of song, by Alva Johnston. (GENE BUCK: Songwriter; President of American Society of Composers, Authors and Publishers; theatrical producer) 8:22-5 D 17 '32; 8:19-22 D 24 '32. 232

The daddy of Sunday painters, by Murdock Pemberton. (CLINTON PETERS: Painter; art teacher) 1:11-12 Jy 11 '25. 233

Dance team, by Margaret Case Harriman. (TONY DeMARCO AND RENÉE DeMARCO: Dancers) 15:22-7 *Ja 6 '40. 234

Dancing Hamlet, by Russell Maloney. (PAUL DRAPER: Tap-dancer) 14:20-5 *Ja 7 '39. 235

Dante and ______, by Ring Lardner. (BEATRICE [Mrs. George S.] KAUFMAN: Wife of playwright) 4:16-17 Jy 7 '28. 236

Dark leader, by Robert Wohlforth. (JAMES WELDON JOHNSON: Author; Executive Secretary, NAACP) 9:20-4 *S 30 '33. 237

Dark ship, by Richard O. Boyer (S.S. MARQUETTE: Troop transport) 20:29-39 D 16 '44; 20:26-36 D 23 '44. 238

D'Artagnan of the courts, by John R. Tunis. (JEAN BOROTRA: Tennis player) 6:24-7 S 6 '30. 239

Daughter of her father, by John McCarten. (HELEN CLAY FRICK: Director, Frick Art Reference Library; philanthropist) 15:21-5 *Jy 15 '39; 15:23-6 *Jy 22 '39. 240

Day-before-yesterday man, by Geoffrey T. Hellman. (BASSETT JONES: Chairman, Committee on Display, New York World's Fair; elevator designer; electrical engineer) 15:24-30 *Ap 29 '39. 241

The days of Duveen, by S.N. Behrman. (JOSEPH DUVEEN: Art dealer) 27:32-61 S 29 '51; 27:41-62 O 6 '51; 27:41-80 O 13 '51; 27:36-59 O 20 '51; 27:38-63 O 27 '51; 27:40-88 N 3 '51. 242

De Medici in Merion, by A.H. Shaw. (ALBERT C. BARNES: Art collector; drug manufacturer) 4:29-34 S 22 '28. 243

De senectute, by Henry F. Pringle. (ELIHU ROOT: Lawyer; U.S. Senator; U.S. Secretary of State; U.S. Ambassador to Russia) 11:21-6 *F 1 '36; 11:21-5 *F 8 '36; 11:22-7 *F 15 '36. 244

The deal, by Sam Boal. (MAYNARD SMITH: Staff sergeant, U.S. Army Air Force) 19:30-40 S 18 '43. 245

Dean of the theatre, by Alva Johnston. (DANIEL FROHMAN: Theatrical producer) 9:21-3 O 28 '33; 9:21-4 N 4 '33. 246

Dearest Edith, by Janet Flanner. (EDITH WHARTON: Novelist) 5:26-8 Mr 2 '29. 247

The deep, tangled Kaufman, by Alexander Woollcott. (GEORGE S. KAUFMAN: Playwright) 5:26-9 My 18 '29. 248

The defense of everybody, by Dwight Macdonald. (ROGER BALDWIN: Founder, American Civil Liberties Union) 29:31-55 Jy 11 '53; 29:29-59 Jy 18 '53. 249

Democracy's friend, by E.J. Kahn, Jr. (LEON MILTON BIRKHEAD: National director, Friends of Democracy, Inc.) 23:28-38 Jy 26 '47; 23:28-39 Ag 2 '47; 23:27-38 Ag 9 '47. 250

Design for a living, by Geoffrey T. Hellman. (NORMAN BEL GEDDES: Stage and industrial designer) 16:24-8 *F 8 '41; 17:22-9 *F 15 '41; 17:26-34 *F 22 '41. 251

Designer for living, by Milton MacKaye. (WALTER B. PITKIN: Author; Professor of Journalism, Columbia University) 10:25-8 My 12 '34; 10:24-8 My 19 '34. 252

Deus ex cinema, by Kenneth Macgowan. (SAMUEL L. [Roxy] ROTHAFEL: Theatre builder and manager) 3:20-2 My 28 '27. 253

Deus ex machina, by Foster Ware. (CHARLES LANIER LAWRANCE: Inventor of airplane engines) 3:16-19 Ag 13 '27. 254

A devout mountebank, by Percy Hammond. (CHANNING POLLOCK: Playwright) 2:17-18 Ap 3 '26. 255

The diamond gardenia, by Wolcott Gibbs. (LUCIUS MORRIS BEEBE: Newspaper society columnist) 13:24-9 *N 20 '37; 13:25-9 *N 27 '37. 256

Diamond Mae, by Thyra Samter Winslow. (MAE WEST: Actress; playwright) 4:26-9 N 10 '28. 257

Die mauer, by John Bainbridge. (BERLIN WALL) 38:57-144 O 27 '62. 258

Dignified meat, by Robert Lewis Taylor. (SAMUEL SLOTKIN: President, Hygrade Food Products Corporation) 22:28-39 Je 15 '46; 22:30-9 Je 22 '46. 259

Diplomat in the doghouse, by Jack Alexander. (HIROSI SAITO: Japanese Ambassador to the United States) 14:22-7 *Ap 30 '38. 260

Directed to the product, by Geoffrey T. Hellman. (RESTAURANT ASSOCIATES AND JOSEPH BAUM: Restaurant chain; originator) 40:59-107 O 17 '64. 261

The director, by Jack Alexander. (JOHN EDGAR HOOVER: Director, U.S. Federal Bureau of Investigation) 13:20-5 *S 25 '37; 13:21-6 *O 2 '37; 13:22-7 *O 9 '37. 262

Directors' director, by E.J. Kahn, Jr. (SIDNEY JAMES WEINBERG: Investment banker; corporation director) 32:39-63 *S 8 '56; 32:49-74 *S 15 '56. 263

Disorder on the rink, by Robert Lewis Taylor. (PHIL WATSON: Professional hockey player) 22:33-46 F 15 '47. 264

District leader, by Jack Alexander. (JAMES J. HINES: Leader, Eleventh Assembly District, New York City) 12:21-6 *Jy 25 '36; 12:18-23 *Ag 1 '36; 12:18-24 *Ag 8 '36. 265

The Dixie Demo Jr., by A.J. Liebling. (DIXIE DEMO CREW: Crew of flying fortress) 18:22-32 N 7 '42. 266

Do or diaphragm, by S.N. Behrman. (FRANCES ROBINSON-DUFF: Drama coach) 11:22-7 *My 25 '35. 267

Doctor of movies, by Arthur Krock. (WILL H. HAYS: Director, Motion Picture Producers and Distributors' Association of America; censor) 2:21-2 My 8 '26. 268

The doctor, the lady, and Columbia University, by Robert Lewis Taylor. (ALFRED MEYER AND ANNIE NATHAN MEYER: Physician; Founder of Barnard College) 19:27-32 O 23 '43; 19:28-37 O 30 '43. 269

Doggy, by E.J. Kahn, Jr. (AMERICAN KENNEL CLUB) 30:30-53 Ag 21 '54; 30:30-53 Ag 28 '54. 270

Dog's best friend, by Geoffrey T. Hellman. (BRUCE BLAIR: Veterinarian) 14:27-33 *D 3 '38. 271

Dolly and Polly, Billy and Cholly, by Margaret Case Harriman. (MAURY H.B. PAUL: Society column writer) 13:23-7 *O 16 '37; 13:22-7 *O 23 '37. 272

Double life, by Helena Huntington Smith. (IGNAZ PADEREWSKI: Concert pianist; Premier of Poland) 6:29-32 N 29 '30. 273

Down the leash, by Angelica Gibbs. (BLANCHE SAUNDERS: Dog obedience trainer) 27:42-64 N 24 '51. 274

Down there, by Joseph Wechsberg. (LEOPOLD LUDWIG: Concert pianist and conductor) 30:36-60 O 2 '54. 275

A downtown Gabriel, by Niven Busch, Jr. (RANDOLPH RAY: Rector, Little Church Around the Corner) 5:20-3 Jy 27 '29. 276

Dragger captain, by Joseph Mitchell. (ELLERY FRANKLIN THOMPSON: Captain in dragger fleet) 22:32-43 Ja 4 '47; 22:30-42 Ja 11 '47. 277

A dream walking, by Margaret Case Harriman. (SALVADOR DALI: Surrealist painter) 15:22-7 *Jy 1 '39. 278

A dreamer of wine, by Joseph Wechsberg. (ALEXIS LICHINE: Vintner, wine merchant) 34:48-86 My 17 '58; 34:37-72 My 24 '58. 279

Drive! drive! drive!, by Richard O. Boyer. (LOU LITTLE: Football coach, Columbia University) 24:37-59 O 9 '48. 280

The duke in his domain, by Truman Capote. (MARLON BRANDO: Stage, motion picture actor) 33:53-100 N 9 '57. 281

Dynamics, by John Brooks. (GENERAL DYNAMICS CORPORATION) 33:29-47 Ja 4 '58. 282

Ear-driven, by Daniel Lang. (EMORY COOK: Sound expert; president, phonograph record company) 32:39-58 *Mr 3 '56; 32:45-65 *Mr 10 '56. 283

The easygoing method, by E.J. Kahn, Jr. (ABE BURROWS: Comedian; playwright; director) 33:51-81 My 11 '57; 33:41-67 My 18 '57. 284

The edge of the sea, by Rachel Carson. (LIFE AT THE EDGE OF THE SEA) 31:34-61 *Ag 20 '55; 31:36-67 *Ag 27 '55. 285

Editorial writer, by John Bainbridge. (REUBEN MAURY: Chief editorial writer, New York Daily News) 23:36-51 My 24 '47; 23:31-41 My 31 '47; 23:38-52 Je 7 '47. 286

The education of a prince, by Alva Johnston. (MICHAEL ALEXANDROVITCH ROMANOFF: Impostor; restaurant owner) 8:19-23 O 29 '32; 8:28-32 N 5 '32; 8:24-8 N 12 '32; 8:24-8 N 19 '32; 8:24-9 N 26 '32. 287

Education of an army, by E.J. Kahn, Jr. (LESLEY JAMES McNAIR: Lieutenant-general, U.S. Army) 20:28-38 O 14 '44; 20:34-47 O 21 '44. 288

Educator, by Geoffrey T. Hellman. (FREDERICK B. ROBINSON: President, College of the City of New York) 9:26-9 *N 18 '33. 289

Edward's grandson, by Anthony Gibbs. (EDWARD, PRINCE OF WALES) 7:27-30 O 3 '31; 7:26-9 O 10 '31. 290

Egg is all, by Eugene Kinkead. (ALEXIS LAWRENCE ROMANOFF: Professor of Chemical Embryology, Cornell University) 29:32-59 Je 20 '53; 29:32-57 Je 27 '53. 291

The egotist, by Janet Flanner. (PAUL POIRET: Couturier) 3:23-5 O 29 '27. 292

Egyptologist, by Geoffrey T. Hellman. (HERBERT E. WINLOCK: Director, Metropolitan Museum; archeologist) 9:16-19 Jy 29 '33. 293

89 Centre Street, by Richard H. Rovere. (HOWE AND HUMMEL: Criminal law office) 22:36-54 N 23 '46; 22:44-57 N 30 '46; 22:46-64 D 7 '46; 22:47-59 D 14 '46. 294

The ekistic world, by Christopher Rand. (CONSTANTINOS DOXIADIS: City planner) 39:49-87 My 11 '63. 295

El único matador, by Lillian Ross. (SIDNEY FRANKLIN: Matador) 25:34-47 Mr 12 '49; 25:34-51 Mr 19 '49; 25:32-56 Mr 26 '49. 296

The elegant tugboater, by Robert Lewis Taylor. (EUGENE F. MORAN: President, Moran Towing & Transport

Company) 21:32-8 N 3 '45; 21:33-43 N 10 '45. 297

The emerald boss, by Niven Busch, Jr. (JOHN H. McCOOEY: Democratic Leader, Kings County, Brooklyn) 3:25-8 Mr 12 '27. 298

Emergencies, advice for, by Brendan Gill. (FREDERIC HUNTINGTON BARTLETT: Pediatrician; author) 20:26-32 Jy 15 '44. 299

An emolument for heliotrope, by Geoffrey T. Hellman. (HOWARD KETCHAM: Color, design and illumination engineer) 28:39-53 Mr 8 '52. 300

The Emperor Jones, by Gilbert Seldes. (ROBERT EDMOND JONES: Stage designer) 7:25-8 My 9 '31. 301

Enemy of gemütlichkeit, by Joseph Wechsberg. (HELMUT QUALTINGER: Actor; playwright) 39:53-95 Ap 20 '63. 302

Enfant terrible, by Geoffrey T. Hellman. (DIEGO RIVERA: Painter) 9:21-4 *My 20 '33. 303

Enfant terrible, by Newman Levy. (SAM FELDMAN: Lawyer) 4:22-5 Ag 25 '28. 304

England's most photographed female, by John R. Tunis. (BETTY NUTHALL: Tennis player) 6:20-2 Ag 23 '30. 305

An enhancing adjunct, by John Brooks. (HENRY HEYDENRYK: Picture framer) 39:49-81 Ap 27 '63. 306

The enigmatic bequest, by Geoffrey T. Hellman. (SMITHSONIAN INSTITUTION: Research institution) 42:66-150 D 3 '66; 42:64-139 D 10 '66; 42:58-112 D 17 '66. 307

Essence of chic Paris, by Ferdinand Tuohy. (SACHA GUITRY AND YVONNE PRINTEMPS: Playwright and actress) 2:29-32 D 18 '26. 308

Even his feet look sad, by Whitney Balliett. CHARLES ELLSWORTH [Pee Wee] RUSSELL: Jazz clarinetist) 38:30-45 Ag 11 '62. 309

Everything is mobile, by Geoffrey T. Hellman. (ALEXANDER CALDER: Maker and seller of mobiles) 17:25-33 *O 4 '41. 310

Evolution of a problem child, by John McCarten. (FRANK HAGUE: Mayor, Jersey City, New Jersey) 13:20-5 *F 12 '38; 14:21-6 *F 19 '38. 311

Evolution of an iron-toed boy, by Robert Lewis Taylor. (RICHARD BARSTOW: Director and choreographer, Ringling Brothers and Barnum & Bailey Circus) 33: 41-76 Ap 20 '57; 33:39-65 Ap 27 '57. 312

Ex-motorman, by Ik Shuman. (JOHN GILLHAUS: Motorman, Sixth Avenue trolley line) 12:23-7 *N 7 '36. 313

The experience of forms, by Donald Hall. (HENRY MOORE: Sculptor) 41:66-141 D 11 '65; 41:59-151 D 18 '65. 314

Family under canvas, by Robert Lewis Taylor. (ARTHUR CONCELLO AND ANTOINETTE CONCELLO: Aerial trapeze artists) 25:31-45 Ap 23 '49; 25:36-51 Ap 30 '49. 315

A farewell to string and sealing wax, by Daniel Lang. (SAMUEL A. GOUDSMIT: Chairman, Physics Department, Brookhaven National Laboratory) 29:47-72 N 7 '53; 29:46-67 N 14 '53. 316

Farm and ringside, by Earl Sparling. (BILL BROWN: Health farm owner; member New York State Athletic Commission) 11:23-8 *My 18 '35. 317

Father Bill, by Henry F. Pringle. (WILLIAM E. CASHIN: Pastor, St. Andrew's Roman Catholic Church; Chaplin, New York State Prison) 3:19-21 Ja 7 '28. 318

A feeling of intense concentration, by Winthrop Sargeant. (JULIUS RUDEL: Conductor, New York City Opera) 38:57-82 O 20 '62. 319

The festive touch, by Geoffrey T. Hellman. (JOSEPH CLARK BALDWIN, III: U.S. Congressman, New York County) 19:22-32 F 27 '43; 19:26-39 Mr 6 '43. 320

Fiendish, by Robert Lewis Taylor. (ROLAND BUTLER: Publicity director, Ringling Brothers and Barnum & Bailey Circus) 29:38-66 Ap 18 '53; 29:37-67 Ap 25 '53. 321

A Fifth Avenue maverick, by William Boardman Knox.

(CORNELIUS VANDERBILT, JR.: Publisher; socialite) 1:11-12 D 26 '25. 322

Fifth Avenue's nize baby, by Niven Busch, Jr. (BENJAMIN WINTER: Real estate speculator) 2:15-17 Jy 3 '26. 323

Fifty per cent, by Barbara Heggie and J.J. O'Malley. (WILLIAM COLSTON LEIGH: Owner, Leigh Bureau of Lectures and Entertainment) 16:23-30 Ja 25 '41. 324

Fifty years of Wall Street, by Matthew Josephson. (HARRY CONTENT: Stock broker) 8:22-6 O 1 '32. 325

Figure in an imaginary landscape, by Calvin Tomkins. (JOHN M. CAGE, JR.: Composer) 40:64-128 N 28 '64. 326

Find 'em, fix 'em, and fight 'em, by A.J. Liebling. (TERRY de la MESA ALLEN: Major-general, U.S. Army) 19:22-6 Ap 24 '43; 19:24-30 My 1 '43. 327

Fire sign, by Niven Busch, Jr. (FANNIE BRICE: Comedienne; actress) 5:25-7 Ap 20 '29. 328

Firebug-catcher, by St. Clair McKelway. (THOMAS PATRICK BROPHY: Chief Fire Marshall, New York City) 11:18-23 *Ja 18 '36; 11:20-4 *Ja 25 '36. 329

The first churchman, by Alva Johnston. (WILLIAM T. MANNING: Bishop, Protestant Episcopal Diocese of New York) 7:24-36 F 28 '31. 330

The first lady, by Paul A. Burns. (GRACE COOLIDGE: Wife, President Calvin Coolidge) 2:17-18 My 15 '26. 331

The five generations, by Andy Logan. (ISSAC FISHBERG: Flutist) 25:32-51 O 29 '49. 332

Five-star schoolmaster, by A.J. Liebling. (OMAR NELSON BRADLEY: General, U.S. Army; Chairman, Joint Chiefs of Staff) 27:38-75 Mr 3 '51; 27:40-77 Mr 10 '51. 333

Flower lover no. 1, by Richard O. Boyer. (JOHN T. SCHEEPERS: Flower bulb broker) 14:18-24 *Je 25 '38. 334

Flying Dutchman, by Doree Smedley and Hollister Noble. (ANTHONY HERMAN GERARD FOKKER: Airplane designer; manufacturer) 6:20-4 F 7 '31. 335

The foolish things of the world, by Dwight Macdonald. (DOROTHY DAY: Author; founder, Catholic Worker movement) 28:37-60 O 4 '52; 28:37-58 O 11 '52. 336

For any occasion, by Margaret Case Harriman. (MAX SCHLING: Florist) 12:18-23 *Jy 18 '36. 337

For city and for Coty, by Geoffrey T. Hellman. (GROVER A. WHALEN: Chairman, Mayor's Reception Committee, New York City) 27:28-45 Jy 14 '51; 27:28-45 Jy 21 '51. 338

For excellence, by Brendan Gill. (SIGMUND M. MOREY: Machine tool manufacturer) 19:25-32 Jy 31 '43. 339

For God, country, Yale, and Garden, by E.J. Kahn, Jr. (JOHN REED KILPATRICK: President, Madison Square Garden) 31:35-51 *Ja 28 '56. 340

For kicks, by Gilbert Millstein. MILTON GABLER: Owner, Commodore Music Shop) 22:30-40 Mr 9 '46; 22:34-43 Mr 16 '46. 341

For the defense, by Milton MacKaye. (EDWARD J. REILLY: Lawyer) 10:22-5 *Ja 12 '35. 342

A forager, by John McPhee. (EUELL THEOPHILUS GIBBONS: Author of books on wild food) 44:45-104 Ap 6 '68. 343

Forecaster to the fliers, by Foster Ware. (JAMES H. KIMBALL: Meteorologist, U.S. Weather Bureau) 4:20-2 Jy 28 '28. 344

Foreign secretary, by Mollie Panter-Downes. (ROBERT ANTHONY EDEN: British foreign minister, prime minister) 20:35-43 D 2 '44; 20:36-43 D 9 '44. 345

The forty-five-minute tempo, by Barbara Heggie. (MARY MARGARET McBRIDE: Radio personality [housewives' program]) 18:27-34 D 19 '42. 346

Forward six, balance six, side gents do-si-do, by Robert

Lewis Taylor. (ELISHA KEELER: Square-dance caller) 32:39-69 F 9 '57. 347

Foundation, by Dwight Macdonald. (FORD FOUNDATION: Philanthropic organization) 31:57-89 *N 26 '55; 31:55-103 *D 3 '55; 31:57-95 *D 10 '55; 31:40-69 *D 17 '55. 348

Founding cadre, by Jane Kramer. (FEMINISTS) 46:52-139 N 28 '70. 349

Four hundred and forty vibrations, by Joseph Wechsberg. (FRANZ ALLERS: Conductor, ballet, opera, symphony, musical comedy) 36:47-80 Ap 2 '60. 350

The four-eyed kid, by Arthur Bartlett. (AUSTIN H. MacCORMICK: Commissioner of Correction; prison reformer) 10:24-7 *My 26 '34. 351

Fourteenth Street and Broadway, by Oliver H. P. Garrett. (JIMMIE WALKER: Politician; Mayor of New York) 1:9-10 Ag 29 '25. 352

The fractured oboist, by Robert Rice. (MITCHELL WILLIAM [Mitch] MILLER: Orchestra leader; oboist) 29:43-63 *Je 6 '53. 353

The French Lily, by Janet Flanner. (LILY PONS: Singer, Metropolitan Opera Company) 7:20-3 Ja 16 '32. 354

Friend of the average man, by Joseph Gollomb. (LOUIS I. DUBLIN: Statistician) 18:20-6 My 23 '42. 355

The friend of the musk ox, by Robert Lewis Taylor. (JOHN J. TEAL, JR.: Associate Professor of Geography and Anthropology, University of Vermont; explorer; author) 34:49-81 O 4 '58; 34:49-84 O 11 '58. 356

The friendly attitude, by E.J. Kahn, Jr. (JAMES WILLIAM JOHNSON: Collector, Internal Revenue Service) 23:36-50 Mr 15 '47. 357

From Madrid to the mirror, by John K. Winkler. (ALEXANDER POLLOCK MOORE: Newspaper publisher; U.S. Ambassador to Peru) 4:23-6 My 26 '28. 358

From sassafras branches, by Winthrop Sargeant. (EDWARD

D. STONE: Architect) 34:32-49 Ja 3 '59. 359

From the record, by Meyer Berger. (WEST FORTY-SEVENTH STREET POLICE STATION) 14:22-7 *N 19 '38; 14:22-8 *N 26 '38. 360

From within to without, by Geoffrey T. Hellman. (CHARLES EDOUARD JEANNERET: Architect) 23:31-45 Ap 26 '47; 23:36-53 My 3 '47. 361

From Yasnaya Polyana to Valley Cottage, by Robert Rice. (ALEXANDRA LVOVNA TOLSTOY: Daughter of Leo Tolstoy; founder of Russian welfare agency) 28:34-47 Mr 15 '52; 28:36-59 Mr 22 '52. 362

Front boy, by Niven Busch, Jr. (LUCIUS BOOMER: President, hotel and restaurant chain) 3:22-4 S 24 '27. 363

The frontal attack, by E.J. Kahn, Jr. (WALTER WHITE: Sociologist; author) 24:28-38 S 4 '48; 24:38-54 S 11 '48. 364

Führer, by Janet Flanner. (ADOLF HITLER: Führer, Third Reich) 12:20-4 *F 29 '36; 12:27-31 *Mr 7 '36; 12:22-6 *Mr 14 '36. 365

Funny-legs, by Waldo Frank. (CHARLIE CHAPLIN: Motion picture actor) 1:9-10 My 23 '25. 366

The fury, by Robert Rice. (MORT SAHL: Comedian) 36:31-53 Jy 30 '60. 367

Gadget-maker, by Henry F. Pringle. (ELMER A. SPERRY: Inventor) 6:24-6 Ap 19 '30. 368

The galloping Hitchcocks, by Herbert Reed. (THOMAS HITCHCOCK, SR., THOMAS HITCHCOCK, JR. AND LOUISE EUSTIS HITCHCOCK: Polo players; horsewoman) 2:17-18 Ag 14 '26. 369

Gene the genteel, by Kelly Coombs. (GENE TUNNEY: Prizefighter) 3:16-19 Ag 20 '27. 370

The General, by Matthew Josephson. (HUGH SAMUEL JOHNSON: Director, National Recovery Administration; General, U.S. Army) 10:19-23 *Ag 18 '34; 10:23-8 Ag 25 '34; 10:22-8 S 1 '34. 371

General director, by Robert A. Simon. (EDWARD JOHNSON: General Director, Metropolitan Opera Company; opera singer) 11:30-3 *D 14 '35. 372

The general manager, by Joseph Wechsberg. (RUDOLF BING: General manager, Metropolitan Opera Company) 42:65-124 S 17 '66. 373

General utility, by Alexander Woollcott. (ALFRED LUNT: Actor) 4:25-7 Ap 28 '28. 374

Generalissimo, by A.J. Liebling. (MAURICE-GUSTAVE GAMELIN: Generalissimo, Allied Armies in France) 16:24-7 *My 11 '40; 16:22-6 *My 18 '40. 375

Genius about town, by Helena Huntington Smith. (JASCHA HEIFETZ: Concert violinist) 4:23-5 F 25 '28. 376

A genius who made art into big business, by Murdock Pemberton. (WALTER L. CLARK: Curator, Grand Central Gallery of Art) 1:9-10 Ag 1 '25. 377

The gentleman from New York, by E.J. Kahn, Jr. (JACOB K. JAVITS: Member, U.S. House of Representatives, U.S. Senate) 25:31-45 Ja 21 '50; 25:30-42 Ja 28 '50. 378

A gentleman from Vienna, by Helena Huntington Smith. (FRITZ KREISLER: Concert violinist) 4:29-32 N 24 '28. 379

The gentleman in politics, by Geoffrey T. Hellman. (HAMILTON FISH, JR.: U.S. Congressman) 9:23-6 *O 7 '33. 380

The gentleman in the pulpit, by Richard O. Boyer. (WALTER RUSSELL BOWIE: Pastor, Grace Episcopal Church) 14:27-33 *O 22 '38. 381

A gentleman with two cauliflower ears, by Marquis James. (JOHN H. CRAIGE: Captain, U.S. Marine Corps) 1:9-10 Ap 4 '25. 382

Geography unshackled, by Geoffrey T. Hellman. (GILBERT H. GROSVENOR: Editor, *National Geographic Magazine*) 19:26-34 S 25 '43; 19:27-37 O 2 '43; 19:27-36 O 9 '43. 383

Geriatrician, by Daniel Lang. (MARTIN GUMPERT: Physician, geriatrics) 26:30-42 Je 10 '50; 26:34-47 Je 17 '50. 384

The ghosting business, by Alva Johnston. (CHRISTY WALSH: Ghost writer [esp. sports]) 11:20-5 *N 23 '35. 385

A giant in her field, by Morton M. Hunt. (HELAINE NEWSTEAD: Professor of English, Hunter College) 33:39-80 Mr 30 '57. 386

The gilded copper, by Alva Johnston. (GROVER A. WHALEN: Chairman, Mayor's Reception Committee; Police Commissioner, New York City) 4:21-4 Ja 12 '29. 387

Glamour boy, by E.J. Kahn, Jr. (RANDOLPH FORREST BURKE: Socialite) 16:23-7 *Ap 6 '40. 388

Glamour, Inc., by Margaret Case Harriman. (ELIZABETH ARDEN: Owner, beauty salon and company) 11:24-30 *Ap 6 '35. 389

A glimpse of heaven, by Hamilton Basso. (CHARLES PRENDERGAST: Artist) 22:24-30 Jy 27 '46; 22:28-37 Ag 3 '46. 390

Glorifier, by Gilbert Seldes. (FLORENZ ZIEGFELD: Theatrical producer) 7:19-22 *Jy 25 '31; 7:18-22 *Ag 1 '31. 391

Glorifier of the alphabet, by Milton MacKaye. (FREDERIC WILLIAM GOUDY: Type designer) 8:20-4 Ja 14 '33. 392

Glove and palette, by Robert Lewis Taylor. (EDWARD PATRICK [Mickey] WALKER: Prizefighter; artist) 31:57-84 *N 12 '55. 393

Godfather to Polymnia, by Deems Taylor. (WALTER DAMROSCH: Conductor, New York Symphony) 5:28-31 N 2 '29. 394

Goethe in Hollywood, by Janet Flanner. (THOMAS MANN: Novelist) 17:31-42 D 13 '41; 17:22-35 D 20 '41. 395

The golden spoon, by Jack Alexander. (WILLIAM VINCENT ASTOR: Real estate owner and manager; investment manager) 14:20-5 *Mr 5 '38; 14:23-7 *Mr 12 '38; 14:21-7 *Mr 19 '38. 396

Golf's Chevalier Bayard, by Herbert Reed. (ROBERT TYRE [Bobby] JONES, JR.: Golfer) 2:17-20 Jy 17 '26. 397

Good and faithful, by Foster Ware. (JOHN J. KIELY: Postmaster, New York City) 3:25-7 D 17 '27. 398

Good at games, by Milton MacKaye. (HAROLD VANDERBILT: Yachtsman; contract bridge authority) 9:21-5 Mr 4 '33. 399

Good citizen, by Richard H. Rovere. (NEWBOLD MORRIS: President, New York City Council) 20:28-36 O 28 '44; 20:28-38 N 4 '44. 400

A good eye, by Winthrop Sargeant. (GIOVANNI MARDERSTEIG: Publisher; printer; literary scholar) 46:32-47 Jy 11 '70. 401

A good hold on the Lord, by Richard O. Boyer. (ANGELINE NAWKINS: Captain, Salvation Army) 22:34-49 S 21 '46. 402

Good humorist, by Max Eastman. (ART YOUNG: Political cartoonist) 11:21-5 *Mr 2 '35. 403

Good manners and common sense, by E.J. Kahn, Jr. (ANGIER BIDDLE DUKE: U.S. Chief of Protocol) 40:34-83 Ag 15 '64. 404

Good morning, Judge, by Milton MacKaye. (JOSEPH E. CORRIGAN: Judge, New York City Criminal Courts) 6:22-5 Ag 30 '30. 405

Goodbye, Mr. Jafsie, by St. Clair McKelway. (JOHN F. CONDON: Public school teacher) 10:20-6 *D 29 '34. 406

Gossip writer, by St. Clair McKelway. (WALTER WINCHELL: Newspaper columnist) 16:26-40 Je 15 '40; 16:24-33 Je 22 '40; 16:23-6 *Je 29 '40; 16:24-30 *Jy 6 '40; 16:21-6 Jy 13 '40; 16:23-8 *Jy 20 '40. 407

The governor, by Milton MacKaye. (FRANKLIN DELANO ROOSEVELT: Governor, New York State; President, United States) 7:18-22 Ag 15 '31; 7:24-9 Ag 22 '31. 408

The governor, by Hickman Powell. (HERBERT HENRY LEHMAN: Governor, New York State) 12:21-6 *My 2 '36; 12:25-30 *My 9 '36. 409

The grace of the moment, by Joseph Wechsberg. (GEORGE SZELL: Conductor, Cleveland Orchestra) 41:59-112 N 6 '65. 410

Grand Sachem, by Frances Warfield. (THOMAS DARLINGTON: Physician; Commissioner of Health, New York City; author; lecturer; Grand Sachem, Society of Tammany) 8:19-23 Ag 6 '32. 411

The great aviculturist, by Geoffrey T. Hellman. (JEAN DELACOUR: Aviculturist; operator, Bronx Zoo) 22:24-33 Ag 10 '46; 22:26-39 Ag 17 '46. 412

The great expurgator, by Alva Johnston. (AL ROSEN: Hollywood agent) 23:40-50 Mr 29 '47. 413

A great green cloud, by Berton Roueché. (AMERICAN ELM) 37:35-53 Jy 15 '61. 414

The great impersonation, by Niven Busch, Jr. (DAVID BELASCO: Theatrical producer) 6:30-3 O 18 '30; 6:30-3 O 25 '30. 415

The great iron ship, by James Dugan. (THE GREAT EASTERN: Ocean liner) 29:34-73 S 19 '53; 29:40-74 S 26 '53; 29:37-76 O 3 '53; 29:45-68 O 10 '53. 416

Great provider, by Mollie Panter-Downes. (FREDERICK JAMES WOOLTON: British Minister of Reconstruction) 20:32-48 My 6 '44. 417

Great simplicity, by Winthrop Sargeant. (DAISETZ TEITARO SUZUKI: Authority on Zen Buddhism) 33:34-53 Ag 31 '57 418

The great spectator, by Stanley Walker. (JAMES EDWARD HAYES: Liaison officer, Democratic Party, New York City) 8:21-5 S 10 '32. 419

The greatest paper-hanger in the world, by Henry Anton Steig. (BEN STEIN: Wallpaper-hanger) 13:22-6 *N 6 '37. 420

Green front, by Stanley Walker. (JAMES BUTLER: Chain-grocery owner; race track owner) 8:20-3 Jy 9 '32. 421

Grim-visaged victory, by Herbert Reed. (EDWARD LEADER: Crew coach, Yale University) 2:17-18 Je 26 '26. 422

Grips and taxes, by Andy Logan. (VIVIEN KELLEMS: Manufacturer of electrical parts) 26:36-54 F 3 '51; 26:39-57 F 10 '51. 423

Groton, Harvard, and Tahiti, by Geoffrey T. Hellman. (GEORGE BIDDLE: Painter) 12:20-6 *My 30 '36. 424

Groton, Harvard, Wall Street, by Matthew Josephson. (RICHARD WHITNEY: President, New York Stock Exchange) 8:19-22 *Ap 2 '32. 425

Grown in Garden City, by Foster Ware. (NELSON DOUBLEDAY: Publisher) 3:21-3 F 18 '28. 426

Guerrilla from Erie, Pa., by A.J. Liebling. (PHILIP COCHRAN: Major, U.S. Army Air Force) 18:22-9 F 13 '43. 427

The Guild, by Cuthbert Wright. (THEATRE GUILD: Theatrical company) 2:17-20 D 25 '26. 428

Hair scientist, by Geoffrey T. Hellman. (CHARLES NESSLER: Inventor, permanent wave machine) 9:20-4 Ap 29 '33. 429

The hand on the pouch, by A.J. Liebling. (WILLIAM O' ROURKE: Diplomatic courier, communications officer, U.S. State Department) 22:30-41 F 1 '47. 430

The hand that feeds you, by Brock Pemberton and Foster Ware. (WILLIAM CHILDS: Owner, Childs' Restaurants) 3:25-8 Ap 9 '27. 431

Hands across the sea, by Milton MacKaye. (EDWARD CORSI: Director, Emergency Home Relief Bureau; Commissioner of Immigration) 11:20-4 *Mr 9 '35; 11:28-33 *Mr 16 '35. 432

Handsprings across the sea, by Janet Flanner. (LADY [Elsie de Wolfe] MENDL: Actress; socialite) 13:25-9 *Ja 15 '38. 433

The happy, happy beggar, by John Hersey. (WALTER P. MORSE: Missionary in China) 22:34-47 My 11 '46. 434

The happy venture, by John Brooks. (HUGH BULLOCK: Investment manager) 34:47-83 Mr 8 '58. 435

Harbor-hopper, by Robert M. Coates. (HILARY F. TURNER: Ferryboat captain) 11:25-9 *S 21 '35. 436

The harp lady, by E.J. Kahn, Jr. (MILDRED DILLING: Concert harpist) 15:25-9 F 3 '40. 437

"A harvest of inventions," by Gilbert Seldes. (JOHN HAYS HAMMOND, JR.: Inventor) 8:16-20 Jy 2 '32. 438

The hat on the roll-top desk, by Matthew Josephson. (LEON FRASER: President, First National Bank) 17:22-6 F 14 '42; 18:21-8 F 21 '42. 439

Hats will be worn, by Margaret Case Harriman. (LILLY DACHÉ: Milliner) 18:20-7 Ap 4 '42. 440

Hausfrau prima donna, by Helena Huntington Smith. (ERNESTINE SCHUMANN-HEINK: Opera singer) 2:17-18 Mr 20 '26. 441

Hawkshaw in the woods, by Eugene Kinkead. (EDWARD T. TOWNSEND: Game warden) 25:42-53 D 10 '49; 25:35-49 D 17 '49. 442

The headmaster, by John McPhee. (FRANK LEAROYD BOYDEN: Headmaster, Deerfield Academy) 42:57-159 Mr 19 '66. 443

Heavier than air, by Eric Hodgins. (ORVILLE WRIGHT: Airplane inventor; manufacturer) 6:29-32 D 13 '30. 444

Her majesty, the Queen, by Janet Flanner. (MARY, QUEEN OF ENGLAND) 11:20-4 *My 4 '35; 11:28-32 *My 11 '35. 445

Here come the clowns, by A.J. Liebling. (BLUCH LANDOLF: Circus clown) 15:25-9 *Ap 15 '39. 446

Hero for business reasons, by Alva Johnston. (GLENN L. MARTIN: Airplane manufacturer) 18:24-32 N 28 '42; 18:26-34 D 5 '42. 447

Hetty Green's son, by John K. Winkler. (E.R.H. GREEN: Owner, Round Hill Experimental Laboratories) 4:24-7 Ja 5 '29. 448

Heureux Noel, by Alexander Woollcott. (NOËL COWARD: Playwright; composer; actor) 4:21-5 Ja 19 '29. 449

Hewer of stone, by Gilbert Seldes. (GASTON LACHAISE: Sculptor) 7:28-31 Ap 4 '31. 450

High railers and full scalers, by Robert Lewis Taylor. (JOSHUA LIONEL COWEN: Chairman, "Lionel Lines," toy electric trains) 23:38-49 D 13 '47. 451

The hit's the thing, by E.J. Kahn, Jr. (ERNEST H. MARTIN [Ernest Markowitz] AND CY FEUER: Theatrical producers) 31:29-47 *Ja 7 '56; 31:33-55 *Ja 14 '56. 452

Hi-yo, platinum! by Margaret Case Harriman. (MOSS HART: Playwright) 19:29-43 S 11 '43. 453

Hoboken must go! by Andy Logan. (WILMA PORTER SOSS: Founder, Federation of Women Shareholders in American Business, Inc.) 27:34-51 Mr 17 '51. 454

Hollywood agent, by Margaret Case Harriman. (LELAND HAYWARD: Theatrical agent) 12:20-4 *Jy 11 '36. 455

The Hollywood Zeus, by Robert E. Sherwood. (CECIL B. DeMILLE: Motion picture director) 1:11-12 N 28 '25. 456

Holy smokestacks, what a mess! by Thomas Whiteside. (DANIEL FRAAD, JR.: President, Allied Maintenance Corporation) 32:39-73 *Mr 24 '56. 457

Home girl, by Joseph Mitchell. (KATE SMITH: Popular singer) 10:25-9 Mr 3 '34. 458

Home of refined dancing, by John Kobler. (LOUIS BRECKER: Owner, Roseland dance hall) 18:22-9 Je 27 '42. 459

Home sweet home, by Winthrop Sargeant. (EILEEN FARRELL: Concert singer) 35:47-71 My 23 '59. 460

Home talent, by Robert A. Simon. (LAWRENCE TIBBETT: Singer, Metropolitan Opera Company) 8:21-5 Ja 21 '33. 461

The honored society, by Norman Lewis. (THE MAFIA: Criminal secret society) 39:42-105 F 8 '64; 39:39-111 F 15 '64; 40:35-91 F 22 '64. 462

Hook, line, and sinker, by E.J. Kahn, Jr. (WILLIAM

MILLS & SON: Fishing tackle store) 14:16-20 *Jy 9 '38. 463

Hors concours, by Joseph Wechsberg. (MARIE-LOUISE MADO POINT: Manager, Restaurant de la Pyramide) 39:57-130 O 5 '63. 464

The hot Bach, by Richard O. Boyer. (EDWARD KENNEDY [Duke] ELLINGTON: Orchestra leader; composer) 20:30-44 Je 24 '44; 20:26-34 Jy 1 '44; 20:26-31 Jy 8 '44. 465

A house called peace, by Joseph Wechsberg. (HERMANN GMEINER: Organizer, SOS Children's Villages) 38: 39-65 D 22 '62. 466

House guest, by Geoffrey T. Hellman. (HARRY L. HOPKINS: Special advisor and assistant to U.S. President) 19:25-31 Ag 7 '43; 19:27-35 Ag 14 '43. 467

A house on Gramercy Park, by Geoffrey T. Hellman. (BENJAMIN SONNENBERG: Public-relations counsellor) 26:40-61 Ap 8 '50. 468

The house that Jack built, by Alexander Woollcott. (ELLIOTT [Jack] HUMPHREY: Head, Seeing eye dog school) 12:20-5 *D 26 '36. 469

How about a little game? by Jeremy Bernstein. (STANLEY KUBRICK: Motion picture director) 42:70-110 N 12 '66. 470

How do you like it now, Gentlemen? by Lillian Ross. (ERNEST HEMINGWAY: Novelist; short story writer) 26:36-56 *My 13 '50. 471

How does it come to be so? by Morton M. Hunt. (ROBERT K. MERTON: Professor of Sociology, Columbia University) 36:39-63 Ja 28 '61. 472

How to be a critic, by Wolcott Gibbs. (KELCEY ALLEN: Drama critic, Women's Wear Daily) 20:30-47 Mr 11 '44. 473

How to win profits and influence literature, by Geoffrey T. Hellman. (RICHARD L. SIMON AND M. LINCOLN SCHUSTER: Publishers) 15:22-8 *S 30 '39; 15:24-30 *O 7 '39; 15:25-9 *O 14 '39. 474

Hu Shih's musketeer, by John Bainbridge. (DANIEL ARNSTEIN: U.S. Ambassador to China; Burma Road expert) 17:22-7 Ja 10 '42; 17:23-32 Ja 17 '42. 475

The human condition, by Janet Flanner. (ANDRÉ MALRAUX: Novelist; French cabinet minister) 30:45-81 N 6 '54; 30:46-100 N 13 '54. 476

The human firecracker, by Geoffrey T. Hellman. (JOHN C. CRAIG: Consultant on pyrotechnics to Board of Display, New York World's Fair) 15:23-8 *Je 17 '39. 477

The human side, by St. Clair McKelway. (BENJAMIN E. GREENSPAN: New York City Magistrate) 10:24-7 Ap 28 '34. 478

The human sound, by Whitney Balliett. (BOBBY SHORT: Popular singer; pianist) 46:28-35 D 26 '70. 479

Humility, concentration, and gusto, by Winthrop Sargeant. (MARIANNE CRAIG MOORE: Poet) 32:38-77 F 16 '57. 480

Hunter of the snark, by Helena Huntington Smith. (ROY CHAPMAN ANDREWS: Explorer; author) 5:22-5 Je 29 '29. 481

Hymns on the harness track, by Richard O. Boyer. (FRANK SAFFORD: Trainer and driver of harness horses) 25:37-53 O 15 '49. 482

Hyper or hypo? by S.N. Berhman. (EMANUEL LIBMAN: Physician; diagnostician) 15:23-9 *Ap 8 '39. 483

"I know my Washington," by Robert S. Allen. (SOL BLOOM: U.S. Congressman, New York State) 8:24-7 *F 20 '32. 484

I was once a 97-pound weakling, by Robert Lewis Taylor. (CHARLES ATLAS: Muscle-builder) 17:21-7 Ja 3 '42. 485

Ice woman, by Barbara Heggie. (MARY ENGLE PENNINGTON: Chief, Food Research Laboratory; refrigeration expert) 17:23-30 *S 6 '41. 486

The iconoclast of the courts, by John K. Winkler. (WILLIAM

TATEM TILDEN, 2nd: Tennis player) 2:27-9 S 18 '26. 487

"I'd give my shirt for Al," by Malcolm Ross. (WILLIAM FRANK KENNY: Industrialist) 4:19-22 Je 23 '28. 488

Idea flourisher, by Barbara Heggie and Robert Lewis Taylor. (ERNO RAPEE: Orchestra conductor, Radio City Music Hall) 19:28-40 F 5 '44. 489

The idea is everything, by Philip Hamburger. (TRYGVE LIE: Secretary-general, United Nations) 23:39-49 O 11 '47; 23:39-52 O 18 '47. 490

Idle hour man, by David B. Campbell. (EDWARD RILEY BRADLEY: Horse breeder; gambling casino owner) 10:21-6 *Ja 19 '35. 491

If trouble can be avoided, by Mark Murphy. (PASQUALE D'AGOSTINO: Grocer) 19:25-34 My 15 '43. 492

The illustrious George, by J. Hansuld. (GEORGE LUKS: Painter) 1:13-14 My 9 '25. 493

The impeccable glass, by Joseph Wechsberg. (FRITZ FREY: Swiss hotel owner) 31:29-46 *Ag 13 '55. 494

Imperturable noble, by Geoffrey T. Hellman. (RENÉ d'HARNONCOURT: Director, Museum of Modern Art) 36:49-112 My 7 '60. 495

In America's image, by Waldo Frank. (SINCLAIR LEWIS: Novelist) 1:10-11 Jy 18 '25. 496

In the mainstream, by Nat Hentoff. (GERRY MULLIGAN: Jazz saxophonist; composer) 35:51-95 Mr 21 '59; 35:39-86 Mr 28 '59. 497

In the outlaw area, by Calvin Tomkins. (RICHARD BUCKMINSTER FULLER: Architect; designer; inventor; engineer) 41:35-97 Ja 8 '66. 498

In tune with the finite, by Waldo Frank. (OTTO H. KAHN: Financier; patron of arts) 2:23-4 F 20 '26. 499

Incredible Mr. Creel, by Harvey O'Higgins. (GEORGE CREEL: Chairman, Committee of Public Information) 1:7-8 Jy 4 '25. 500

Independent cop, by Jack Alexander. (LEWIS J. VALENTINE: Police Commissioner, New York City) 12:21-7 *O 3 '36; 12:24-8 *O 10 '36; 12:28-34 *O 17 '36. 501

Industrial classicist, by Gilbert Seldes. (WALTER DORWIN TEAGUE: Industrial designer) 10:28-32 *D 15 '34. 502

The infinitesimal and the infinite, by Robert Simpson. (WILLIAM L. LAURENCE: Science reporter, New York Times) 21:26-35 Ag 18 '45. 503

Inhabitant of the air, by Barbara Heggie. (ALICIA MARKOVA: Ballerina) 20:33-44 Ap 15 '44. 504

The inland sea, by Morton M. Hunt. (LONG ISLAND SOUND) 40:37-86 Ag 22 '64; 40:37-77 Ag 29 '64; 40:37-105 S 5 '64. 505

The innocents abroad, by Geoffrey T. Hellman. (ARMAND HAMMER: Jewelry collector) 9:18-21 D 23 '33. 506

Inquisitor, by Richard O. Boyer. (SAMUEL SEABURY: Politician; judge) 7:20-3 *Je 27 '31. 507

Inside, by Richard H. Rovere. (JOHN GUNTHER: Author; geographer) 23:30-40 Ag 23 '47. 508

Insurance man, by St. Clair McKelway. (ROBERT J. JOHNSON, pseud.: Insurance salesman) 10:20-6 Jy 7 '34. 509

Isadora, by Janet Flanner. (ISADORA DUNCAN: Dancer) 2:17-19 Ja 1 '27. 510

The island of the crofter and the laird, by John McPhee. (COLONSAY ISLAND) 45:69-165 D 6 '69; 45:61-112 D 13 '69. 511

The it girl, by Margaret Case Harriman. (DOROTHY THOMPSON: Newspaper columnist) 16:24-30 *Ap 20 '40; 16:23-9 *Ap 27 '40. 512

It pays to preach, by Richard F. Warner. (BRUCE BARTON: Author; advertising executive) 6:21-4 N 1 '30. 513

Italian table d'hôte, by Henry F. Pringle. (FIORELLO H. La GUARDIA: Politician; Mayor of New York City) 5:26-9 Ag 31 '29. 514

It's all anthropology, by Winthrop Sargeant. (MARGARET MEAD: Anthropologist; author) 37:31-44 D 30 '61. 515

It's de-lovely, by Russell Maloney. (MONTY WOOLEY: Actor) 15:25-9 *Ja 20 '40. 516

It's detestable when you live it, by Whitney Balliett. (RAY CHARLES: Popular singer; pianist; composer; publisher) 46:44-76 Mr 28 '70. 517

It's nice out there this morning, by Mark Murphy. (RICHARD OLNEY HART: Head, window-washing crew, Empire State Building) 24:35-49 Ap 24 '48. 518

The janitor's boy, by Henry F. Pringle. (ROBERT F. WAGNER, SR.: Member, U.S. Senate, New York State Senate, Supreme Court) 3:24-6 Mr 5 '27. 519

Joe Gould's secret, by Joseph Mitchell. (JOSEPH FERDINAND GOULD: Bohemian; author of unpublished book) 40:61-125 S 19 '64; 40:53-159 S 26 '64. 520

The Jollity Building, by A.J. Liebling. (JOLLITY BUILDING) 17:22-30 *Ap 26 '41; 17:22-31 *My 3 '41; 17:22-9 *My 10 '41. 521

Jolly bear, by Matthew Josephson. (BERNARD E. SMITH: Stock broker) 8:22-5 *My 14 '32; 8:21-5 *My 21 '32. 522

Joyful wisdom, by Waldo Frank. (ABRAHAM ARDEN BRILL: Psychiatrist) 1:11-12 O 17 '25. 523

The judicious observer will be disgusted, by Kenneth Tynan. (VALENCIA) 46:33-53 Jy 25 '70. 524

Jumbo, by Alva Johnston. (WALLACE BEERY: Motion picture actor; comedian) 11:22-7 *N 9 '35. 525

Jurist, by Matthew Josephson. (FELIX FRANKFURTER: U.S. Supreme Court Justice) 16:24-32 *N 30 '40; 16:34-44 *D 7 '40; 16:24-34 *D 14 '40. 526

Just a débutante, by E.J. Kahn, Jr. (BRENDA DIANA DUFF FRAZIER: Socialite; débutante) 15:23-8 *Je 10 '39. 527

Just a little off the top, by William Whitworth. (PAUL MOLÉ: Barber) 43:63-78 O 21 '67. 528

Just the old-time religion, by Richard O. Boyer. (CHRISTIAN F. REISNER: Methodist Episcopal minister, Broadway Temple) 15:32-8 *D 16 '39. 529

Kentucky-fried, by William Whitworth. (HARLAND SANDERS: Founder, restaurant chain) 45:40-52 F 14 '70. 530

Kewpie doll, by Alexander King. (ROSE O'NEILL: Designer of Kewpie Doll) 10:22-6 *N 24 '34. 531

A kind man, by Waldo Frank. (WILLIAM LYON PHELPS: Professor of English, Yale University) 1:11-12 O 24 '25. 532

The king, by Alva Johnston. (W. KINGSLAND MACY: Leader, Republican Party, New York State) 7:25-8 S 12 '31. 533

King of Harlem, by Mildred Gilman. (PAUL ROBESON: Actor; concert singer) 4:26-9 S 29 '28. 534

King of the Bronx, by Robert M. Coates. (J. CLARENCE DAVIES: Real estate developer) 5:33-5 D 7 '29. 535

King of the gypsies, by Joseph Mitchell. (JOHNNY NIKANOV: Gypsy king) 18:21-34 Ag 15 '42. 536

King of the wild beasts, by Janet Flanner. (HENRI MATISSE: Artist) 27:30-46 D 22 '51; 27:26-49 D 29 '51. 537

Kings of the talkies, by Alva Johnston. (HARRY WARNER, JACK WARNER, ALBERT WARNER AND SAM WARNER: Motion picture producers) 4:21-4 D 22 '28. 538

Kingsman, by Mollie Panter-Downes. (EDWARD MORGAN FORSTER: Novelist) 35:51-86 S 19 '59. 539

Klondike Stef, by Robert Lewis Taylor. (VILHJALMUR STEFANSSON: Arctic explorer) 17:26-36 *O 18 '41; 17:23-34 *O 25 '41. 540

Knight with the rueful countenance, by Alexander Woollcott. (LLOYD PAUL STRYKER: Lawyer) 14:23-6 *Ja 21 '39. 541

La belle dame sans merci, by Robert Lewis Taylor. (HUR-

RICANE DONNA AND CECIL GREEN: Hurricane; Fishing guide, Florida Keys) 36:39-70 F 11 '61; 37: 45-90 F 18 '61. 542

La France et le vieux, by Janet Flanner. (HENRI PHILIPPE PÉTAIN: Marshall of France; head, Vichy France government) 19:27-40 F 12 '44; 20:27-43 F 19 '44; 20:28-41 F 26 '44; 20:27-41 Mr 4 '44. 543

La, La, Inc., by A.J. Liebling. (CLIFFORD C. FISCHER: Producer of revues) 13:27-32 *My 15 '37. 544

Ladies in uniform, by Janet Flanner. (ALICE THROCKMORTON McLEAN: Founder, American Women's Voluntary Services) 18:21-9 Jy 4 '42. 545

Lady bountiful, by Arthur Bartlett. (MARJORIE POST CLOSE HUTTON DAVIES: Wife, U.S. Ambassador to Russia; socialite) 14:21-6 *F 4 '39; 14:23-7 *F 11 '39; 15:24-7 *F 18 '39. 546

Lady Chesterfield, by Helena Huntington Smith. (EMILY POST: Author; authority on etiquette) 6:22-5 Ag 16 '30. 547

Lady in crêpe, by Meyer Berger. (ANNA LONERGAN: Head, stevedore union) 11:28-32 *O 5 '35; 11:25-9 *O 12 '35. 548

Lady into dynamo, by Margaret K. Leech. (ANNE MORGAN: Club woman; philanthropist) 3:21-3 O 22 '27. 549

Lady of an antique world, by Margaret K. Leech. (RITA de ALBA de ACOSTA LYDIG: Socialite; author) 3: 28-30 N 19 '27. 550

Lady of Fourteenth Street, by Djuna Barnes. (EVA LE GALLIENNE: Actress; director; translator) 5:29-32 Ap 6 '29. 551

Lady of the cats, by Wolcott Gibbs and E. F. Kinkead. (RITA ROSS: Cat-catcher) 14:21-6 *My 14 '38. 552

Lady of the stars, by Alva Johnston. (EVANGELINE ADAMS: Astrologer) 4:29-32 O 27 '28. 553

Lady Olga, by Joseph Mitchell. (JANE BARNELL: Bearded lady in circus sideshow) 16:20-8 *Ag 3 '40. 554

A lady who writes, by Harvey O'Higgins. (ALICE DUER MILLER: Novelist) 3:25-7 F 19 '27. 555

Lady with a cause, by Geoffrey T. Hellman. (ELIZABETH ACHELIS: Advocate of permanent calendar) 15:21-5 *D 30 '39. 556

Laird of Woodley, by Henry F. Pringle. (HENRY L. STIMSON: U.S. Secretary of State) 6:30-3 O 4 '30. 557

Last of the prosecutors, by Alva Johnston. (GEORGE Z. MEDALIE: U.S. District Attorney) 9:18-22 Ag 19 '33. 558

Last of the species, by Geoffrey T. Hellman. (FRANK CROWNINSHIELD: Editor, Vanity Fair) 18:22-33 S 19 '42; 18:24-31 S 26 '42. 559

The law and the prophets, by Russell Maloney. (A.J. TOWNSEND AND WILLIAM TOWNSEND: Advertising consultants) 15:21-6 *S 16 '39. 560

The lawns of Wimbledon, by John McPhee. (ROBERT TWYNAM: Groundskeeper) 44:32-57 Je 22 '68. 561

Le gamin, by Janet Flanner. (BERNARD BUFFET: Painter) 35:57-112 N 21 '59. 562

Le meneur de jeu, by Penelope Gilliatt. (JEAN RENOIR: Motion picture director) 45:34-61 Ag 23 '69. 563

Lead player, by William Whitworth. (BERNIE GLOW: Trumpet player) 45:43-54 D 20 '69. 564

Learned lyricist, by A.J. Liebling. (OTTO HARBACH: Author, musical comedies) 13:22-7 *F 27 '37. 565

The leaves of a tree, by Winthrop Sargeant. (ROSINA LHEVINNE: Piano teacher) 38:37-72 Ja 12 '63. 566

Legend of a sport, by Alva Johnston. (WILSON MIZNER: Confidence man; promoter; Broadway personality) 18:21-8 O 10 '42; 18:26-34 O 17 '42; 18:25-32 O 24 '42; 18:25-8 O 31 '42; 26:39-67 F 25 '50; 26:30-45 Jy 22 '50; 26:26-41 Jy 29 '50; 26:28-39 D 23 '50; 26:26-41 D 30 '50. 567

Legitimate nonchalance, by Alva Johnston. (W. C. FIELDS:

Comedian; actor; juggler) 10:23-6 F 2 '35; 10:25-8 F 9 '35; 11:22-6 F 16 '35. 568

Leprechaun on the Palisades, by Matthew Josephson. (JOHN MARIN: Painter) 18:26-35 Mr 14 '42. 569

Let freedom ring, by Alva Johnston. (SAMUEL S. LEIBOWITZ: Lawyer) 8:21-4 Je 4 '32; 8:18-23 Je 11 '32. 570

Let's find out, by Robert Lewis Taylor. (FRANK STANTON: President, Columbia Broadcasting System) 22:32-42 Ja 18 '47; 22:28-38 Ja 25 '47. 571

The level head, by Robert Lewis Taylor. (RICHARD STODDARD ALDRICH: Summer-theatre producer) 31:31-41 *Jy 30 '55; 31:27-43 *Ag 6 '55. 572

Levels of the game, by John McPhee. (ARTHUR ASHE AND CLARK GRAEBNER: Tennis players) 45:45-111 Je 7 '69; 45:44-81 Je 14 '69. 573

Lights, lights, lights, by E.J. Kahn, Jr. (DOUGLAS LEIGH: Designer, luminous signs and neon signs) 17:23-31 *Je 7 '41. 574

Lights, please! by Geoffrey T. Hellman. (WILLIAM NORMAN GUTHRIE: Rector, St. Mark's-in-the-Bouwerie) 6:22-5 Ja 31 '31. 575

Like a homesick angel, by John Bainbridge. (HAROLD FREDERIC BLACKBURN: Pilot, Trans World Airlines) 38:61-145 N 10 '62. 576

Lilt, by Angelica Gibbs. (MAY GADD: Authority on folk dancing) 28:36-55 F 7 '53. 577

The line, by A.J. Liebling. (AUGUSTINE J. GRENET: Horse racing bookmaker) 13:20-5 *Jy 24 '37. 578

Linksland and Meadowland, by Herbert Warren Wind. (ROBERT TRENT JONES: Golf course architect) 27:28-43 Ag 4 '51. 579

Little giant, by Alva Johnston. (SAMUEL UNTERMYER: Lawyer) 6:29-32 My 17 '30; 6:24-7 My 24 '30. 580

The little Heinie, by Niven Busch, Jr. (LOUIS HENRY GEHRIG: Baseball player) 5:22-5 Ag 10 '29. 581

Little magazine, by John Bainbridge. (DeWITT WALLACE: Editor, Reader's Digest) 21:33-42 N 17 '45; 21:36-44 *N 24 '45; 21:40-51 D 1 '45; 21:38-51 *D 8 '45; 21:38-54 *D 15 '45. 582

Little monarch, by Andrew A. Freeman. (PRAJADHIPOK, KING OF SIAM) 7:24-6 Ap 18 '31. 583

Little Narcissus, by Henry F. Pringle. (LILY DAMITA: Motion picture actress) 5:30-3 O 26 '29. 584

The little room, by Anthony Bailey. (THE NETHERLANDS) 46:34-57 Ag 8 '70; 46:32-63 Ag 15 '70. 585

Living well is the best revenge, by Calvin Tomkins. (GEORGE MURPHY AND SARA MURPHY: President of Mark Cross, and wife; prototypes of leading characters in Fitzgerald's Tender is the Night) 38:31-69 Jy 28 '62. 586

Local boy makes good, by Henry F. Pringle. (JOHN FRANCIS CURRY: Leader, New York County Democratic Party) 5:21-4 Ag 3 '29. 587

The lone prospector: thirty years after, by Elmer Davis. (ADOLPH SIMON OCHS: Publisher, New York Times) 1:11-12 N 21 '25. 588

Long after Bligh, by John McCarten. (FREDERICK JOHNSON: Captain, S.S. Josiah Crabtree) 20:27-37 S 30 '44. 589

The long phrase, by Joseph Wechsberg. (ISAAC STERN: Concert violinist) 41:49-117 Je 5 '65. 590

The long road to Roxy, by Gilbert Seldes. (DONALD DESKEY: Furniture manufacturer) 9:22-6 F 25 '33. 591

Lord Fauntleroy in Hollywood, by Alva Johnston. (W.S. VAN DYKE: Motion picture director) 11:20-4 *S 28 '35. 592

A lover of cities, by Bernard Taper. (CHARLES ABRAMS: City planner) 42:39-91 F 4 '67; 42:45-115 F 11 '67. 593

Lucky Cochet, by John R. Tunis. (HENRI COCHET: Tennis player) 4:28-30 S 15 '28. 594

No entry. 595

The lucky stiff, by Arthur Krock. (A. CHARLES SCHWARTZ: Financier) 2:15-17 Jy 24 '26. 596

Luxury, Inc., by Lois Long and Nancy Hardin. (HATTIE CARNEGIE: Couturière) 10:23-7 Mr 31 '34. 597

The mad hatter of Hollywood, by Alva Johnston. (CHARLES BUTTERWORTH: Comedian; motion picture actor) 11:20-6 *Jy 27 '35. 598

Madam, by Mollie Panter-Downes. (NINETTE de VALOIS: Director, Sadler's Wells Ballet) 26:32-54 S 16 '50. 599

Madame Secretary, by Russell Lord. (FRANCES PERKINS: U.S. Secretary of Labor; sociologist) 9:16-19 S 2 '33; 9:20-3 S 9 '33. 600

Madness and music, by Waldo Frank. (ERNEST BLOCH: Composer) 2:25-6 S 11 '26. 601

Maestrissimo! by Gilbert W. Gabriel. (GIULIO GATTI-CASAZZA: Impresario, Metropolitan Opera Company) 1:9-10 F 21 '25. 602

Maestro di costruzione, by Winthrop Sargeant. (PIER LUIGI NERVI: Architect; engineer) 36:40-64 Je 11 '60. 603

Maestro on a mountaintop, by Richard O. Boyer. (DIMITRI MITROPOULOS: Conductor, New York Philharmonic) 26:38-60 Ap 15 '50. 604

The magnificent touch, by Eugene Kinkead and Russell Maloney. (WILLIAM BERNARD OKIE, JR.: Window display designer) 18:20-31 My 30 '42. 605

The mahatma, by Milton MacKaye. (LOUIS MICHEL EILSHEMIUS: Artist) 11:24-8 *S 14 '35. 606

Maker of castles, by Foster Ware. (CHARLES VINCENT PATERNO: Building contractor) 3:19-20 Jy 2 '27. 607

A man, a museum--and their secret vice, by Murdock Pemberton. (RICHARD F. BACH: Architect; Associate in Industrial Arts, Metropolitan Museum of Art) 1:12-13 S 12 '25. 608

Man against the sky, by Allene Talmey. (RAYMOND HOOD: Architect) 7:24-7 Ap 11 '31. 609

The man behind Prometheus, by Geoffrey T. Hellman. (JOHN R. TODD: Co-manager, Rockefeller Center) 12:31-4 *N 14 '36; 12:23-6 *N 21 '36. 610

The man behind the gun, by John McCarten. (JOHN C. GARAND: Inventor, semi-automatic rifle) 18:22-8 F 6 '43. 611

Man in a blue suit, by Niven Busch, Jr. (BILL KLEM: Baseball umpire) 5:31-3 O 5 '29. 612

The man in the corner, by A.J. Liebling. (MORRIS BIMSTEIN: Prizefight second) 13:28-33 *Mr 20 '37. 613

Man of ideas, by H.K. Rigg. (W. STARLING BURGESS: Racing yacht designer) 13:20-6 *Jy 31 '37. 614

Man of means, by E.J. Kahn, Jr. (JOHN HAY [Jock] WHITNEY: Foundation director; philanthropist) 27:32-49 Ag 11 '51; 27:36-57 Ag 18 '51. 615

A man this country needed, by Sanderson Vanderbilt. (ARTHUR WALSH: Cigar store owner) 13:24-9 *S 11 '37. 616

The man who answers telephones, by Jack Alexander. (SHERMAN C. AMSDEN: Head, Telephone Answering Service) 15:21-7 *Ap 22 '39. 617

The man who changed the course of Chinese history, by John Kirkpatrick. (MAURICE WILLIAM: Historian; author; dentist) 18:20-6 Ag 22 '42. 618

Man who is happening now, by Jane Kramer. (ROBERT COOPER SCULL: Art dealer; owner of taxicab company) 42:64-120 N 26 '66. 619

The man who is not his cousin, by Geoffrey T. Hellman. (CORNELIUS VANDERBILT WHITNEY: Corporation director; polo player; racing stables owner) 17:21-9 *Je 21 '41. 620

The man who made us what we are, by Waldo Frank. (JOHN DEWEY: Philosopher; educator; author) 1:15-16 My 22 '26. 621

The man who ruined Paris, by Alexander Woollcott. (EDWIN L. JAMES: European correspondent, New York Times) 2:25-6 O 2 '26. 622

Man with a thumb, by Robert Lewis Taylor. (JOE FALCARO: Bowler) 17:23-32 *Ap 5 '41. 623

Man with camera, by Gilbert Seldes. (MERIAN COOPER: Motion picture photographer) 7:21-5 *My 30 '31. 624

The man with the squeege, by Russel Crouse. (STANLEY NORRIS: Window washer) 8:21-4 *My 7 '32. 625

The mantle of Rockne, by Joel Sayre. (JOHN FRANCIS [Chick] MEEHAN: Football coach, New York University) 7:23-7 N 14 '31. 626

The markee, by Joseph Mitchell. (JOE MADDEN: Saloonkeeper) 15:20-7 *N 4 '39. 627

The mascot of the troop, by Alice Frankforter. (FRITZI SCHEFF: Opera and light-opera singer) 5:30-3 N 16 '29. 628

Mass entertainment, by Alva Johnston. (BILLY ROSE: Stage show producer) 11:22-9 *Ap 27 '35. 629

Master, by Janet Flanner. (GEORGES BRAQUE: Painter) 32:49-89 O 6 '56; 32:50-97 O 13 '56. 630

The master, by Geoffrey T. Hellman. (ELMER G. LETERMAN: Insurance salesman) 16:24-8 *My 4 '40. 631

A master ditch digger, by Russell Owen. (SAM ROSOFF: Contractor, Eighth Avenue Subway) 3:19-21 Je 4 '27. 632

Master hinter, by Alva Johnston. (ROYAL S. COPELAND: Member, U.S. Senate) 4:21-4 Ag 18 '28. 633

Master of ceremonies, by James Thurber. (MYRON T. HERRICK: U.S. Ambassador to France) 4:19-22 Jy 21 '28. 634

A master of her art, by John R. Tunis. (ELIZABETH [Bunny] RYAN: Tennis player) 1:9-10 Ag 22 '25. 635

Master of masters, by Helena Huntington Smith. (LEOPOLD

AUER: Concert violinist; music teacher) 5:24-7 Ap 27 '29. 636

Master of the before and the after, by Andy Logan. (VALENTINO SARRA: Photographer; president of advertising agency) 27:29-42 *S 1 '51. 637

Masterpieces and mummies, by Geoffrey T. Hellman. (METROPOLITAN MUSEUM OF ART) 16:36-42 *Mr 16 '40; 16:25-30 Mr 23 '40; 16:23-9 Mr 30 '40. 638

Masters of the midway, by A.J. Liebling. (LEW DUFOUR AND JOE ROGERS: Midway concessionaires, New York World's Fair) 15:22-5 *Ag 12 '39; 15:23-7 *Ag 19 '39. 639

May I just step inside? by John Bainbridge. (ALFRED CARL FULLER: President, Fuller Brush Company) 24:36-59 N 13 '48. 640

The mayor, by Philip Hamburger. (ROBERT F. WAGNER, JR.: Mayor, New York City) 32:39-67 Ja 26 '57; 32:39-69 F 2 '57. 641

The mayor, by Nat Hentoff. (JOHN V. LINDSAY: Mayor, New York City) 43:58-128 O 7 '67; 43:61-148 O 14 '67; 45:44-104 My 3 '69; 45:42-118 My 10 '69. 642

The mayor of Futani, by John Lardner. (TONY CUDA: Mayor of Futani, Italy) 20:32-9 My 27 '44. 643

The mayor of the fish market, by Joseph Mitchell. (HUGH G. FLOOD: House-wrecking contractor [retired]) 19:25-34 Ja 1 '44. 644

Mazie, by Joseph Mitchell. (MAZIE P. GORDON: Ticket seller, Venice Theatre on Bowery) 16:22-31 *D 21 '40. 645

"Me," by Richard O. Boyer. (MEYER DAVIS: Orchestra leader) 15:26-32 *Mr 11 '39. 646

Me--Mutt! by Kelly Coombs. (HARRY CONWAY [Bud] FISHER: Cartoonist [Mutt and Jeff]) 3:27-9 N 26 '27. 647

The measure of man, by Robert Coles. (ERIK H. ERIKSON:

Psychoanalyst) 46:51-131 N 7 '70; 46:59-138 N 14 '70. 648

The meddlers, by E. J. Kahn, Jr. (AMNESTY INTERNATIONAL: Society for freeing political prisoners) 46: 44-57 Ag 22 '70. 649

Mediator, by Fred C. Shapiro. (THEODORE KHEEL: Lawyer; labor mediator) 46:36-58 Ag 1 '70. 650

The Medici on Washington Square, by Geoffrey T. Hellman. (ALBERT EUGENE GALLATIN: Founder, manager, Museum of Living Art) 16:25-32 *Ja 18 '41. 651

The meshuggah of Manhattan, by Stanley Walker. (JOHN ROACH STRATON: Fundamentalist minister) 3:25-7 Ap 16 '27. 652

Metamorphic merchant, by Dwight Macdonald. (WILLIAM SCHLEMMER: Head, Hammacher Schlemmer & Co. [hardware]) 15:25-31 *Jy 8 '39. 653

Metamorphosis, by Joseph Wechsberg. (ARTUR RUBINSTEIN: Concert pianist) 34:47-95 N 1 '58. 654

Mickey-Mouse maker, by Gilbert Seldes. (WALT DISNEY: Motion picture cartoonist) 7:23-7 D 19 '31. 655

Middle-aged man without a horn, by Robert Lewis Taylor. (ARTIE SHAW: Jazz clarinetist; orchestra leader) 38:47-98 My 19 '62. 656

Middlewoman, by Richard O. Boyer. (ANNA ROSENBERG: Labor mediator; Regional Director, Social Security Board; Head, New York State National Recovery Administration) 14:24-9 *Ap 23 '38. 657

Mighty dealer in dollars, by John K. Winkler. (J. PIERPONT MORGAN: Financier) 4:23-6 F 2 '29; 4:27-36 F 9 '29. 658

Milkman, by Russell Lord. (HENRY WILLIAM JEFFERS: Milk distributor) 8:22-6 D 3 '32. 659

The millionaire, by Lillian Ross. (HENRY JONAS ROSENFELD: Dress manufacturer) 25:30-41 Ja 7 '50; 25: 32-44 Ja 14 '50. 660

Miss Fixit, by Margaret Case Harriman. (FANNY HOLTZ-

MANN: Lawyer for theatrical profession) 12:21-5 *Ja 30 '37; 12:22-5 *F 6 '37. 661

Miss Lily of New Orleans, by Margaret Case Harriman. (LILLIAN HELLMAN: Playwright) 17:22-33 *N 8 '41. 662

Mr. Ambassador, by Janet Flanner. (WILLIAM CHRISTIAN BULLITT: U.S. Ambassador to France) 14:32-5 *D 10 '38; 14:22-7 *D 17 '38. 663

Mr. Chairman, by Geoffrey T. Hellman. (GEORGE GORDON BATTLE: Lawyer; philanthropist; money raiser) 9: 21-5 Mr 11 '33. 664

Mr. Hunter's grave, by Joseph Mitchell. (GEORGE H. HUNTER: Chairman, Board of Trustees, African Methodist Church) 32:50-95 S 22 '56. 665

Mr. Jaeckel and a few hides, by S.N. Behrman. (RICHARD JAECKEL: Furrier) 8:22-5 *Ap 9 '32. 666

Mr. Miller and Mr. Hyde, by Margaret Case Harriman. (GILBERT MILLER: Playwright) 19:25-30 My 29 '43; 19:26-36 Je 5 '43. 667

Mister Muggsy, by William Slavens McNutt. (JOHN McGRAW: Manager, New York Giants) 1:9-10 Mr 28 '25. 668

Mr. President, by John Hersey. (HARRY S. TRUMAN: U.S. President) 27:42-56 Ap 7 '51; 27:38-55 Ap 14 '51; 27:36-61 Ap 21 '51; 27:36-55 Ap 28 '51; 27:36-53 My 5 '51. 669

Mr. President, by Henry F. Pringle. (JAMES BRYANT CONANT: President, Harvard University) 12:20-4 *S 12 '36; 12:23-7 *S 19 '36. 670

Mr. Public Printer, by Geoffrey T. Hellman. (AUGUSTUS E. GIEGENGACK: Head, U.S. Government Printing Office) 19:24-33 Je 12 '43; 19:28-39 Je 19 '43; 19: 24-30 Je 26 '43. 671

Mr. Secretary, by Philip Hamburger. (DEAN GOODERHAM ACHESON: U.S. Secretary of State) 25:39-53 N 12 '49; 25:40-61 N 19 '49. 672

Mr. X and mankind's greatest blessing, by George R. Leighton and Strother Holland Walker. (MORRIS SIEGEL:

Insurance expert) 17:19-27 *Je 28 '41 673

Mrs. Firebrand, by John S. Martin. (MABEL WALKER WILLEBRANDT: Reformer; lawyer; Assistant U.S. Attorney-General) 4:23-6 F 16 '29. 674

Mnemonist, by Richard H. Rovere. (BRUNO FURST: Mnemonist; hypnotist; handwriting expert) 22:32-43 F 23 '46. 675

Model T, by Niven Busch, Jr. (HENRY FORD: Automobile manufacturer) 4:29-31 Mr 3 '28; 4:29-31 Mr 10 '28; 4:33-8 Mr 17 '28; 4:26-8 Mr 24 '28. 676

No entry 677

Modern, by Robert M. Coates. (WILLIAM LESCAZE: Architect) 12:28-34 *D 12 '36. 678

The mongoose, by Jack Murphy. (ARCHIBALD LEE [Archie] MOORE: Prizefighter) 37:61-112 N 11 '61. 679

The moon's best friend, by E.J. Kahn, Jr. (CLYDE FISHER: Curator-in-Chief, Hayden Planetarium) 16:23-8 *D 28 '40. 680

More bounce to the ounce, by E.J. Kahn, Jr. (WALTER S. MACK, JR.: Chairman, Pepsi-Cola Company) 26:32-49 Jy 1 '50; 26:28-43 Jy 8 '50. 681

A mousetrap in the Bronx, by Creighton Peet. (HALSEY WILLIAM WILSON: Publisher, Readers' Guide to Periodical Literature) 14:25-8 *O 29 '38. 682

Moviemaker, by Robert Lewis Taylor. (ROBERT J. FLAHERTY: Documentary film producer) 25:30-45 Je 11 '49; 25:28-41 Je 18 '49; 25:28-43 Je 25 '49. 683

Moving out, by Calvin Tomkins. (ROBERT RAUSCHENBERG: Artist) 40:39-105 F 29 '64. 684

The M-S-M, by Alva Johnston. (ALPHEUS GEER: Philanthropist; reformer; Director of Marshall Stillman Movement) 5:23-6 My 11 '29. 685

The music is more important, by Whitney Balliett. (KEN-

NETH [Red] NORVO: Vibraharp player) 44:36-47 D 28 '68. 686

Music with meals, by Gilbert Seldes. (EMIL COLEMAN: Orchestra leader) 11:26-30 *O 19 '35. 687

Musical mornings, by Mary Van Rensselaer Thayer. (ALBERT MORRIS BAGBY: Patron of arts; socialite) 14:19-25 *D 31 '38. 688

Musician, by Robert Lewis Taylor. (PERCY GRAINGER: Composer; concert pianist) 23:29-37 Ja 31 '48; 23:32-9 *F 7 '48; 23:32-40 *F 14 '48. 689

Music's faithful servant, by César Saerchinger. (ARTUR SCHNABEL: Concert pianist) 14:21-5 *Ap 2 '38. 690

"My lawyer," by Alva Johnston. (MAX D. STEUER: Lawyer) 7:24-7 My 16 '31; 7:21-4 My 23 '31. 691

The mysteries of Rudolfo, by Alexander Woollcott. (RUDOLF K. KOMMER: Theatrical producer) 9:20-3 Mr 18 '33. 692

Nagelmacker's way, by Joseph Wechsberg. (LEO CESOLI: European train conductor) 32:29-49 *Ag 11 '56. 693

A name is made, by Elizabeth Armstrong. (MARION TALLEY: Singer, Metropolitan Opera Company) 3:18-20 F 11 '28. 694

Napoleon of books, by Avery Strakosch. (A.S.W. ROSENBACH: Book dealer) 4:25-8 Ap 14 '28. 695

The national idea man, by Alva Johnston. (BEARDSLEY RUML: Economist; author; government advisor) 20:28-35 F 10 '45; 21:26-34 F 17 '45; 21:30-41 F 24 '45. 696

Neanderthal, by Dwight Macdonald. (LEONOR F. LOREE: President, Delaware & Hudson Railroad) 9:18-21 *Je 3 '33. 697

The new crusade, by Milton MacKaye. (PAULINE MORTON SABIN: Politician; President, Women's Organization for National Prohibition Reform) 8:20-4 O 22 '32. 698

The new theologian, by Ved Mehta. (NEW THEOLOGY AND THEOLOGIANS) 41:63-153 N 13 '65; 41:60-144 N 20 '65; 41:65-169 N 27 '65. 699

New woman, by Helena Huntington Smith. (ELEANOR SMITH: Aviatrix) 6:28-31 My 10 '30. 700

New York or bust, by William McGuire and Mark Murphy. (U.S.S. NEW YORK: Battleship) 21:28-41 O 27 '45. 701

A New Yorker who sings, by Clare Peeler. (REINALD WERRENRATH: Concert singer) 1:9-10 O 3 '25. 702

News photographer, by Alva Johnston. (EDWARD N. JACKSON: Photographer, New York Daily News) 10:28-31 *D 1 '34; 10:28-31 *D 8 '34. 703

Nize Sam, ett opp all the G. O. P., by Oliver H. P. Garrett. (SAM KOENIG: Politician) 2:15-16 Mr 6 '26. 704

No feeling of falling, by Robert Lewis Taylor. (JACQUES ANDRÉ ISTEL: Parachutist) 34:42-73 Ja 24 '59. 705

No hero, by Henry F. Pringle. (CHARLES E. ROSENDAHL: Aviator, lighter-than-air) 8:22-5 *Mr 26 '32. 706

No more lawyers, by Alva Johnston. (GEORGE WASHINGTON OLVANY: Judge, New York Court of General Sessions) 7:22-5 Ja 9 '32. 707

No suave inflections, by A.J. Liebling. (OLE OLSEN AND CHIC JOHNSON: Comedians, stagers of Hellz-a-Poppin) 14:20-5 *Ja 28 '39. 708

Noble merchandise, by Alva Johnston. (JOSEPH DUVEEN: Art dealer) 4:29-31 Ap 21 '28. 709

Noblesse oblige, by Helena Huntington Smith. (ELEANOR ROOSEVELT [Mrs. Franklin D.]: Author; lecturer; statesman) 6:23-5 Ap 5 '30. 710

North of Boston, by Raymond Holden. (ROBERT FROST: Poet) 7:24-7 *Je 6 '31. 711

Not like taking the waters, by Robert Shaplen. (BRUCE SMITH: Director, Institute of Public Administration) 30:39-65 *F 27 '54. 712

Not seen and/or less seen, by Calvin Tomkins. (MARCEL DUCHAMP: Artist) 40:37-93 F 6 '65. 713

Notes on a soldier, by Marquis James. (JOHN J. PERSHING: General, U.S. Army) 1:11-12 N 7 '25. 714

Notes on a well-known citizen, by John K. Winkler. (JOHN D. ROCKEFELLER: Industrialist) 2:16-20 Ja 22 '27; 2:24-9 Ja 29 '27. 715

Notes on an American phenomenon, by John K. Winkler. (WILLIAM RANDOLPH HEARST: Newspaper publisher) 3:25-7 Ap 23 '27; 3:25-8 Ap 30 '27; 3:23-6 My 7 '27; 3:24-7 My 14 '27; 3:23-6 My 21 '27. 716

Nothing much to it, by Richard H. Rovere. (EDWARD JOSEPH FLYNN: Lawyer; Chairman, Democratic National Committee) 21:28-41 S 8 '45. 717

Nothing up his sleeve, by E.J. Kahn, Jr. (JOSEPH DUNNENGER: Magician) 17:26-36 N 29 '41. 718

No. 11 Downing Street, by Mollie Panter-Downes. (STAFFORD CRIPPS: British statesman) 18:19-29 Ag 8 '42. 719

No. 1 picaroon, by Richard O. Boyer. (ARTHUR URBANE DILLEY: Oriental rug dealer; author) 15:24-30 *S 2 '39. 720

Odd man, by Geoffrey T. Hellman. (ROBERT L. RIPLEY: "Believe it or Not" cartoonist; radio personality) 16:20-4 *Ag 31 '40; 16:27-30 *S 7 '40. 721

The odyssey of the oblong blur, by Philip Hamburger. (NORMAN CORWIN: Radio script writer and director) 23:36-49 Ap 5 '47. 722

Of thee I sing, Baby, by John O'Hara. (GRAYCE [no last name given]: Chorus girl) 8:23-5 O 15 '32. 723

Office-boy of destiny, by Alexander Woollcott. (SAM ZOLOTOW: Publisher, Advance Theatrical Guide) 4:28-30 O 13 '28. 724

Oh, hawk of mercy! by Robert Lewis Taylor. (ROSALIE BARROW EDGE: Chairman, Emergency Conservation Committee) 24:31-45 Ap 17 '48. 725

Old Dick and young Dick, by Robert F. Kelley. (RICHARD

G. GLENDON, SR. AND RICHARD G. GLENDON, JR.: Crew coach, U.S. Naval Academy; crew coach, Columbia University) 4:25-7 Je 16 '28. 726

The old house at home, by Joseph Mitchell. (McSORLEY'S: Saloon) 16:20-6 *Ap 13 '40. 727

The old man, by John Hersey. (BERNARD MANNES BARUCH: Financier; speculator; government advisor) 23:28-37 Ja 3 '48; 23:30-40 Ja 10 '48; 23:30-41 Ja 17 '48. 728

The Old Man, by John R. Tunis. (A COLLEGE FOOTBALL COACH [composite portrait]) 5:30-2 N 23 '29. 729

The old Max, by Margaret Case Harriman. (MAX GORDON: Theatrical producer) 17:22-30 *Mr 29 '41. 730

Old monotonous, by S.N. Behrman. (ROBERT EMMET SHERWOOD: Playwright) 16:33-41 *Je 1 '40; 16:23-36 Je 8 '40. 731

Old reliable, by Richard O. Boyer. (THOMAS DAVID HENRICH: Baseball player) 25:33-45 Je 4 '49. 732

The omelet of A. MacLeish, by Edmund Wilson. (ARCHIBALD MacLEISH: Poet) 14:23-4 *Ja 14 '39. 733

The omnibus diplomat, by A.J. Liebling. (ANTHONY J. DREXEL BIDDLE, JR.: U.S. Ambassador to Polish, Belgian, Netherlands and Norwegian governments in London) 18:22-30 Je 6 '42; 18:23-35 Je 13 '42; 18:23-32 Je 20 '42. 734

On the formula, by Andy Logan. (HOWARD BERKEY BISHOP: Crusader against tobacco habit) 21:25-35 S 1 '45. 735

On the square, by Milton MacKaye. (S. KLEIN: Clothing manufacturer, distributor) 8:17-21 Je 25 '32. 736

On the tide of the times, by William Whitworth. (HOMER A. TOMLINSON: Bishop, Church of God) 42:67-108 S 24 '66. 737

On the up, by Richard F. Warner. (GEORGE UPTON HAR-

VEY: Borough President, New York City) 6:24-7 My 31 '30. 738

One beat to the bar, by Robert Lewis Taylor. (MERLE EVANS: Band leader, Ringling Brothers and Barnum & Bailey Circus) 31:47-73 Ap 16 '55; 31:39-64 Ap 23 '55. 739

The one big name, by Robert Lewis Taylor. (MURRAY KORMAN: Photographer) 18:19-29 O 3 '42. 740

One hundred per cent American, by Waldo Frank. (HORACE B. LIVERIGHT: Publisher) 1:9-10 O 10 '25. 741

One jump to four miles, by A.J. Liebling. (EDDIE ARCARO: Jockey) 14:16-21 *Jy 30 '38. 742

One of the boys, by Oliver H.P. Garrett. (RUTH PRATT [Mrs. John T.]: Member, New York City Board of Aldermen) 2:21-2 Ap 24 '26. 743

One sweet little business, by Angelica Gibbs. (VERONICA DENGEL: Beautician) 24:26-37 Jy 31 '48. 744

One thing led to another, by Robert Rice. (MARY STINSON PILLSBURY LORD: U.S. representative to U.N. Commission on Human Rights) 29:37-56 My 16 '53. 745

One-man group, by Janet Flanner. (PABLO RUIZ y PICASSO: Painter) 15:28-33 *D 9 '39. 746

One-man lobby, by Robert Shaplen. (SIRDAR JAGJIT SINGH: Interpreter; president, India League of America) 27:35-55 Mr 24 '51. 747

One-man think tank, by William Whitworth. (RICHARD M. SCAMMON: Statistician; political scientist) 45:50-89 S 20 '69. 748

The one-ton pencil, by Thomas Whiteside. (FRED W. FRIENDLY: Television producer) 37:41-88 F 17 '62. 749

Ooff!! (sob!) eep!! (gulp!) zowie!!! by E.J. Kahn, Jr. (AL CAPP: Comic strip cartoonist) 23:45-57 N 29 '47; 23:46-61 D 6 '47. 750

Ooty, by Mollie Panter-Downes. (OOTACAMUND, INDIA) 43:48-131 Mr 4 '67; 43:57-124 Mr 11 '67. 751

Opera and the dean, by Hollister Noble. (WILLIAM JAMES HENDERSON: Music critic) 2:23-5 O 30 '26. 752

Orchestra, by Joseph Wechsberg. (CLEVELAND ORCHESTRA) 46:38-68 My 30 '70. 753

Organizer, by Peter Matthiessen. (CESAR CHAVEZ: Farm labor organizer) 45:42-85 Je 21 '69; 45:43-71 Je 28 '69. 754

Orlando in Mount Kisco, by Winthrop Sargeant. (GIAN CARLO MENOTTI: Opera composer) 39:49-89 My 4 '63. 755

'Orrible woman, by Joseph Bryan, III. (ROSA LEWIS: Proprietor, Cavendish Hotel) 9:23-6 *S 16 '33. 756

Our own Lenin, by Alva Johnston. (WILLIAM ZEBULON FOSTER: Presidential candidate, U.S. Communist Party) 6:19-22 Je 28 '30. 757

Out here again, by Whitney Balliett. (MARY LOU WILLIAMS: Jazz pianist; composer) 40:52-85 My 2 '64. 758

Out of the dark, by Brendan Gill. (GEORGES SIMENON: Novelist) 28:35-53 Ja 24 '53. 759

Out of the ego chamber, by Jeremy Bernstein. (ARTHUR C. CLARKE: Science fiction author) 45:40-65 Ag 9 '69. 760

Out of the past, by Milton MacKaye. (GEORGE BRINTON McCLELLAN: Mayor, New York City; historian) 8:21-5 My 28 '32. 761

Over Babel, by Niven Busch, Jr. (IRVING T. BUSH: Originator, director, Bush Terminal) 3:26-8 Ap 2 '27. 762

The owner of Ben Finney, by Alexander Woollcott. (EGON [German shepherd dog]) 4:25-8 My 12 '28. 763

Paddy of the R.A.F., by A.J. Liebling. (BRENDAN FINUCANE: Flight Lieutenant, Royal Air Force) 17:37-49 D 6 '41. 764

The paid piper, by Niven Busch, Jr. (PAUL WHITEMAN: Orchestra leader) 2:25-7 N 27 '26. 765

The Palm Beach architect, by Alva Johnston. (ADDISON

MIZNER: Architect) 28:46-93 N 22 '52; 28:46-94 N 29 '52; 28:48-64 D 6 '52; 28:42-85 D 13 '52. 766

Pandora and the doctor, by Niven Busch, Jr. (JOHN FREDERICK ERDMANN: Surgeon) 2:32-4 D 4 '26. 767

Parachute jumper, by Geoffrey T. Hellman. (JOE CRANE: National champion parachute jumper) 8:16-19 D 31 '32. 768

Paramount's patriarch, by Niven Busch, Jr. (ADOLPH ZUKOR: President, Paramount Famous-Lasky) 5:29-33 S 7 '29. 769

Partners, by E.J. Kahn, Jr. (EDWARD GREEN HARRIGAN AND TONY HART, pseud.: Variety-show, musical comedy team) 31:42-67 Mr 19 '55; 31:39-72 Mr 26 '55; 31:45-67 Ap 2 '55; 31:41-81 Ap 9 '55. 770

Party linesman, by John McCarten. (EARL BROWDER: General Secretary, U.S. Communist Party) 14:20-4 *S 24 '38; 14:22-7 *O 1 '38. 771

The passionate professor, by Heywood Broun. (CHARLES TOWNSEND COPELAND: Professor of Rhetoric and Oratory, Harvard University) 3:20-2 Ja 21 '28. 772

Paterfamilias, by Jane Kramer. (ALLEN GINSBERG: Poet) 44:32-73 Ag 17 '68; 44:38-91 Ag 24 '68. 773

Patron of the preemies, by A.J. Liebling. (MARTIN A. COUNEY: Physician; specialist in premature births) 15:20-4 *Je 3 '39. 774

Pause for reflection, by Berton Roueché. (LOUIS HAFT: Owner, Haft Glass Company) 29:39-55 My 23 '53. 775

A peaceable town, by Berton Roueché. (STAPLETON, NEBRASKA) 46:29-40 Ja 2 '71. 776

Peacemaker, by Robert Shaplen. (ARTHUR JOSEPH GOLDBERG: Lawyer; U.S. Secretary of Labor; United Nations representative; Justice, U.S. Supreme Court) 38:49-112 Ap 7 '62; 38:49-105 Ap 14 '62. 777

Peasant by paradox, by Waldo Frank. (CARL SANDBURG: Poet) 1:13-14 N 14 '25. 778

Pedagogue, by Helena Huntington Smith. (GEORGE J. RYAN: Member, New York City Board of Education) 6:29-32 F 22 '30. 779

Penny-arcade philanthropist, by Robert Rice. (WILLIAM RABKIN: Manufacturer of coin-operated amusement machines) 24:36-48 O 16 '48. 780

The perennial freshman, by Robert E. Sherwood. (HAROLD LLOYD: Motion picture actor) 1:15-16 Ja 30 '26. 781

The perfect glow, by Philip Hamburger. (OSCAR HAMMERSTEIN, II: Song writer; musical comedy writer) 27:35-48 My 12 '51; 27:45-63 My 19 '51. 782

Perfume and politics, by Janet Flanner. (FRANÇOIS COTY: Perfume maker; journalist; politician) 6:22-5 My 3 '30. 783

The pervasive musician, by Robert Rice. (LEONARD BERNSTEIN: Conductor, New York Philharomic; composer) 33:37-63 Ja 11 '58; 33:36-65 Ja 18 '58. 784

Phenomenon, by E.J. Kahn, Jr. (FRANCIS ALBERT [Frank] SINATRA: Popular singer) 22:36-48 O 26 '46; 22:37-54 N 2 '46; 22:36-53 N 9 '46. 785

Philosopher, by Hamilton Basso. (JEAN WAHL: Philosopher) 21:27-41 My 12 '45. 786

Philosopher in a new key, by Winthrop Sargeant. (SUSANNE K. LANGER: Philosopher of aesthetics; author) 36:67-100 D 3 '60. 787

Philosophy and figure eights, by Robert Lewis Taylor. (PIERRE BRUNET: Senior professional, New York Skating Club) 30:28-41 D 25 '54. 788

Physical culture, by Robert Lewis Taylor. (BERNARR MacFADDEN: Publisher; physical fitness advocate) 26:39-51 O 14 '50; 26:39-52 O 21 '50; 26:37-51 O 28 '50. 789

Physician in the flower beds, by Eugene Kinkead. (CYNTHIA WESTCOTT: Plant pathologist) 28:26-43 Jy 26 '52. 790

Piano man, by Bruce Bliven, Jr. (WILLIAM HUPFER:

Piano tone regulator) 29:39-63 My 9 '53. 791

Pigeon man's progress, by G. F. T. Ryall. (HIRSCH JACOBS: Racehorse trainer) 15:20-4 *Ag 5 '39. 792

Pilgrim's progress, by Morton M. Hunt. (PILGRIM STATE HOSPITAL, NEW YORK: Mental institution) 37:51-116 S 30 '61; 37:67-124 O 7 '61. 793

The Pine Barrens, by John McPhee. (PINE BARRENS: New Jersey forest land) 43:67-147 N 25 '67; 43:66-144 D 2 '67. 794

Pioneer, by Janet Flanner. (MAIN BOCHER: Couturier) 15:24-8 *Ja 13 '40. 795

Place and leave with, by St. Clair McKelway. (HARRY GROSSMAN: Process-server) 11:23-6 *Ag 24 '35; 11:21-4 *Ag 31 '35. 796

The playboy of politics, by John K. Winkler. (NICHOLAS LONGWORTH: Speaker, U.S. House of Representatives) 2:15-16 Ap 10 '26. 797

The player, by Lillian Ross. (KIM STANLEY, MICHAEL REDGRAVE, ELI WALLACH, INGRID BERGMAN, WILLIAM HOLDEN, HUME CRONYN, VLADIMIR SOKOLOF: Actors) 37:59-124 O 21 '61. 798

The player, by Lillian Ross. (HENRY FONDA, MAURINE STAPLETON, ROD STEIGER, KATHARINE CORNELL, ZERO MOSTEL, MARIA SCHELL, CEDRIC HARDWICKE: Actors) 37:61-132 O 28 '61. 799

The player, by Lillian Ross. (RICHARD WIDMARK, GERALDINE PAGE, JASON ROBARDS, SIMONE SIGNORET, ANTHONY PERKINS, JOHN GIELGUD, WALTER MATTHAU: Actors) 37:60-125 N 4 '61. 800

Playwright, by S.N. Behrman. (FERENC MOLNÁR: Playwright) 22:28-41 My 25 '46; 22:32-46 Je 1 '46; 22:32-47 Je 8 '46. 801

Please, darling, bring three to seven, by Winthrop Sargeant. (JEAN ROSENTHAL: Theatre lighting expert) 31:33-53 *F 4 '56. 802

Plenipotentiary, by E.J. Kahn, Jr. (WILLIAM AVERELL

HARRIMAN: U.S. statesman) 28:41-67 My 3 '52; 28:36-57 My 10 '52. 803

Plush and gaslight, by Joseph Gollomb. (B.L.M. BATES: Owner and manager, Murray Hill Hotel) 5:23-6 Je 15 '29. 804

The plywood baron, by Alva Johnston. (LAWRENCE OTTINGER: President, United States Plywood Corporation) 21:28-35 D 22 '45; 21:24-33 D 29 '45. 805

Poet in steel, by Milton MacKaye. (OTHMAR HERMANN AMMANN: Chief Engineer, Port of New York Authority) 10:23-7 Je 2 '34. 806

Poet's progress, by Murdock Pemberton. (HARRY KEMP: Poet) 1:9-10 Ag 8 '25. 807

Polo's little man, by Meyer Berger. (PETE BOSTWICK: Polo player) 14:16-20 *S 3 '38. 808

Polymers everywhere, by Morton M. Hunt. (HERMAN F. MARK: Scientist; Professor of Organic Chemistry, Polytechnic Institute of Brooklyn) 34:48-72 S 13 '58; 34:46-83 S 20 '58. 809

Poor little rich boy, by Waldo Frank. (HENDRIK WILLEM Van LOON: Author; historian) 2:19-20 Je 19 '26. 810

Portrait in black paint, with a very sparing use of whitewash, by Elinor Wylie. (ELINOR WYLIE: Poet) 3:24 Mr 19 '27; 4:20 D 29 '28. 811

Portrait of a Dutchman, by Niven Busch, Jr. (WALTER HAGEN: Golfer) 3:17-19 Je 11 '27. 812

"Portrait of a man with red hair," by Alexander Woollcott. (HARPO MARX: Comedian; actor) 4:33-6 D 1 '28. 813

Powder your face with sunshine, by E.J. Kahn, Jr. (GUY LOMBARDO: Popular orchestra leader) 32:35-49 Ja 5 '57; 32:35-57 Ja 12 '57. 814

A powerful cue, by Robert Lewis Taylor. (WILLIAM FREDERICK HOPPE: Professional billiard player) 16:24-33 *N 16 '40. 815

A powerful sense of his duty, by Thomas Whiteside. (HEN-

RIK KURT CARLSEN: Merchant ship captain) 34:49-103 D 13 '58. 816

Powerful sword, by Winthrop Sargeant. (ZUBIN MEHTA: Symphony orchestra conductor) 43:53-92 D 16 '67. 817

Powers model, by E.J. Kahn, Jr. (CELESTE GHEEN: Model) 16:26-33 *S 14 '40. 818

Practical Orpheus, by Samuel Chotzinoff. (LEOPOLD STOKOWSKI: Conductor, Philadelphia Orchestra) 7:22-6 Mr 21 '31. 819

A prelude, by Edmund Wilson. (EDMUND WILSON: Author; critic) 43:50-131 Ap 29 '67; 43:52-149 My 6 '67; 43:54-157 My 13 '67. 820

The President, by Henry F. Pringle. (HERBERT HOOVER: U.S. President) 6:20-3 D 27 '30; 6:22-5 Ja 3 '31; 6:22-5 Ja 10 '31. 821

The President, by Henry F. Pringle. (FRANKLIN DELANO ROOSEVELT: U.S. President) 10:20-5 Je 16 '34; 10:20-4 Je 23 '34; 10:20-4 Je 30 '34. 822

Prexy, by Robert Lewis Taylor. (MICHAEL JOSEPH DELEHANTY: President, Civil Service school) 17:24-30 *My 24 '41. 823

Prime Minister/Premier Ministre, by Edith Iglauer. (PIERRE TRUDEAU: Prime Minister, Canada) 45:36-60 Jy 5 '69. 824

A prince of Broadway, by Brock Pemberton. (JOE LEBLANG: Theatrical ticket agent) 1:11-12 Ja 2 '26. 825

A prince of the city, by Joseph Wechsberg. (SIEGMUND G. WARBURG: Merchant banker) 42:45-78 Ap 9 '66. 826

Princess Alice, by Marquis James. (ALICE ROOSEVELT LONGWORTH: Socialite) 1:9-10 F 28 '25. 827

The principal, by Nat Hentoff. (ELLIOTT SHAPIRO: Elementary school principal) 42:52-119 My 7 '66. 828

Printer, by Geoffrey T. Hellman. (BERTRAM A. POWERS: President, New York Typographical Union No. 6) 46:43-81 Mr 7 '70. 829

Private detective, by Alva Johnston. (RAYMOND C. SCHINDLER: Head, private detective agency) 19: 26-36 Jy 3 '43; 19:26-37 Jy 10 '43; 19:27-33 Jy 17 '43. 830

Prizefighter to gentleman--en route, by Paul Gallico. (MAX ADALBERT BAER: Prizefighter) 10:20-4 *Je 9 '34. 831

The prodigal father, by Alexander Woollcott. (FRANK LLOYD WRIGHT: Architect) 6:22-5 Jy 19 '30. 832

Prodigy's progress, by Winthrop Sargeant. (YEHUDI MENUHIN: Concert violinist) 31:50-85 *O 8 '55; 31:49-68 *O 15 '55. 833

Production man, by Matthew Josephson. (WILLIAM S. KNUDSEN: President, General Motors Corporation; Member, Advisory Commission to Council of National Defense) 17:22-32 *Mr 8 '41; 17:26-36 *Mr 15 '41; 17:25-36 *Mr 22 '41. 834

Professor in politics, by Milton MacKaye. (JOSEPH D. McGOLDRICK: Comptroller, New York City; Professor of Government, Columbia University) 10:19-22 Ag 11 '34. 835

Professor sea gull, by Joseph Mitchell. (JOE GOULD: Bohemian) 18:28-43 D 12 '42. 836

No entry 837

Professor's progress, by Helena Huntington Smith. (JOHN ERSKINE: Professor of English, Columbia University; author) 3:27-9 D 10 '27. 838

Prometheus bound, by Geoffrey T. Hellman. (JOSEPH P. DAY: Real estate auctioneer) 9:18-22 My 27 '33. 839

Prophet, 1931, by Geoffrey T. Hellman. (STEPHEN S. WISE: Rabbi, Jewish Institute of Religion) 7:22-5 N 7 '31. 840

Prophet of doom, by Henry F. Pringle. (ROGER W. BABSON: Economist; Director, Babson Park) 5:23-5 F 15 '30. 841

A Proust in Wall Street, by John Brooks. (WALTER KNOWLTON GUTMAN: Investment counselor; art critic) 35:41-70 Je 20 '59. 842

The prudent pioneer, by Robert Rice. (ALLEN BALCOM DuMONT: Inventor; pioneer in television industry) 26:35-53 Ja 27 '51. 843

The public be served, by J. M. Flagler. (STANLEY M. ISAACS: New York City Council member) 35:59-96 D 12 '59; 35:41-71 *D 19 '59. 844

Public man, by Milton MacKaye. (PAUL DRENNAN CRAVATH: Lawyer; corporation director) 7:21-4 Ja 2 '32. 845

Public relations, by Alva Johnston. (RUSSELL BIRDWELL: Press agent; publicity man) 20:26-32 Ag 19 '44; 20:26-34 Ag 26 '44; 20:24-8 S 2 '44; 20:30-8 S 9 '44. 846

Public servant, by Milton MacKaye. (ROBERT MOSES: Chairman, New York State Council of Parks) 10:24-6 *Mr 10 '34. 847

Publisher, by Geoffrey T. Hellman. (BENNETT A. CERF: President, Random House; radio and television personality) 35:48-92 My 9 '59; 35:49-84 My 16 '59. 848

Publisher, by Geoffrey T. Hellman. (ALFRED A. KNOPF: Publisher) 24:44-57 N 20 '48; 24:36-52 N 27 '48; 24:40-53 D 4 '48. 849

Publisher, by Geoffrey T. Hellman. (DOROTHY SCHIFF: Owner and publisher, New York Post) 44:37-65 Ag 10 '68. 850

Publisher, by A. J. Liebling. (ROY WILSON HOWARD: Publisher, Scripps-Howard Newspapers) 17:19-26 *Ag 2 '41; 17:20-9 *Ag 9 '41; 17:20-7 *Ag 16 '41; 17:23-30 *Ag 23 '41. 851

The Pullman Theseus, by Joel Sayre. (JIM LONDOS: Professional wrestler) 8:26-9 *Mr 5 '32. 852

Pulse on the public, by Howard Whitman. (JACK KAPP: President, Decca Records) 16:22-6 *Ag 24 '40. 853

Quest for Mollie, by A. J. Liebling. (KARL WARNER:

American soldier) 21:28-36 My 26 '45; 21:24-35 Je 2 '45. 854

A question of parity, by Jeremy Bernstein. (TSUNG-DAO LEE AND CHEN NING YANG: Theoretical physicists; Nobel Prize winners) 38:49-104 My 12 '62. 855

Quiet, beneficient things, by Ved Mehta. (B.H. BLACKWELL, LTD. AND BASIL BLACKWELL: Book store; owner) 40:63-126 O 31 '64. 856

The quiet guy in Lindy's, by E.J. Kahn, Jr. (ABE LASTFOGEL: Theatrical agent, U.S.O. shows) 22:34-46 Ap 20 '46; 22:27-41 Ap 27 '46. 857

The rabbit that bit the bulldog, by Heywood Broun. (HEYWOOD BROUN: Newspaper columnist) 3:18-22 O 1 '27. 858

Rampant but respectable, by Helena Huntington Smith. (LILLIAN D. WALD: Philanthropist; Founder, Henry Street Settlement) 5:32-5 D 14 '29. 859

Rare as music, by Waldo Frank. (LEO ORNSTEIN: Concert pianist) 1:9-10 D 19 '25. 860

Razor on horseback, by John Bainbridge. (HIDEKI TOJO: Premier of Japan) 19:26-38 Ap 17 '43. 861

Realtor, by Robert M. Coates. (FRED F. FRENCH: Realtor; building contractor) 5:22-5 Je 1 '29. 862

Recurrent and irreducible, by Angelica Gibbs. (JESSICA GARRETSON COSGRAVE: Educator; founder of Finch Junior College) 22:35-51 Ap 13 '46. 863

The red and the blue, by S.N. Behrman. (AVRAAM ELIA [Joe] KAZAN: Author; rug merchant) 21:30-45 Ap 21 '45. 864

Red hot, by Niven Busch, Jr. (HARRY S. STEVENS: Concessionaire) 4:23-5 Ag 11 '28. 865

Red, white, and blue, by Henry F. Pringle. (HARRY LAITY BOWLBY: Protestant minister; General Secretary, Lord's Day Alliance) 5:30-3 S 28 '29. 866

Reformed spellbinder, by Alva Johnston. (MARTIN J. LIT-

TLETON: Orator) 8:18-22 Ag 20 '32. 867

The regular, by George Woodward. (JOSEPH P. PRENDIVILLE: Staff-sergeant, U.S. Army) 20:23-31 Ag 5 '44. 868

A reputation in swans, by Mark Murphy. (GEORGE DUDLEY TILLEY: Operator, ornamental-bird farm) 18:21-7 Jy 11 '42. 869

Resources and responsibilities, by E.J. Kahn, Jr. (DAVID ROCKEFELLER: President, Chase Manhattan Bank) 40:37-83 Ja 9 '65; 40:40-73 Ja 16 '65. 870

The restless baker, by Robert Lewis Taylor. (PAUL DEAN ARNOLD: Owner of bakery) 33:49-80 D 14 '57. 871

The revel of the earth, by Mary McCarthy. (VENICE) 32:27-58 *Jy 7 '56; 32:29-64 *Jy 14 '56. 872

Revolution's number one boy, by John McCarten. (CLIFFORD ODETS: Playwright) 13:21-7 *Ja 22 '38. 873

Rhythm in my mind, by Whitney Balliett. (EARL [Father] HINES: Jazz pianist; orchestra leader) 40:39-57 Ja 2 '65. 874

Rickard rounds up the rubes, by W.O. McGeehan. (GEORGE L. [Tex] RICKARD: Director, Madison Square Garden) 1:17-18 D 12 '25. 875

The right light, by Joseph Wechsberg. (ABE H. FEDER: Lighting designer) 36:49-84 O 22 '60. 876

The rivermen, by Joseph Mitchell. (HARRY LYONS: Barge and small boat owner) 35:42-111 Ap 4 '59. 877

Robin Hood, 1930, by Samuel Chotzinoff. (ABRAHAM FLEXNER: Educator; philanthropist; Secretary, Rockefeller Foundation General Education Board) 6:29-32 N 22 '30. 878

The rolling historian, by Robert Lewis Taylor. (BRYAN HANNON: Historian; author; streetcar driver) 22:28-39 Mr 2 '46. 879

Romance, incorporated, by Margaret K. Leech. (ALICE

FOOTE MacDOUGALL: Restaurant owner) 3:21-3 F 4 '28. 880

A roomful of Hovings, by John McPhee. (THOMAS P. F. HOVING: Parks Commissioner, New York City; Director, Metropolitan Museum of Art) 43:49-137 My 20 '67. 881

The Roper complex, by Herbert Reed. (WILLIAM W. ROPER: Football coach, Princeton University; politician) 2:25-7 N 13 '26. 882

Rouge, impair, et manque, by Joseph Wechsberg. (GASTON RAYMOND: Croupier at Monte Carlo) 25:25-36 Jy 9 '49. 883

Roughneck and romancer, by Maxwell Bodenheim. (EUGENE O'NEILL: Playwright) 1:17-18 F 6 '26. 884

Roumania's royal saleslady, by John K. Winkler. (MARIE, QUEEN OF ROUMANIA) 2:26-7 O 23 '26. 885

Route salesman, by Robert M. Coates. (WALTER REISELIN: Milk delivery man) 11:18-22 *Je 22 '35. 886

The rules of the game, by Francine du Plessix Gray. (IVAN ILLICH: Roman Catholic priest; educator; author) 46:40-92 Ap 25 '70. 887

Run, Helen! by Herbert Warren Wind. (HAZEL HOTCHKISS WIGHTMAN: Tennis player; coach; author) 28:31-49 Ag 30 '52. 888

Rural New Yorker, by Arthur Bartlett. (JOHN J. DILLON: Publisher, Rural New-Yorker) 14:25-9 *My 21 '38. 889

Rural New Yorker, by Russell Lord. (REXFORD GUY TUGWELL: U.S. Under-Secretary of Agriculture; Professor of Economics, Columbia University) 11:20-4 *Mr 23 '35; 11:22-6 *Mr 30 '35. 890

Rushville's renowned son-in-law, by Janet Flanner. (WENDELL LEWIS WILLKIE: U.S. Presidential candidate; business executive; lawyer) 16:27-42 *O 12 '40. 891

Russian firebird, by Janet Flanner. (IGOR STRAVINSKY: Composer; conductor) 10:23-8 *Ja 5 '35. 892

Sailmaker, by Anthony Bailey. (FREDERICK E. HOOD: Sailmaker) 43:34-73 Ag 26 '67. 893

Saint Al, by Percy Hammond. (A.H. WOODS: Theatrical producer) 3:25-7 F 26 '27. 894

St. George and the dragnet, by Wolcott Gibbs and John Bainbridge. (THOMAS EDMUND DEWEY: District attorney, New York City; Governor, New York State; Presidential candidate) 16:24-38 *My 25 '40. 895

St. George of Manhattan, by Milton MacKaye. (WILLIAM TRAVERS JEROME: Reformer; District Attorney, Manhattan) 7:19-23 Ja 30 '32. 896

Saint in politics, by Alva Johnston. (CHARLES H. TUTTLE: U.S. District Attorney; lawyer) 5:23-6 Mr 23 '29. 897

Salome redivivus, by John K. Winkler. (MARY GARDEN: Opera singer) 2:31-3 D 11 '26. 898

Sam Drebin, by William Slavens McNutt. (SAM DREBIN: Soldier of fortune) 1:13-14 My 2 '25. 899

The sassafras hawk, by Geoffrey T. Hellman. (J. OTIS SWIFT: Nature Editor, *New York World-Telegram*) 17:21-9 *My 31 '41. 900

The scholar in politics, by Alva Johnston. (JOHN P. O'BRIEN: Mayor, New York City) 9:18-21 Jy 1 '33; 9:17-20 Jy 8 '33. 901

The scholarly skipper, by James Robbins. (CHARLES FRANCIS ADAMS: Lawyer; politician; Treasurer of Harvard University; yachtsman) 2:17-18 S 4 '26. 902

A scientific Santa Claus, by John K. Winkler. (JOHN D. ROCKEFELLER, JR.: Industrialist; philanthropist) 4:27-31 Je 2 '28; 4:20-4 Je 9 '28. 903

Scientist and mob idol, by Alva Johnston. (ALBERT EINSTEIN: Mathemetician; scientist) 9:23-6 D 2 '33; 9:29-32 D 9 '33. 904

A scientist's advice, by Daniel Lang. (JEROME BERT WIESNER: Professor of Electrical Engineering, Massachusetts Institute of Technology; President's Special Assistant for Science and Technology) 38:39-59 Ja

19 '63; 38:38-71 Ja 26 '63. 905

Sculptors are different, by Ferdinand Tuohy. (JO DAVIDSON: Sculptor) 3:27-9 Mr 26 '27. 906

Sculpture, not machinery, by Babette Deutsch. (GEORGE GREY BARNARD: Sculptor) 6:26-9 Ja 17 '31. 907

The sea, by Rachel L. Carson. (THE SEA) 27:32-59 Je 2 '51; 27:34-65 Je 9 '51; 27:35-68 Je 16 '51. 908

Second city, by A.J. Liebling. (CHICAGO) 27:29-37 Ja 12 '52; 27:32-55 Ja 19 '52; 27:33-48 Ja 26 '52. 909

A second sort of life, by John Brooks. (DAVID ELI LILIENTHAL: Financier; corporation director; author; Chairman, U.S. Atomic Energy Commission) 37:45-90 Ap 29 '61. 910

Second-hand hot spots, by Joseph Mitchell. (I. ARTHUR GANGER: Head, bar equipment business) 16:24-31 *S 21 '40. 911

A sense of where you are, by John McPhee. (WILLIAM WARREN BRADLEY: Basketball player) 40:40-91 Ja 23 '65. 912

Seven centuries late, by Helena Huntington Smith. (RALPH ADAMS CRAM: Architect) 2:15-16 Mr 13 '26. 913

Seventy years young, by Margaret K. Leech. (ELISABETH MARBURY: National Democratic Committeewoman, New York City) 3:19-21 D 24 '27. 914

Shore whaler, by Berton Roueché. (EVERETT JOSHUA EDWARDS: Shore whaler) 25:37-48 *S 24 '49. 915

A short, squat island, by Robert Rice. (ANDREW GUNNAR HAGSTROM: Cartographer) 25:39-52 Ap 9 '49. 916

Sidewalk fisherman, by Meyer Berger. (SAM SCHULTZ: Sidewalk grate "fisherman") 14:16-20 *Jy 23 '38. 917

Significant Sig and the funnies, by John Bainbridge. (MILTON CANIFF: Comic-strip cartoonist) 19:25-37 Ja 8 '44. 918

Silk and leather, by Niven Busch, Jr. (EARL SANDE: Jockey) 3:15-18 Jy 30 '27. 919

Silver-tongue, by Charles Willis Thompson. (WILLIAM JENNINGS BRYAN: Politician) 1:9-10 Je 13 '25. 920

Since 1818, by Russell Maloney. (BROOKS BROTHERS: Clothing store) 14:20-3 *My 7 '38. 921

685 voices, by Robert A. Simon. (CHANNING LEFEBVRE: Choirmaster, organist, Trinity Church) 13:24-7 *My 1 '37. 922

Six, two, and even, by Niven Busch, Jr. ("POP": Bookmaker) 9:18-21 Je 24 '33. 923

Sixteenth-century style, by Helena Huntington Smith. (WILLIAM J. FINN: Roman Catholic priest; leader of Paulist choristers) 6:26-8 D 20 '30. 924

The sizzle, by John McNulty. (ELMER WHEELER: Head, Tested Selling Institute) 14:19-23 *Ap 16 '38. 925

Skybinder, by Niven Busch, Jr. (IRWIN S. CHANIN: Realtor; architectural engineer) 4:20-4 Ja 26 '29. 926

The slave of Hebrew, by Dwight Macdonald. (DANIEL PERSKY: Hebrew scholar; member, Herzliah Institute) 35:57-105 N 28 '59. 927

A small package, by Henry F. Pringle. (MILLER HUGGINS: Manager, New York Yankees) 3:25-7 O 8 '27. 928

Snow man, by Niven Busch, Jr. (URBAIN ["Mr. Zero"] LEDOUX: Philanthropist) 2:27-9 F 5 '27. 929

Socko! by Philip Hamburger. (MARTIN BLOCK: Radio "disc jockey") 20:27-37 Jy 29 '44. 930

Socrates afloat, by Brendan Gill. (HARTWELL STUART SHIPPEY: Barge captain) 21:25-32 Ag 25 '45. 931

Soldier in mufti, by E.J. Kahn, Jr. (LUCIUS DU BIGNON CLAY: General, U.S. Army; Head, Office of Defense Mobilization) 26:29-41 Ja 13 '51. 932

Something for a lawyer to do, by Fred Powledge. (CHARLES

MORGAN, JR.: Lawyer for American Civil Liberties Union) 45:63-134 O 25 '69. 933

Something out there, by John Brooks. (EDWARD RUSSELL DEWEY: Director, Foundation for the Study of Cycles) 37:37-69 F 3 '62. 934

Something to say, by James Thurber. (ELLIOT VEREKER: Author; dilettante) 8:17-19 Jy 30 '32. 935

Somnambulistic certainty, by Joseph Wechsberg. (OTTO MOLDEN: Founder, European Forum; political visionary) 37:51-84 S 16 '61. 936

Song and dance man, by Gilbert Seldes. (GEORGE M. COHAN: Playwright; song writer; dancer; actor) 10:27-31 Mr 17 '34; 10:23-7 Mr 24 '34. 937

Song and sentiment, by Marcia Davenport. (LOTTE LEHMANN: Singer, Metropolitan Opera Company) 11:18-22 *F 23 '35. 938

Soul surgeon, by Alva Johnston. (FRANK BUCHMAN: Evangelistic minister) 8:22-5 *Ap 23 '32. 939

The sound and the fury, by Robert Lewis Taylor. (ERNEST HENRY PEABODY: President, Peabody Engineering Corporation; anti-noise campaigner) 17:28-36 N 22 '41. 940

"South Pole Charlie," by Alva Johnston. (CHARLES V. BOB: Promoter; financier) 7:22-5 *Jy 4 '31. 941

Space-age maestro, by Winthrop Sargeant. (HERBERT VON KARAJAN: Symphony orchestra conductor) 36:35-62 Ja 7 '61. 942

Sparring partner, by A.J. Liebling. (GEORGE NICHOLSON: Prizefight sparring partner) 15:25-8 *Je 24 '39. 943

Spartacus in Westchester, by Stanley Walker. (WILLIAM MULDOON: Owner, Hygenic Institute; Member, New York State Boxing Commission) 3:18-21 Jy 16 '27. 944

Specialist in snakes, by Cameron Rogers. (RAYMOND DITMARS: Supervisor, Bronx Zoo Snake House) 4:24-7 Jy 14 '28. 945

Specialties, by Richard H. Rovere. (HENRY BLACKMAN SELL: Maker of canned meat products) 24:32-44 Mr 27 '48; 24:34-47 Ap 3 '48; 24:34-47 Ap 3 '48; 24: 33-47 Ap 10 '48. 946

The spinner of bomb bay, by St. Clair McKelway. (ALBERT HOLLINS: Worker in bomb factory) 18:20-6 Mr 7 '42. 947

Spiritual refuge, by Geoffrey T. Hellman. (COOPER UNION: Educational institution) 13:20-6 *Ag 21 '37; 13:18-22 *Ag 28 '37. 948

A spism and a spasm, by Joseph Mitchell. (JAMES JEFFERSON DAVIS HALL: Street preacher) 19:23-37 Jy 24 '43. 949

Spokesman with a temperature, by Rogers E. M. Whitaker. (ALBERT EDWIN [Eddie] CONDON: Jazz guitarist) 21:28-37 Ap 28 '45; 21:28-41 My 5 '45. 950

Sports model, misses', by Niven Busch, Jr. (GLENNA COLLETT: Golfer) 3:27-8 S 17 '27. 951

Spread eagle, by Niven Busch, Jr. (WILLIAM CAREY: Contractor; Director, Madison Square Garden) 5:21-4 Jy 13 '29. 952

Square deal among the fungi, by Geoffrey T. Hellman. (WILLIAM J. ROBBINS: Director, New York Botanical Gardens) 23:30-41 Jy 19 '47. 953

Squaring away and turning to, by Lillian Ross. (CHARLES FOUNTAIN WILLIS, JR.: President, non-scheduled airlines) 23:28-36 Jy 5 '47. 954

Star, by Robert Lewis Taylor. (LILLIAN LEITZEL: Aerialist, Ringling Brothers and Barnum & Bailey Circus) 32:45-66 *Ap 21 '56; 32:47-69 *Ap 28 '56. 955

Steel, by John K. Winkler. (CHARLES M. SCHWAB: President, United States Steel Corporation) 7:23-6 Ap 25 '31; 7:26-35 My 2 '31. 956

Stentor, by Meyer Berger. (JOSEPH E. HUMPHREYS: Prizefight announcer) 9:24-7 O 14 '33; 9:27-30 O 21 '33. 957

The steward of Strawberry Hill, by Geoffrey T. Hellman. (WILMARTH SHELDON LEWIS: Author; Horace Walpole scholar) 25:26-37 Ag 6 '49; 25:31-41 Ag 13 '49. 958

Stirrup and leather, by Margaret Case Harriman. (F. AMBROSE CLARK: Horse breeder; President, United Hunts) 10:20-4 S 29 '34. 959

The story of everything, by Richard O. Boyer. (HENDRICK WILLEM Van LOON: Author; historian) 19:24-31 *Mr 20 '43; 19:24-30 Mr 27 '43; 19:24-36 Ap 3 '43. 960

Striking a blow for Grandma, by John Bainbridge. (MARGARET RUDKIN: President, Pepperidge Farms, Inc. [bakery]) 24:38-51 My 22 '48. 961

Student of the spontaneous, by J.M. Flagler. (ALLEN FUNT: Radio, television personality; cameraman) 36:59-92 D 10 '60. 962

Summoned by bells, by John Betjeman. (JOHN BETJEMAN: Poet) 36:31-42 Ag 27 '60. 963

The super-American state, by John Bainbridge. (TEXAS) 37:47-111 Mr 11 '61; 37:51-120 Mr 18 '61; 37:40-99 Ap 1 '61; 37:62-131 Ap 8 '61; 37:48-115 Ap 22 '61; 37:49-120 My 6 '61; 37:49-117 My 20 '61. 964

The surprise of the century, by Janet Flanner. (PABLO RUIZ Y PICASSO: Painter) 33:37-63 Mr 9 '57; 33:39-74 Mr 16 '57. 965

The swan in the mirror, by John McCarten. (NICK KENNY: Columnist, New York Daily Mirror) 29:35-54 Mr 7 '53. 966

Swat the fly! by Robert Lewis Taylor. (SAMUEL J. CRUMBINE: Physician; public health worker) 24:31-8 Jy 17 '48; 24:28-36 Jy 24 '48. 967

Sweetheart, by Margaret Case Harriman. (MARY PICKFORD: Motion picture actress) 10:29-33 Ap 7 '34. 968

A symbol in pugilism, by James Kevin McGuinness. (JACK DEMPSEY: Prizefighter) 1:15-16 Mr 14 '25. 969

A symbol of justice, by Alva Johnston. (MAX D. STEUER: Lawyer) 1:13-14 My 16 '25. 970

Talker, by Robert Lewis Taylor. (NATE EAGLE: Side-show manager, Ringling Brothers and Barnum & Bailey Circus) 34:47-71 Ap 19 '58; 34:39-73 Ap 26 '58. 971

The talking stockbroker, by John Bainbridge. (LEWIS DUSENBERY GILBERT: Minority stockholder) 24:40-54 D 11 '48; 24:33-47 D 18 '48. 972

Tammany in modern clothes, by Oliver H. P. Garrett. (GEORGE V. McLAUGHLIN: Police Commissioner, New York City) 1:11-12 Ja 16 '26. 973

The tax, by John Brooks. (U.S. INCOME TAX) 41:52-84 Ap 3 '65; 41:51-83 Ap 10 '65. 974

Tax angler, by E.J. Kahn, Jr. (JACOB KAY LASSER: Author; income tax expert) 29:36-58 Mr 14 '53. 975

T-bars and I-dots, by Angelica Gibbs. (SHIRLEY SPENCER: Graphologist, New York Daily News) 25:26-36 D 24 '49. 976

The temperamental Suzanne, by Ferdinand Tuohy. (SUZANNE LENGLEN: Tennis player) 2:15-17 F 27 '26. 977

Tempest in a kitchen, by Joseph Wechsberg. (ALEXANDRE DUMAINE: Chef) 31:32-64 Je 18 '55. 978

Templex, by John McPhee. (TEMPLE HORNADAY FIELDING: Author of guidebooks) 43:32-67 Ja 6 '68. 979

10 1/2, by Lillian Ross. (FEDERICO FELLINI: Motion picture director) 41:63-107 O 30 '65. 980

The terrible joys, by Winthrop Sargeant. (ENZO FERRARI: Automobile designer, manufacturer) 41:40-66 Ja 15 '66. 981

The terrible midget, by Robert Lewis Taylor. (LOUIS PAGLIARO: Ping-pong champion) 17:20-6 Ja 31 '42. 982

The testimony of a sinner, by Matthew Josephson and Russell Maloney. (J.B. MATTHEWS: Consulting expert, Dies Committee, U.S. House of Representatives) 20: 30-41 Ap 22 '44. 983

That sad young man, by John Chapin Mosher. (F. SCOTT FITZGERALD: Novelist) 2:20-1 Ap 17 '26. 984

There's no place, by Philip Hamburger. (JOHN P. MARQUAND: Novelist) 28:37-57 Mr 29 '52; 28:43-67 Ap 5 '52; 28:39-64 Ap 12 '52. 985

These things are fated, by Russell Maloney. (LEONARD LYONS: Newspaper gossip columnist) 21:28-39 Ap 7 '45. 986

They bought it! by Geoffrey T. Hellman. (STANLEY N. ARNOLD: Marketing and sales-management consultant) 36:51-85 O 29 '60. 987

No entry. 988

They were eleven, by Helena Huntington Smith. (MARGARET SANGER: Author; birth control advocate) 6:22-5 Jy 5 '30. 989

A thing among things, by Calvin Tomkins. (RICHARD LIPPOLD: Sculptor) 39:47-107 Mr 30 '63. 990

Thinker in Hollywood, by Geoffrey T. Hellman. (FRANK CAPRA: Motion picture director) 16:23-8 *F 24 '40. 991

The third most important day, by E.J. Kahn, Jr. (JOHN COLQUHOUN TYSEN: President, real estate firm) 32:57-92 N 17 '56. 992

The thirteenth labor of Hercules, by Margaret Case Harriman and John Bainbridge. (ROBERT A. LOVETT: U.S. Assistant Secretary of War for Air) 19:30-9 N 6 '43; 19:29-34 N 13 '43. 993

Thirty-five years of Balzac, by Alva Johnston. (WILLIAM H. ROYCE: Scholar [Balzac]; author) 9:18-21 Ap 1 '33. 994

31, Rue Cambon, by Janet Flanner. (GABRIELLE CHANEL: Couturière) 7:25-8 Mr 14 '31. 995

"This ageless soul," by Russell Maloney. (ORSON WELLES: Actor; director; radio personality) 14:20-5 *O 8 '38. 996

This girl of the Channel, by Lurton Blassingame. (GERTRUDE EDERLE: Swimmer) 2:15-16 Ag 28 '26. 997

Thor plays polo, by Herbert Reed. (DEVEREUX MILBURN: Polo player; lawyer) 2:23-4 Je 5 '26. 998

Those were the days, by Janet Flanner. (WORTH et CIE.: Couturier) 9:17-20 Ja 20 '34. 999

Thoughts on baseball, by Robert Rice. (BRANCH RICKEY: President, Brooklyn Dodgers) 26:32-46 My 27 '50; 26:30-47 Je 3 '50. 1000

The thousand silver threads, by Robert Rice. (FRANK CHARLES LAUBACH: Congregational minister; educator) 27:38-57 F 16 '52. 1001

The Three, by E.J. Kahn, Jr. (DC-3: Airplane) 36:49-75 S 10 '60. 1002

Three cheers for the blue, white and red, by E.J. Kahn, Jr. (GRIDLEY ADAMS: Chairman, National Flag Code Committee) 28:29-44 Jy 5 '52. 1003

A three dimensional person, by Edna Ferber. (WILLIAM ALLEN WHITE: Newspaper editor) 1:9-10 My 30 '25. 1004

Three men and the horse, by John McCarten and Robert Lewis Taylor. (IKE KAUFFMAN, JAKE KAUFFMAN AND BERNIE KAUFFMAN: Owners, Kauffman Saddlery Company) 19:24-34 S 4 '43. 1005

Through the great city, by Anthony Bailey. (NORTHEAST CORRIDOR, U.S.A.) 43:35-69 Jy 22 '67; 43:35-69 Jy 29 '67; 43:32-63 Ag 5 '67. 1006

A tilted insight, by Robert Rice. (MICHAEL [Mike] NICHOLS AND ELAINE MAY: Comedy team. Motion picture director. Playwright) 37:47-75 Ap 15 '61. 1007

Time...Fortune...Life...Luce, by Wolcott Gibbs. (HENRY ROBINSON LUCE: Publisher) 12:20-5 *N 28 '36. 1008

The time is twenty-one after, by Thomas Whiteside. (DAVID GARROWAY: Television personality) 35:39-75 S 5 '59. 1009

A timid little man, by R. Hale. (ARTHUR HOPKINS: Theatrical producer) 1:9-10 Mr 21 '25. 1010

The tiny landscape, by Eugene Kinkead. (ROMAN VISHNIAC: Photographer of microscopic life; zoologist; physician) 31:28-42 *Jy 2 '55; 31:31-56 Jy 9 '55. 1011

To spare the obedient beast, by Brendan Gill. (CHARLES BRADY KING: Automobile designer, builder, racer) 22:30-40 My 18 '46. 1012

To touch and not be touched, by Robert Lewis Taylor. (GEORGE [Giorgio] SANTELLI: Fencing master) 28:30-42 Ja 10 '53; 28:32-48 Ja 17 '53. 1013

Tobacco, tunnels, arsenic, and old lace, by Geoffrey T. Hellman. (HOWARD J. CULLMAN: Theatrical investor; President, Beekman Hospital; partner, Cullman Brothers [tobacco]) 21:28-38 F 9 '46; 22:36-44 F 16 '46. 1014

Tong leader, by St. Clair McKelway. (MOCK SAI WING: Tong leader) 9:18-22 D 30 '33. 1015

The tooth, by Joseph Mitchell. (COMMODORE DUTCH, pseud.: Confidence man; Broadway character) 17:24-37 *N 1 '41. 1016

Toots's world, by John Bainbridge. (BERNARD [Toots] SHOR: Restaurant owner) 26:50-76 N 11 '50; 26:54-74 N 18 '50; 26:42-61 N 25 '50. 1017

Torna! Torna! by Winthrop Sargeant. (GUIDO CHIGI SARACINI: Italian count; music patron) 36:37-77 S 3 '60. 1018

The touch, by Robert Rice. (ANNE HONE ROGERS: Professional show dog handler; breeder) 36:49-87 Ap 9 '60. 1019

The tough guy and the soft guy, by E.J. Kahn, Jr. (JOSHUA LOCKWOOD LOGAN: Playwright; director; producer) 29:38-65 Ap 4 '53; 29:37-67 Ap 11 '53. 1020

The tragic sense, by Hamilton Basso. (EUGENE O'NEILL: Playwright) 24:34-45 F 28 '48; 24:34-49 Mr 6 '48; 24:37-47 Mr 13 '48. 1021

The train had just arrived at Malgudi Station, by Ved Mehta. (RASIPURAM KRISHASWAMI NARAYAN: Novelist) 38:51-90 S 15 '62. 1022

The treatment of patients, by Nat Hentoff. (MARIE NYSWANDER: Psychiatrist, psychoanalyst for narcotics addicts) 41:32-77 Je 26 '65; 41:32-57 Jy 3 '65. 1023

The trinity--and a dog, by Lurton Blassingame. (SAMUEL KNOPF, ALFRED KNOPF AND BLANCHE KNOPF: Publishers) 2:15-17 Ag 21 '26. 1024

The triumph of hoopla, by Robert Lewis Taylor. (JOHN RINGLING NORTH: President, Ringling Brothers and Barnum & Bailey Circus) 30:39-59 Ap 10 '54; 30:39-60 Ap 17 '54. 1025

Troubadour, by S. N. Behrman. (GEORGE GERSHWIN: Composer) 5:27-9 My 25 '29. 1026

Troublemaker, by Max Eastman. (CARLO TRESCA: Labor organizer; revolutionist) 10:31-6 S 15 '34; 10:26-9 S 22 '34. 1027

The true mobility, by John Brooks. (DAVID SIDNEY JACKSON: Specialist, New York Stock Exchange) 31:41-66 *O 1 '55. 1028

Trustee in Fiddledale, by Joseph Wechsberg. (EMIL HERRMANN: Violin dealer) 29:38-59 O 17 '53; 29:39-63 O 24 '53. 1029

Trust-gobbler, by Geoffrey T. Hellman. (FLOYD B. ODLUM: Director, investment trust) 9:20-4 Ag 26 '33. 1030

Trustworthy, loyal, helpful, friendly, by St. Clair McKelway. (THEODORE PETZOLD: Boy Scout) 18:19-24 Jy 25 '42. 1031

Tummler, by A. J. Liebling. (HYMIE KATZ, pseud.: Night-club owner) 14:24-9 *F 26 '38. 1032

Turf and gridiron, by A. J. Liebling. (TIMOTHY JAMES

MARA: Founder, Turf and Gridiron Club [Bookmakers]) 13:25-9 *S 18 '37. 1033

A twentieth century puritan, by Lurton Blassingame. (HARRY EMERSON FOSDICK: Minister; author) 3:18-20 Je 18 '27. 1034

Two authors in an attic, by Robert Lewis Taylor. (JOHN DICKSON CARR: Mystery writer) 27:39-48 S 8 '51; 27:36-51 S 15 '51. 1035

291, by Waldo Frank. (ALFRED STIEGLITZ: Photographer) 1:9-10 Ap 18 '25. 1036

"Two on the aisle," by Kenneth Macgowan. (JOHN McBRIDE: Theatrical ticket agent) 3:18-21 Ag 6 '27. 1037

Two waiters and a chef, by Margaret Case Harriman. (COLONY RESTAURANT: Ernest Cerutti; Gene Cavallero; Alfred Hartmann) 11:20-4 *Je 1 '35; 11:22-6 *Je 8 '35. 1038

Two-eyed Connelly, by Alexander Woollcott. (MARCUS COOK [Marc] CONNELLY: Playwright) 6:29-32 Ap 12 '30. 1039

A two-Ringling circus, by Helena Huntington Smith. (JOHN RINGLING AND CHARLES RINGLING: Owners, Ringling Brothers Circus) 2:19-20 My 1 '26. 1040

Two-star general, by E.J. Kahn, Jr. (EDWIN FORREST HARDING: Major-general, U.S. Army) 18:21-32 D 26 '42; 18:24-31 Ja 2 '43. 1041

Type model, by Lurton Blassingame. (WALTER P. CHRYSLER: Automobile manufacturer) 2:21-4 Ja 8 '27. 1042

Typhoid carrier no. 36, by Stanley Walker. (MARY [Typhoid Mary] MALLON: Cook; typhoid carrier) 10:21-5 *Ja 26 '35. 1043

U.S. artist, by Rufus Jarman. (NORMAN ROCKWELL: Artist; illustrator) 21:34-45 Mr 17 '45; 21:36-47 Mr 24 '45. 1044

Ugly duckling, by Helena Huntington Smith. (GLORIA SWANSON: Motion picture actress) 5:24-7 Ja 18 '30. 1045

Ukrainian shadow, by John Fischer. (PAVEL PETROVICH PUROBAYEV: Secret agent) 23:36-45 Ap 12 '47. 1046

The ultimate city, by Christopher Rand. (LOS ANGELES) 42:56-116 O 1 '66; 42:64-115 O 8 '66; 42:64-117 O 15 '66. 1047

Ulysses ashore--for a while, by Arthur Krock. (BERNARD M. BARUCH: Financier) 2:15-16 Ag 7 '26. 1048

Uncle Don, by Margaret Case Harriman. (DON CARNEY: Radio broadcaster for children) 9:22-7 *D 16 '33. 1049

Under the rug, by Robert Lewis Taylor. (ARTHUR UPHAM POPE: Authority on Iran; author; philosophy professor) 21:28-34 Jy 14 '45; 21:22-9 Jy 21 '45. 1050

Union president, by Richard O. Boyer. (JOSEPH CURRAN: President, National Maritime Union) 22:24-33 Jy 6 '46; 22:30-40 Jy 13 '46; 22:26-37 Jy 20 '46. 1051

The universal drink, by E.J. Kahn, Jr. (COCA-COLA COMPANY) 34:37-67 F 14 '59; 35:39-95 F 21 '59; 35:35-65 F 28 '59; 35:39-79 Mr 7 '59. 1052

Unshaken friend, by Malcolm Cowley. (MAXWELL EVARTS PERKINS: Editor; vice-president, Charles Scribner's Sons) 20:32-42 Ap 1 '44; 20:30-43 Ap 8 '44. 1053

The unusually nice necktie, by Geoffrey T. Hellman. (LUCILLA MARA de VESCOVI WHITMAN: Owner of men's shop [Countess Mara]) 25:34-47 F 26 '49. 1054

Up from Amherst, by Wolcott Gibbs. (BURGESS MEREDITH: Actor) 13:24-30 *Ap 3 '37. 1055

Up from Corker, by Morton M. Hunt. (OLIN STEPHENS AND RODERICK STEPHENS: Yacht designers and builders) 33:39-71 S 7 '57; 33:49-88 S 14 '57. 1056

Up from Fifth Avenue, by Carl Brandt. (HARRY PAYNE WHITNEY: Socialite; polo player) 1:8-9 Jy 25 '25. 1057

Up from Harvard, by Robert S. Allen. (OGDEN LIVINGSTON MILLS: Financier; U.S. Undersecretary of the Treasury) 7:25-8 D 12 '31. 1058

Up from Hell's Kitchen, by Charles Robbins. (ALVIN [Shipwreck] KELLY: Flagpole sitter) 6:22-5 Ap 26 '30. 1059

Urgent! rush! by Daniel Lang. (IRVING SEIDEN: President, Mercury Service Systems) 34:29-51 Jy 5 '58. 1060

Useful on the grand scale, by Robert Shaplen. (ROBERT W. DOWLING: Architect; Head, Advisory Arts Committee for National Cultural Center) 36:61-113 N 5 '60. 1060a

V.A., by Alexander Woollcott. (CARR VATELL VAN ANDA: Managing editor, New York Times) 1:7-8 Mr 7 '25. 1061

Vamp in violet, by Sinclair Lewis. (EFFIE KAYSHUS: Shoe manufacturer) 12:20-5 *Ja 16 '37. 1062

Vanishing American, by Joel Sayre. (DANIEL CARTER BEARD: National Commissioner, Boy Scouts of America; book and magazine illustrator) 8:17-20 Jy 23 '32. 1063

Vaudeville to television, by Alva Johnston. (JOHN F. ROYAL: Vice-president, National Broadcasting Company) 22:32-43 S 28 '46; 22:36-47 O 5 '46; 22:36-46 O 12 '46. 1064

Veni, vidi, Vicky, by Margaret Case Harriman. (HELEN HAYES: Actress) 15:24-30 *My 20 '39; 15:28-35 *My 27 '39. 1065

Versatility personified, by Newman Levy. (DEEMS TAYLOR: Music critic) 1:9-10 Je 6 '25. 1066

A very active type man, by Wolcott Gibbs. (RALPH INGERSOLL: Editor of PM) 18:21-30 My 2 '42; 18:21-30 My 9 '42. 1067

Very old party, by Hamilton Basso. (WILLIAM SOMERSET MAUGHAM: Novelist; playwright) 20:24-34 D 30 '44; 20:28-38 Ja 6 '45. 1068

The very rich hours of Joe Levine, by Calvin Tomkins. (JOSEPH E. LEVINE: Motion picture producer) 43:55-136 S 16 '67. 1069

Very terrific, very divine, by Margaret Case Harriman. (NETTIE ROSENSTEIN: Couturière) 16:28-36 *O 19 '40. 1070

Very, very cordial, by Geoffrey T. Hellman. (CLAUDIUS CHARLES PHILIPPE: Vice-president, catering, Waldorf-Astoria Hotel) 31:37-75 F 19 '55. 1071

A victim of noblesse oblige, by Robert Rice. (ROBERT JOSEPH COUSY: Basketball player) 36:38-60 F 4 '61. 1072

Viennese tomboy, by Pitts Sanborn. (MARIA JERITZA: Singer, Metropolitan Opera Company) 6:21-4 Ja 24 '31. 1073

Viennese visitor, by Lola Jean Simpson. (ALFRED ADLER: Psychologist) 4:29-31 My 5 '28. 1074

Viewer from the 14th floor, by Geoffrey T. Hellman. (ARTHUR OCHS SULZBERGER: President and publisher, New York Times) 44:40-71 Ja 18 '69. 1075

Villain of villains, by George White Garland. (ANTONIO SCOTTI: Singer, Metropolitan Opera Company) 1:15-16 F 13 '26. 1076

"Vincent," by Griffin Barry. (EDNA ST. VINCENT MILLAY: Poet) 2:25-7 F 12 '27. 1077

The vocal mission, by Joseph Wechsberg. (GEORGE LONDON: Singer, Metropolitan Opera Company) 33:49-92 O 26 '57; 33:47-81 N 2 '57. 1078

The voice, by Richard O. Boyer. (RAYMOND GRAM SWING: Radio commentator) 18:24-31 N 14 '42; 18:24-35 N 21 '42. 1079

The voice, by Margaret Case Harriman. (MARION SAYLE TAYLOR: Radio "Voice of Experience") 11:26-9 *O 26 '35; 11:24-8 *N 2 '35. 1080

Voices, by Barbara Heggie. (GEORGE ROBERT VINCENT: Collector, voices of famous persons) 17:24-31 *My 17 '41. 1081

Vox populi, by Jack Alexander. (JOSEPH MEDILL PATTERSON: Publisher, New York Daily News) 14:16-21 *Ag 6 '38; 14:19-24 *Ag 13 '38; 14:19-23 *Ag 20 '38. 1082

The wahoo boy, by Alva Johnston. (DARRYL FRANCIS

ZANUCK: Motion picture producer) 10:24-8 N 10 '34; 10:24-9 *N 17 '34. 1083

A walk to the Park, by Whitney Balliett. (ELVIN JONES: Jazz drummer) 44:45-70 My 18 '68. 1084

The wallflower's friend, by Milton MacKaye. (ARTHUR MURRAY: Dance instructor) 9:27-30 Ja 6 '34. 1085

A way of life, by C. Lester Walker. (HANNES SCHNEIDER: Inventor of skiing techniques) 18:21-7 F 28 '42. 1086

We, by Barbara Heggie. (MARGARET WEBSTER: Actress; director) 20:32-43 My 20 '44. 1087

Wet hope, by Henry F. Pringle. (HENRY HASTINGS CURRAN: Lawyer; politician; President, American Association Against the Prohibition Amendment) 6:22-5 Je 14 '30. 1088

Wham! Pow! Zowie! by Joel Sayre. (JOHN J. BRODERICK: Detective, New York City Police) 7:18-21 D 26 '31. 1089

What a moment! What a feeling! by Morton M. Hunt. (MARY A. BENJAMIN: Autograph dealer) 35:57-92 D 5 '59. 1090

What can I do for you, gentlemen? by E.J. Kahn, Jr. (ARTHUR SIMON MEYER: Chairman, New York State Board of Mediation) 22:34-49 F 8 '47. 1091

"What happens after that," by Russell Maloney. (ALFRED HITCHCOCK: Motion picture director) 14:24-8 *S 10 '38. 1092

"What is a merchant?" by Babette Deutsch. (AUGUST HECKSCHER: Industrialist; philanthropist) 6:20-3 Ag 2 '30. 1093

What is permitted to Jove, by Hannah Arendt. (BERTOLT BRECHT: Playwright) 42:68-122 N 5 '66. 1094

Wheels in his head, by Henry F. Pringle. (FRANK HEDLEY: President, Interborough Rapid Transit Company) 3:17-19 D 31 '27. 1095

Whistling in the darkroom, by Joseph Wechsberg. (LEOPOLD

GODOWSKY: Co-inventor, Kodachrome process; concert violist) 32:61-109 *N 10 '56. 1096

A white hot tamale, by Joseph T. Scarry. (HUDSON MAXIM: Inventor) 2:25-7 O 16 '26. 1097

White sales and Aristotle, by Dwight Macdonald. (RICHARD WEIL, JR.: President, R. H. Macy) 27:30-47 F 2 '52; 27:39-55 F 9 '52. 1098

Who is this king of glory? by St. Clair McKelway and A. J. Liebling. (GEORGE [Father Divine] BAKER: Leader, religious cult) 12:21-8 *Je 13 '36; 12:22-8 *Je 20 '36; 12:22-32 *Je 27 '36. 1099

Who you are and what you think you're doing, by Robert Rice. (HUGH K. JOHNSON: Anthropologist; social worker) 37:32-56 D 23 '61. 1100

The whole thing is all with lights, by John Kobler. (JACOB BUCHTER: Chief electrician, Metropolitan Opera Company) 23:38-53 N 15 '47. 1101

Whooping it up, by Geoffrey T. Hellman. (ROBERT W. SERVICE: Poet) 22:34-41 Mr 30 '46; 22:32-45 Ap 6 '46. 1102

Why don't we just hum for a while? by William Whitworth. (ROGER MILLER: Popular songwriter; singer) 45:38-66 Mr 1 '69. 1103

Why fight it? by John Brooks. (SIDNEY JANIS: Art dealer) 36:59-101 N 12 '60. 1104

The winged - S, by Geoffrey T. Hellman. (IGOR IVANOVITCH SIKORSKY: Airplane designer, engineer, executive) 16:21-9 *Ag 10 '40; 16:20-8 *Ag 17 '40. 1105

Wings over America, by William Weimar. (GIUSEPPE MARIO BELLANCA: Airplane designer, manufacturer) 5:22-5 Mr 30 '29. 1106

Winning against time, by John R. Tunis. (RENE LACOSTE: Tennis player) 1:10-11 S 5 '25. 1107

With palette knife and skillet, by Angelica Gibbs. (DIANE WILSON LUCAS: Owner of cooking school) 25:34-53 My 28 '49. 1108

With the meat in their mouth, by Joel Sayre. (JOHN CORDES: Detective, New York Police Department) 29:37-61 S 5 '53; 29:39-59 S 12 '53. 1109

Without benefit of tin foil, by Oliver H. P. Garrett. (FRANK G. SHATTUCK: Owner, Schraffts Restaurants) 4:29-31 My 19 '28. 1110

The wizard, by Alva Johnston. (THOMAS ALVA EDISON: Inventor) 5:21-4 D 28 '29; 5:24-6 Ja 4 '30; 5:22-5 Ja 11 '30. 1111

A woman entering a taxi in the rain, by Winthrop Sargeant. (RICHARD AVEDON: Fashion photographer) 34:49-84 N 8 '58. 1112

A woman in the house, by Janet Flanner. (CHERYL CRAWFORD: Musical comedy producer) 24:34-51 My 8 '48. 1113

Woomera has it! by Calvin Tomkins. (JOHN R. PIERCE: Executive Director of Communications Research, Bell Telephone Laboratories) 39:49-110 S 21 '63. 1114

Words and music, by Franklin P. Adams. (JEROME KERN: Song writer; musical comedy writer) 5:21-3 F 8 '30. 1115

Words and music, by Margaret Case Harriman. (RICHARD RODGERS AND LORENZ HART: Song writers; musical comedy writers) 14:19-23 *My 28 '38; 14:21-5 *Je 4 '38. 1116

Words and music, by Margaret Case Harriman. (COLE PORTER: Song writer; musical comedy writer) 16:24-34 *N 23 '40. 1117

The world and Sauk Center, by W. E. Woodward. (SINCLAIR LEWIS: Novelist) 9:24-7 Ja 27 '34; 9:24-7 F 3 '34. 1118

The world of Caspar Milquetoast, by Hamilton Basso. (HAROLD TUCKER WEBSTER: Comic strip cartoonist) 25:40-61 N 5 '49. 1119

The world on his back, by Charles Wertenbaker. (EDWARD R. MURROW: Radio and television news commentator) 29:28-45 D 26 '53. 1120

Xerox Xerox Xerox Xerox, by John Brooks. (XEROX CORPORATION: Manufacturers of photocopying machinery) 43:46-90 Ap 1 '67. 1121

Yankee horse trader, by Arthur Bartlett. (WALTER COX: Horse trainer) 11:19-24 *Ag 10 '35. 1122

Yea, verily, by A.J. Liebling. (JOHN R. STINGO, pseud.: Columnist, New York Enquirer) 28:46-72 S 13 '52; 28:45-71 S 20 '52; 28:34-61 S 27 '52. 1123

The years alone, by E.J. Kahn, Jr. (ELEANOR ROOSEVELT [Mrs. Franklin D.]: Author; lecturer; statesman) 24:30-43 Je 12 '48; 24:30-42 Je 19 '48. 1124

Yes, Mr. Mayer, by Henry F. Pringle. (LOUIS B. MAYER: Motion picture executive) 12:26-31 *Mr 28 '36; 12:26-30 *Ap 4 '36. 1125

You can't force it, by Winthrop Sargeant. (RICHARD RODGERS: Song writer; musical comedy writer) 37:58-95 N 18 '61. 1126

You come and go, by John Bainbridge. (HAROLD F. BLACKBURN: Trans World Airlines pilot) 32:38-78 *My 5 '56. 1127

You never learn to say goodbye, by Lillian Ross. (M.S. SAGAFJORD: Ocean liner) 42:65-177 N 19 '66. 1128

Young Captain Chips, by John Kirkpatrick. (DANIEL SNYDER: Captain, U.S. Army Air Forces) 19:23-30 My 8 '43. 1129

Young man behind plexiglass, by Brendan Gill. (JOSEPH THEODORE HALLOCK: 1st Lieutenant, U.S. Army Air Forces) 20:26-37 Ag 12 '44. 1130

Young man from Dubuque, by Jo Swerling. (LOUIS [Frisco] JOSEPHS: Jazz dancer) 1:9-10 S 26 '25. 1131

Young man of affairs, by Morris Markey. (CHARLES AUGUSTUS LINDBERGH: Aviator) 6:26-9 S 20 '30; 6:30-3 S 27 '30. 1132

Young man with a viola, by E.J. Kahn, Jr. (JOHN HENRY HAMMOND, JR.: Popular music critic; Director, Columbia Recording Corporation) 15:19-24 *Jy 29 '39. 1133

The young monk of Siberia, by Alexander Woollcott. (CHARLES GORDON MacARTHUR: Playwright) 5: 23-6 Mr 9 '29. 1134

Yrs. truly, A. Lincoln, by John Kobler. (JOSEPH COSEY, pseud.: Forger) 32:38-85 *F 25 '56. 1135

Part II

NAME INDEX

NAME INDEX

A. Profiles of Individuals

ABRAMS, Charles. City planner. 593
ACHELIS, Elisabeth. Advocate of permanent calendar. 556
ACHESON, Dean Gooderham. U.S. Secretary of State. 672
ADAMS, Charles Francis. Lawyer; politician; Treasurer of Harvard University; yachtsman. 902
ADAMS, Evangeline. Astrologer. 553
ADAMS, Gridley. Chairman, National Flag Code Committee. 1003
ADLER, Alfred. Psychologist. 1074
ADLER, Larry. Harmonica player. 102
ALDRICH, Richard Stoddard. Summer-theatre producer. 572
ALLEN, Henry (Red). Jazz trumpet player. 111
ALLEN, Kelcey. Drama critic, Women's Wear Daily. 473
ALLEN, Terry de la Mesa. Major-general, U.S. Army. 327
ALLERS, Franz. Conductor: ballet, opera, symphony, musical comedy. 350
AMES, Winthrop. Theatrical producer. 122
AMMANN, Othmar Hermann. Chief Engineer, Port of New York Authority. 806
AMSDEN, Sherman C. Head, Telephone Answering Service. 617
ANDREWS, Roy Chapman. Explorer; author. 481
ANTOINE. see Cierplikowski, Antoine.
ARCARO, Eddie. Jockey. 742
ARDEN, Elizabeth. Owner, beauty salon and company. 389
ARNOLD, Paul Dean. Owner of bakery. 871
ARNOLD, Stanley N. Marketing and sales-management consultant. 987
ARNSTEIN, Daniel. U.S. Ambassador to China; Burma Road expert. 475
ARSHAWSKY, Arthur. see Shaw, Artie.
ASHE, Arthur. Tennis player. 573
ASTOR, William Vincent. Real estate owner and manager;

investment manager. 396
ATLAS, Charles. Muscle-builder. 485
AUER, Leopold. Concert violinist; music teacher. 636
AVEDON, Richard. Fashion photographer. 1112
AVINOFF, Andrey. Lepidopterist; painter. 109

BABSON, Roger W. Economist; Director, Babson Park. 841
BACH, Richard F. Architect; Associate in Industrial Arts, Metropolitan Museum of Art. 608
BACKER, Dorothy. see Schiff, Dorothy.
BAER, Max Adalbert. Prizefighter. 831
BAGBY, Albert Morris. Patron of arts; socialite. 688
BAKER, George (Father Divine). Leader, religious cult. 1099
BALANCHINE, George. Chief choreographer, New York City Ballet. 176
BALDWIN, Joseph Clark, III. U.S. Congressman, New York County. 320
BALDWIN, Roger. Founder, American Civil Liberties Union. 249
BARNARD, George Grey. Sculptor. 907
BARNELL, Jane. Bearded lady in circus sideshow. 554
BARNES, Albert C. Art collector; drug manufacturer. 243
BARR, Alfred H., Jr. Director of Collections, Museum of Modern Art. 7
BARSTOW, Richard. Director and choreographer, Ringling Brothers and Barnum & Bailey Circus. 312
BARTLETT, Frederic Huntington. Pediatrician; author. 299
BARTON, Bruce. Author; advertising executive. 513
BARUCH, Bernard Mannes. Financier; speculator; government advisor. 728, 1048
BATES, B.L.M. Owner and manager, Murray Hill Hotel. 804
BATTLE, George Gordon. Lawyer; philanthropist; money raiser. 664
BAUM, Joseph. Originator, Restaurant Associates. 261
BEARD, Daniel Carter. National Commissioner, Boy Scouts of America; book and magazine illustrator. 1063
BEEBE, Lucius Morris. Newspaper society columnist. 256
BEERBOHM, Henry Maximilian (Max). Caricaturist; author; critic. 212
BEERY, Wallace. Motion picture actor; comedian. 525
BELASCO, David. Theatrical producer. 415
BELLANCA, Giuseppe Mario. Airplane designer, manufacturer. 1106
BELLET, Robert. Chief purser, S.S. Liberté. 222

BENEDICK, Billy. see Paul, Maury H.B.
BENJAMIN, Mary A. Autograph dealer. 1090
BENNETT, Robert Russell. Orchestrator for musical comedies. 49
BERGMAN, Ingrid. Actress. 798
BERLE, Adolf Augustus, Jr. U.S. Assistant Secretary of State. 69
BERLIN, Elaine. see May, Elaine.
BERNSTEIN, Leonard. Conductor, New York Philharomic; composer. 784
BERRIGAN, Daniel. Roman Catholic priest; militant pacifist leader; author. 10
BERRIGAN, Philip. Roman Catholic priest; militant pacifist leader; author. 10
BETJEMAN, John. Poet. 963
BIDDLE, Anthony J. Drexel, Jr. U.S. Ambassador to Polish, Belgian, Netherlands and Norwegian governments in London. 734
BIDDLE, George. Painter. 425
BIMSTEIN, Morris. Prizefight second. 613
BING, Rudolf. General manager, Metropolitan Opera Company. 373
BIRDWELL, Russell. Press agent; publicity man. 846
BIRKHEAD, Leon Milton. National director, Friends of Democracy, Inc. 250
BISHOP, Howard Berkey. Crusader against tobacco habit. 735
BLACKBURN, Harold Frederic. Trans World Airlines pilot. 576, 1127
BLACKWELL, Basil. Book store owner. 856
BLAIR, Bruce. Veterinarian. 271
BLOCH, Ernest. Composer. 601
BLOCK, Martin. Radio "disc jockey." 930
BLOOM, Sol. U.S. Congressman, New York State. 484
BLUMENTHAL, Alfred Cleveland. Real estate, theatrical promoter. 112
BOB, Charles V. Promoter; financier. 941
BOCHER, Main. Couturier. 795
BODANZKY, Artur. Conductor, Metropolitan Opera Company. 30
BOGDANOV, Peter Alexyevitch. Chairman, Amtorg Corporation. 114
BOOMER, Lucius. President, hotel and restaurant chain. 363
BOOTH, Evangeline. Commander, Salvation Army. 200
BOOTHE, Clare. Playwright; actress; U.S. Ambassador to Italy. 148

BORGE, Victor. Comedian; pianist; poultry breeder. 104
BORGES, Jorge Luis. Novelist; poet; short story writer. 71
BOROTRA, Jean. Tennis player. 239
BOROWITZ, Abram Solman. see Burrows, Abe.
BOSTWICK, Pete. Polo player. 808
BOWIE, Walter Russell. Pastor, Grace Episcopal Church. 381
BOWLBY, Harry Laity. Protestant minister; General Secretary, Lord's Day Alliance. 866
BOWMAN, John McEntee. Director, Bowman Biltmore Hotels Corporation. 41
BOYDEN, Frank Learoyd. Headmaster, Deerfield Academy. 443
BRADLEY, Edward Riley. Horse breeder; gambling casino owner. 491
BRADLEY, Omar Nelson. General, U.S. Army; Chairman, Joint Chiefs of Staff. 333
BRADLEY, William Warren. Basketball player. 912
BRANDO, Marlon. Stage, motion picture actor. 281
BRAQUE, Georges. Painter. 630
BRECHT, Bertolt. Playwright. 1094
BRECKER, Louis. Owner, Roseland dance hall. 459
BREDER, Charles M., Jr. Director, New York Aquarium. 86
BRICE, Fannie. Comedienne; actress. 328
BRILL, Abraham Arden. Psychiatrist. 523
BRINKLEY, David. Television news commentator. 5
BRODERICK, John J. Detective, New York City Police. 1089
BROKAW, Clare Boothe. see Boothe, Clare.
BROPHY, Thomas Patrick. Chief Fire Marshall, New York City. 329
BROUN, Heywood. Newspaper columnist. 858
BROWDER, Earl. General Secretary, U.S. Communist Party. 771
BROWN, Bill. Health farm owner; member New York State Athletic Commission. 317
BROWN, Joe E. Comedian; actor. 198
BROWN, John Mason. Drama critic; editor; author; lecturer. 180
BROWN, William Montgomery. Bishop of Arkansas. 88
BRUBECK, David. Jazz pianist; orchestra leader. 185
BRUNDAGE, Avery. President, International Olympic Committee. 31
BRUNET, Pierre. Senior professional, New York Skating Club. 788

BRYAN, William Jennings. Politician. 920
BUCHMAN, Frank. Evangelistic minister. 939
BUCHTER, Jacob. Chief electrician, Metropolitan Opera Company. 1101
BUCK, Gene. Songwriter; President of American Society of Composers, Authors and Publishers; theatrical producer. 232
BUCKNER, Emery R. Lawyer. 219
BUFFET, Bernard. Painter. 562
BULLITT, William Christian. U.S. Ambassador to France. 663
BULLOCK, Hugh. Investment-manager. 435
BURGESS, W. Starling. Racing yacht designer. 614
BURKE, Randolph Forrest. Socialite. 388
BURNSTEIN, George. see London, George.
BURROWS, Abe. Comedian; playwright; director. 284
BUSH, Irving T. Originator, director, Bush Terminal. 762
BUTLER, James. Chain-grocery owner; race track owner. 421
BUTLER, Nicholas Murray. President, Columbia University; author. 215
BUTLER, Roland. Publicity director, Ringling Brothers and Barnum & Bailey Circus. 321
BUTTERWORTH, Charles. Comedian; motion picture actor. 598

CABOT, John Moors. U.S. Ambassador to Brazil. 33
CAGE, John M., Jr. Composer. 326
CALDER, Alexander. Maker and seller of mobiles. 310
CAMPBELL, Frank E. Mortician. 196
CAMPION, Daniel J. New York City Police detective. 83
CANIFF, Milton. Comic-strip cartoonist. 918
CANNON, Anthony. see Hart, Tony.
CANTOR, Eddie. Comedian; actor. 178
CAPP, Al. Comic-strip cartoonist. 750
CAPRA, Frank. Motion picture director. 991
CARDOZO, Benjamin Nathan. Chief Justice, New York Supreme Court. 186
CAREY, William. Contractor; Director, Madison Square Garden. 952
CARLSEN, Henrik Kurt. Merchant ship captain. 816
CARNEGIE, Hattie. Couturière. 597
CARNEY, Don. Radio broadcaster for children. 1049
CARR, John Dickson. Mystery writer. 1035
CASALS, Pablo. Concert cellist. 159
CASEY, James E. President, United Parcel Service. 17
CASHIN, William E. Pastor, St. Andrew's Roman Catholic Church; Chaplin, New York State Prison. 318

CATHER, Willa. Novelist. 36
CAVALLERO, Gene. Waiter, Colony Restaurant. 1038
CERF, Bennett A. President, Random House; radio and television personality. 849
CERUTTI, Ernest. Waiter, Colony Restaurant. 1038
CESOLI, Leo. European train conductor. 693
CHALIAPIN, Feodor C. Singer, Metropolitan Opera Company. 63
CHANEL, Gabrielle. Couturière. 995
CHANIN, Irwin S. Realtor; architectural engineer. 926
CHAPLIN, Charlie. Motion picture actor. 366
CHAPMAN, Frank M. Curator of Ornithology, American Museum of Natural History. 127
CHARLES, Ray. Popular singer; pianist; composer; publisher. 517
CHAVEZ, Cesar. Farm labor organizer. 754
CHERNE, Leo M. Executive Secretary, Research Institute of America. 154
CHILDS, William. Owner, Childs' Restaurants. 431
CHRYSLER, Walter P. Automobile manufacturer. 1042
CIERPLIKOWSKI, Antoine. Coiffeur. 189
CLARK, Bobby. Comedian. 197
CLARK, F. Ambrose. Horse breeder; President, United Hunts. 959
CLARK, Walter L. Curator, Grand Central Gallery of Art. 377
CLARKE, Arthur C. Science fiction writer. 760
CLAY, Lucius Du Bignon. General, U.S. Army; Head, Office of Defense Mobilization. 932
CLOSE, Marjorie Post. see Davies, Marjorie Post Close Hutton.
COCHET, Henri. Tennis player. 594
COCHRAN, Philip. Major, U.S. Army Air Forces. 427
COHAN, George M. Playwright; song writer; dancer; actor. 937
COLEMAN, Emil. Orchestra leader. 687
A COLLEGE FOOTBALL COACH (composite portrait). 729
COLLETT, Glenna. Golfer. 951
COMMODORE DUTCH. see Dutch, Commodore.
CONANT, James Bryant. President, Harvard University. 670
CONCELLO, Antoinette. Aerial trapeze artist. 315
CONCELLO, Arthur. Aerial trapeze artist. 315
CONDON, Albert Edwin (Eddie). Jazz guitarist. 950
CONDON, John F. Public school teacher. 406
CONEELY, Martin. see Cosey, Joseph.

CONNELLY, Marcus Cook (Marc). Playwright. 1039
CONTENT, Harry. Stock broker. 325
COOK, Emory. Sound expert; President, phonograph record company. 283
COOK, Joe. Vaudeville performer. 126
COOLIDGE, Grace. Wife, President Calvin Coolidge. 331
COOPER, Merian. Motion picture photographer. 624
COPELAND, Charles Townsend. Professor of Rhetoric and Oratory, Harvard University. 772
COPELAND, Royal S. Member, U.S. Senate. 633
CORDES, John. Detective, New York Police Department. 1109
CORNELL, Katharine. Actress. 9, 799
CORRIGAN, Joseph E. Judge, New York City Criminal Courts. 405
CORSI, Edward. Director, Emergency Home Relief Bureau; Commissioner of Immigration. 432
CORWIN, Norman. Radio script writer and director. 722
COSEY, Joseph (pseud.). Forger. 1135
COSGRAVE, Jessica Garretson. Educator; founder of Finch Junior College. 863
COTY, François. Perfume maker; journalist; politician. 783
COUGHLIN, John D. Police inspector. 213
COUNEY, Martin A. Physician; specialist in premature births. 774
COUNTESS MARA. see Whitman, Lucilla Mara de Vescovi.
COUSY, Robert Joseph. Basketball player. 1072
COWARD, Noël. Playwright; composer; actor. 449
COWEN, Joshua Lionel. Chairman, "Lionel Lines," toy electric trains. 451
COX, Walter. Horse trainer. 1122
CRAIG, John C. Consultant on pyrotechnics to Board of Display, New York World's Fair. 477
CRAIGE, John H. Captain, U.S. Marine Corps. 382
CRAM, Ralph Adams. Architect. 913
CRANE, Joe. National champion parachute jumper. 768
CRAVATH, Paul Drennan. Lawyer; corporation director. 845
CRAWFORD, Cheryl. Musical comedy producer. 1113
CREEL, George. Chairman, Committee of Public Information. 500
CRIPPS, Stafford. British statesman. 719
CRONYN, Hume. Actor. 798
CROWNINSHIELD, Frank. Editor, Vanity Fair. 559
CRUMBINE, Samuel J. Physician; public health worker. 967

CUDA, Tony. Mayor of Futani, Italy. 643
CULLMAN, Howard J. Theatrical investor; President, Beekman Hospital; partner, Cullman Brothers (tobacco). 1014
CUNNINGHAM, Merce. Choreographer. 55
CURLEY, Jack. Sports promoter. 157
CURRAN, Henry Hastings. Lawyer; politician; President, American Association Against the Prohibition Amendment. 1088
CURRAN, Joseph. President, National Maritime Union. 1051
CURRY, John Francis. Leader, New York County Democratic Party. 587

DACHÉ, Lilly. Milliner. 440
D'AGOSTINO, Pasquale. Grocer. 492
DALE, Chester. President, National Gallery of Art; investment banker. 229
DALI, Salvador. Surrealist painter. 278
DAMITA, Lily. Motion picture actress. 584
DAMROSCH, Walter. Conductor, New York Symphony. 394
DARLINGTON, Thomas. Physician; Commissioner of Health, New York City; author; lecturer; Grand Sachem, Society of Tammany. 411
DAVIDSON, Jo. Sculptor. 906
DAVIES, J. Clarence. Real estate developer. 535
DAVIES, Marjorie Post Close Hutton. Wife, U.S. Ambassador to Russia; socialite. 546
DAVIS, Bette. Motion picture actress. 216
DAVIS, Meyer. Orchestra leader. 646
DAY, Dorothy. Author; founder, Catholic Worker movement. 336
DAY, Joseph P. Real estate auctioneer. 839
de FLOREZ, Luis. Captain, U.S. Naval Reserve; mechanical engineer; inventor of synthetic training devices. 150
de MILLE, Agnes. Theatrical choreographer. 175
De SICA, Vittorio. Motion picture director; actor. 133
de VALOIS, Ninette. Director, Sadler's Wells Ballet. 599
de WOLFE, Elsie. see Mendl, Lady.
DeZEMBLER, Charles. Barber shop owner. 77
DELACOUR, Jean. Aviculturist; operator, Bronx Zoo. 412
DELEHANTY, Michael Joseph. President, Civil Service school. 823
DeMARCO, Renée. Dancer. 234
DeMARCO, Tony. Dancer. 234
DeMILLE, Cecil B. Motion picture director. 456
DEMPSEY, Jack. Prizefighter. 969

DENGEL, Veronica. Beautician. 744
DENISON, Frank Emerson. Tea grader and blender. 167
DESKEY, Donald. Furniture manufacturer. 591
DEWEY, Edward Russell. Director, Foundation for the Study of Cycles. 934
DEWEY, John. Philosopher; educator; author. 621
DEWEY, Thomas Edmund. District attorney, New York City; Governor, New York State; Presidential candidate. 895
d'HARNONCOURT, René. Director, Museum of Modern Art. 495
DIAMOND, Jack (Legs). Gambler, racketeer. 100
DICKSON, Carter. *see* Carr, John Dickson.
DILLEY, Arthur Urbane. Oriental rug dealer; author. 720
DILLING, Mildred. Concert harpist. 437
DILLON, Clarence. Banker. 103
DILLON, John J. Publisher, *Rural New-Yorker*. 890
DISNEY, Walt. Motion picture cartoonist. 655
DITMARS, Raymond. Supervisor, Bronx Zoo Snake House. 945
DIVINE, Father. *see* Baker, George.
DR. SEUSS. *see* Geisel, Theodor Seuss.
DONON, Joseph. Private chef. 92
DOUBLEDAY, Nelson. Publisher. 426
DOWLING, Robert W. Architect; Head, Advisory Arts Committee for National Cultural Center. 1060
DOXIADIS, Constantinos. City planner. 295
DRAPER, Paul. Tap-dancer. 235
DREBIN, Sam. Soldier of fortune. 899
DREISER, Theodore. Novelist. 193
DREYFUS, Max. Music publisher. 6
DREYFUSS, Henry. Theatrical designer. 62
DUBLIN, Louis I. Statistician. 355
DUCHAMP, Marcel. Artist. 713
DUFF, Peter (pseud.). Auctioneer. 70
DUFOUR, Lew. Midway concessionaire, New York World's Fair. 639
DUKE, Angier Biddle. U.S. Chief of Protocol. 404
DUKENFIELD, Claude William. *see* Fields, W.C.
DUMAINE, Alexandre. Chef. 978
DuMONT, Allen Balcom. Inventor; pioneer in television industry. 843
DUNCAN, Isadora. Dancer. 510
DUNNENGER, Joseph. Magician. 718
DUTCH, Commodore (pseud.). Confidence man; Broadway character. 1016
DUVEEN, Joseph. Art dealer. 242, 709

DYLAN, Bob. Popular music composer, singer. 220

EAGLE, Nate. Sideshow manager, Ringling Brothers and Barnum & Bailey Circus. 971
EASTMAN, George. Inventor; industrialist. 147
EDEN, Robert Anthony. British foreign minister, prime minister. 345
EDERLE, Gertrude. Swimmer. 997
EDGE, Rosalie Barrow. Chairman, Emergency Conservation Committee. 725
EDISON, Thomas Alva. Inventor. 1111
EDWARD, Prince of Wales. 290
EDWARDS, Everett Joshua. Shore whaler. 915
EILSHEMIUS, Louis Michel. Artist. 606
EINSTEIN, Albert. Mathematician; scientist. 904
ELIOT, George Fielding. Military analyst; author. 143
ELLINGTON, Edward Kennedy (Duke). Orchestra leader; composer. 465
ELLIOTT, James W. Sales promoter. 192
ELLIS, Abraham. Hat check concessionaire. 28
ERDMANN, John Frederick. Surgeon. 767
ERIKSON, Erik H. Psychoanalyst. 648
ERSKINE, John. Professor of English, Columbia University; author. 838
EVANS, Merle. Band leader, Ringling Brothers and Barnum & Bailey Circus. 739

FAIRCHILD, Sherman Mills. Airplane manufacturer; authority on aerial photography. 20
FALCARO, Joe. Bowler. 623
FARLEY, James A. Politician; U.S. Postmaster General. 96
FARRELL, Eileen. Concert singer. 460
FATHER DIVINE. see Baker, George.
FEDER, Abe H. Lighting designer. 876
FELDMAN, Sam. Lawyer. 304
FELLINI, Federico. Motion picture director. 980
FERRARI, Enzo. Automobile designer, manufacturer. 981
FEUER, Cy. Theatrical producer. 452
FIELDING, Temple Hornaday. Author of guidebooks. 979
FIELDS, W.C. Comedian; actor; juggler. 568
FINCH, Mrs. James Wells. see Cosgrave, Jessica Garretson.
FINN, William J. Roman Catholic priest; leader of Paulist choristers. 924
FINUCANE, Brendan. Flight Lieutenant, Royal Air Force. 764

FISCHER, Clifford C. Producer of revues. 544
FISH, Hamilton, Jr. U. S. Congressman. 380
FISHBERG, Isaac. Flutist. 332
FISHER, Clyde. Curator-in-Chief, Hayden Planetarium. 680
FISHER, Harry Conway (Bud). Cartoonist (Mutt and Jeff). 647
FITZGERALD, F. Scott. Novelist. 984
FLAHERTY, Robert J. Documentary film producer. 683
FLEXNER, Abraham. Educator; philanthropist; Secretary, Rockefeller Foundation General Education Board. 878
FLOOD, Hugh G. House-wrecking contractor. 644
FLYNN, Edward Joseph. Lawyer; Chairman, Democratic National Committee. 717
FOKKER, Anthony Herman Gerard. Airplane designer, manufacturer. 335
FONDA, Henry. Actor. 799
FORD, Henry. Automobile manufacturer. 676
FORSTER, Edward Morgan. Novelist. 539
FOSDICK, Harry Emerson. Minister. 1034
FOSTER, William Zebulon. Presidential candidate, U. S. Communist Party. 757
FRAAD, Daniel, Jr. President, Allied Maintenance Corporation. 457
FRANKFURTER, Felix. U. S. Supreme Court Justice. 526
FRANKLIN, Marty (pseud.). Confidence man. 137
FRANKLIN, Sidney. Matador. 296
FRASER, Leon. President, First National Bank. 439
FRAZIER, Brenda Diana Duff. Socialite; débutante. 527
FRENCH, Fred F. Realtor; building contractor. 862
FREY, Fritz. Swiss hotel owner. 494
FRICK, Helen Clay. Director, Frick Art Reference Library; philanthropist. 240
FRIENDLY, Fred W. Television producer. 749
FROHMAN, Daniel. Theatrical producer. 246
FROST, Robert. Poet. 711
FULLER, Alfred Carl. President, Fuller Brush Company. 640
FULLER, Richard Buckminster. Architect; designer; inventor; engineer. 498
FUNT, Allen. Radio, television personality; cameraman. 962
FURST, Bruno. Mnemonist; hypnotist; handwriting expert. 675

GABLER, Milton. Owner, Commodore Music Shop. 341
GADD, May. Authority on folk dancing. 577

GALLATIN, Albert Eugene. Founder, manager, Museum of Living Art. 651
GALLUP, George Horace. Public opinion poll taker. 105
GAMELIN, Maurice-Gustave. Generalissimo, Allied Armies in France. 375
GANGER, I. Arthur. Head, bar equipment business. 911
GARAND, John C. Inventor, semi-automatic rifle. 611
GARBO, Greta. Motion picture actress. 39
GARDEN, Mary. Opera singer. 898
GARRETSON, Jessica. see Cosgrave, Jessica Garretson.
GARROWAY, David. Television personality. 1009
GATTI-CASAZZA, Giulio. Impresario, Metropolitan Opera Company. 602
GEDDES, Norman Bel. Stage and industrial designer. 251
GEER, Alpheus. Philanthropist; reformer; Director of Marshall Stillman Movement. 685
GEHRIG, Louis Henry. Baseball player. 581
GEISEL, Theodor Seuss (Dr. Seuss). Author, illustrator of children's books. 174
GERSHWIN, George. Composer. 1026
GEST, Morris. Theatrical producer. 108
GHEEN, Celeste. Model. 818
GIBBONS, Euell Theophilus. Author of books on wild food. 343
GIBBS, William Francis. Naval architect. 89
GIEGENGACK, Augustus E. Head, U.S. Government Printing Office. 671
GIELGUD, John. Actor. 800
GIFFORD, Walter Sherman. President, American Telephone & Telegraph Company. 171
GILBERT, Alfred Carlton. Founder, A.C. Gilbert Co. (toys). 35
GILBERT, Eugene. Advertising researcher for teen culture; author. 155
GILBERT, Lewis Dusenbery. Minority stockholder. 972
GILLESPIE, John Birks (Dizzy). Orchestra leader; trumpet player. 116
GILLHAUS, John. Motorman, Sixth Avenue trolley line. 313
GINSBERG, Allen. Poet. 773
GLENDON, Richard G., Sr. Crew coach, U.S. Naval Academy. 726
GLENDON, Richard G., Jr. Crew coach, Columbia University. 726
GLOW, Bernie. Trumpet player. 564
GMEINER, Hermann. Organizer, SOS Children's Villages. 466

GODOWSKY, Leopold. Co-inventor, Kodachrome process; concert violist. 1096
GOLDBERG, Arthur Joseph. Lawyer; U.S. Secretary of Labor; United Nations representative; Justice, U.S. Supreme Court. 777
GOLDWIN, Samuel. Motion picture producer. 160
GOODMAN, Benny. Orchestra leader; clarinetist. 26
GOODMAN, Edwin. Owner, Bergdorf Goodman. 118
GORDON, Max. Theatrical producer. 730
GORDON, Mazie P. Ticket seller, Venice Theatre on Bowery. 645
GOUDSMIT, Samuel A. Chairman, Physics Department, Brookhaven National Laboratory. 316
GOUDY, Frederic William. Type designer. 392
GOULD, Glenn. Concert pianist. 53
GOULD, Joseph Ferdinand. Bohemian; author of unpublished book. 520, 837
GOULD, Samuel B. Chancellor, State University of New York. 164
GRAEBNER, Clark. Tennis player. 573
GRAHAM, Martha. Dancer. 1
GRAINGER, Percy. Composer; concert pianist. 689
GRANGE, Harold E. (Red). Football player. 25
GRAYCE (no last name given). Chorus girl. 723
GREEN, Cecil. Fishing guide, Florida Keys. 542
GREEN, E.R.H. Owner, Round Hill Experimental Laboratories. 448
GREENSPAN, Benjamin E. New York City Magistrate. 478
GRENET, Augustine J. Horse racing bookmaker. 578
GROSSMAN, Harry. Process-server. 796
GROSVENOR, Gilbert H. Editor, National Geographic Magazine. 383
GROSZ, George. Artist. 61
GUITRY, Sacha. Playwright. 308
GUMPERT, Martin. Physician, geriatrics. 384
GUMPERTZ, Samuel W. Director, Ringling Brothers and Barnum & Bailey Circus. 119
GUNTHER, John. Author; geographer. 508
GUSWELLER, James A. Episcopal minister. 177
GUTHRIE, William Norman. Rector, St. Mark's-in-the-Bouwerie. 575
GUTMAN, Walter Knowlton. Investment-counselor; art critic. 842

HAFT, Louis. Owner, Haft Glass Company. 775
HAGEN, Joseph Francis. see O'Brien, (Philadelphia) Jack.
HAGEN, Walter. Golfer. 812

HAGSTROM, Andrew Gunnar. Cartographer. 916
HAGUE, Frank. Mayor, Jersey City, New Jersey. 311
HALDEMAN-JULIUS, E. Publisher. 14
HALL, Dorothy. see Schiff, Dorothy.
HALL, James Jefferson Davis. Street preacher. 949
HALLETT, George Hervey, Jr. Executive Secretary, Citizens Union; reformer. 181
HALLOCK, Joseph Theodore. 1st Lieutenant, U. S. Army Air Forces. 1130
HAMID, George A. President, amusement park booking agency. 15
HAMMER, Armand. Jewelry collector. 506
HAMMERSTEIN, Oscar, II. Song writer; musical comedy writer. 782
HAMMOND, John Hays, Jr. Inventor. 438
HAMMOND, John Henry, Jr. Popular music critic; Director, Columbia Recording Corporation. 1133
HANNON, Bryan. Historian; author; streetcar driver. 879
HARBACH, Otto. Author, musical comedies. 565
HARBURGER, John. Milliner. 131
HARDING, Edwin Forrest. Major-general, U. S. Army. 1041
HARDWICKE, Cedric. Actor. 799
HARRIGAN, Edward Green. Variety-show, musical comedy performer. 770
HARRIMAN, William Averell. U. S. statesman; governor, New York State. 803
HARRISON, Wallace Kirkman. Director of planning, U. N. headquarters. 57
HART, Lorenz. Song writer; musical comedy writer. 1115
HART, Moss. Playwright. producer. 453
HART, Richard Olney. Head, window-washing crew, Empire State Building. 518
HART, Tony (pseud.). Variety-show, musical comedy performer. 770
HARTMANN, Alfred. Chef. 1038
HARVEY, George Upton. Borough President, New York City. 738
HAYES, Helen. Actress. 1065
HAYES, James Edward. Liaison officer, Democratic Party, New York City. 419
HAYES, Patrick Joseph. Cardinal, Archdiocese of New York. 152
HAYS, Will H. Director, Motion Picture Producers and Distributors' Association of America; Censor. 231, 268.
HAYWARD, Leland. Theatrical agent. 455

HEARST, William Randolph. Newspaper publisher. 716
HEATTER, Gabriel. Radio commentator. 224
HECKSCHER, August. Industrialist; philanthropist. 1093
HEDLEY, Frank. President, Interborough Rapid Transit Company. 1095
HEIFETZ, Jascha. Concert violinist. 376
HELBURN, Theresa. Director, The Theatre Guild. 87
HELLMAN, Lillian. Playwright. 662
HEMINGWAY, Ernest. Novelist; short story writer. 64, 471
HENDERSON, Mary Avezzana Benjamin. see Benjamin, Mary A.
HENDERSON, William James. Music critic. 752
HENRICH, Thomas David. Baseball player. 732
HERRICK, Myron T. U.S. Ambassador to France. 634
HERRMANN, Emil. Violin dealer. 1029
HERTZ, Mr. and Mrs. John D. Horse breeders. 221
HEWITT, Edward Ringwood. Director, International Motor Company; fisherman; inventor. 204
HEYDENRYK, Henry. Picture framer. 306
HILDRETH, Samuel. Racehorse trainer. 24
HINES, Earl (Father). Jazz pianist; orchestra leader. 874
HINES, James J. Leader, Eleventh Assembly District, New York City. 265
HITCHCOCK, Alfred. Motion picture director. 1092
HITCHCOCK, Louise Eustis. Horsewoman. 369
HITCHCOCK, Thomas, Sr. Polo player. 369
HITCHCOCK, Thomas, Jr. Polo player. 369
HITLER, Adolf. Führer, Third Reich. 365
HODGE, Paul. Chief Petty Officer, U.S. Navy. 146
HOFFER, Eric. Philosopher; author; longshoreman. 223
HOLDEN, William. Actor. 798
HOLLINS, Albert. Worker in bomb factory. 947
HOLTZMANN, Fanny. Lawyer for Theatrical Profession. 661
HOOD, Frederick E. Sailmaker. 893
HOOD, Raymond. Architect. 609
HOOPINGARNER, Newman Leander. Professor of Business Psychology, New York University. 226
HOOVER, Herbert. U.S. President. 821
HOOVER, John Edgar. Director, U.S. Federal Bureau of Investigation. 262
HOPKINS, Arthur. Theatrical producer. 1010
HOPKINS, Harry L. Special advisor and assistant to U.S. President. 467
HOPPE, William Frederick. Professional billiard player. 815

HOTCHKISS, Hazel. see Wightman, Hazel Hotchkiss.
HOVING, Thomas P. F. Parks Commissioner, New York City; Director, Metropolitan Museum of Art. 881
HOWARD, Roy Wilson. Publisher, Scripps-Howard Newspapers. 851
HOWE, William F. Criminal lawyer. 294
HUGGINS, Miller. Manager, New York Yankees. 928
HUGHES, Charles Evans. U.S. Supreme Court Chief Justice. 169
HUMMEL, Abraham H. Criminal lawyer. 294
HUMPHREY, Elliott (Jack). Head, Seeing eye dog school. 469
HUMPHREYS, Joseph E. Prizefight announcer. 957
HUNTER, George H. Chairman, Board of Trustees, African Methodist Church. 665
HUNTLEY, Chet. Television news commentator. 5
HUPFER, William. Piano tone regulator. 791
HURST, Frederic. Milliner. 131
HUTTON, Marjorie Post Close. see Davies, Marjorie Post Close Hutton.

ILLICH, Ivan. Roman Catholic priest; educator; author. 887
INGBER, Lou. see Stillman, Lou.
INGERSOLL, Ralph. Editor of PM. 1067
ISAACS, Stanley M. New York City Council member. 844
ISTEL, Jacques André. Parachutist. 705

JACKSON, David Sidney. Specialist, New York Stock Exchange. 1028
JACKSON, Edward N. Photographer, New York Daily News. 703
JACOBS, Hirsch. Racehorse trainer. 792
JAECKEL, Richard. Furrier. 666
JAMES, Edwin L. European correspondent, New York Times. 622
JANIS, Sidney. Art dealer. 1104
JANNINGS, Emil. Motion picture actor. 179
JANSSEN, Werner. Conductor, New York Philharmonic Orchestra. 37
JAVITS, Jacob K. Member, U.S. House of Representatives, U.S. Senate. 378
JEANNERET, Charles Edouard (Le Corbusier). Architect. 361
JEFFERS, Henry William. Milk distributor. 659
JERITZA, Maria. Singer, Metropolitan Opera Company. 1073

JEROME, William Travers. Reformer; District Attorney, Manhattan. 896
JOHNSON, Chic. Comedian; stager of Hellz-a-Poppin. 708
JOHNSON, Edward. General Director, Metropolitan Opera Company; opera singer. 372
JOHNSON, Frederick. Captain, S. S. Josiah Crabtree. 589
JOHNSON, Hugh K. Anthropologist; social worker. 1100
JOHNSON, Hugh Samuel. Director, National Recovery Administration; General, U. S. Army. 371
JOHNSON, James Weldon. Author; Executive Secretary, NAACP. 237
JOHNSON, James William. Collector, Internal Revenue Service. 357
JOHNSON, Robert J. (pseud.) Insurance salesman. 509
JOHNSTON, James Jay. Boxing promoter; Assistant to President, Madison Square Garden. 205
JONES, Bassett. Chairman, Committee on Display, New York World's Fair; elevator designer; electrical engineer. 241
JONES, Elvin. Jazz drummer. 1084
JONES, Robert Edmond. Stage designer. 301
JONES, Robert Trent. Golf course architect. 579
JONES, Robert Tyre (Bobby), Jr. Golfer. 397
JOSEPHS, Louis (Frisco). Jazz dancer. 1131
JULIAN, Hubert. Aviator; parachute jumper; Minister of Air, Abyssinia. 107

KAHN, Otto H. Financier; patron of arts. 499
KAPP, Jack. President, Decca Records. 853
KATZ, Hymie (pseud.). Night-club owner. 1032
KAUFMAN, Beatrice (Mrs. George S.). Wife of playwright. 236
KAUFMAN, George S. Playwright. 248
KAUFFMAN, Bernie. Owner, Kauffman Saddlery Company. 1005
KAUFFMAN, Ike. Owner, Kauffman Saddlery Company. 1005
KAUFFMAN, Jake. Owner, Kauffman Saddlery Company. 1005
KAYSHUS, Effie. Shoe manufacturer. 1062
KAZAN, Avraam Elia (Joe). Author; rug merchant. 864
KEELER, Elisha. Square-dance caller. 346
KELLEMS, Vivien. Manufacturer of electrical parts. 423
KELLER, Helen. Author; lecturer. 110
KELLY, Alvin (Shipwreck). Flagpole sitter. 1059
KEMP, Harry. Poet. 807
KENLON, John. Chief, New York City Fire Department. 188

KENNY, Nick. Columnist, New York Daily Mirror. 966
KENNY, William Frank. Industrialist. 488
KERN, Jerome. Song writer; musical comedy writer. 1116
KETCHAM, Howard. Color, design and illumination engineer. 300
KHEEL, Theodore. Lawyer; labor mediator. 650
KIELY, John J. Postmaster, New York City. 398
KILPATRICK, John Reed. President, Madison Square Garden. 340
KIMBALL, James H. Meteorologist, U.S. Weather Bureau. 344
KING, Charles Brady. Automobile designer; builder; racer. 1012
KLEIN, S. Clothing manufacturer, distributor. 736
KLEM, Bill. Baseball umpire. 612
KNAUTH, Susanne Katherina. see Langer, Susanne K.
KNOPF, Alfred A. Publisher. 849, 1024
KNOPF, Blanche. Publisher. 1024
KNOPF, Samuel. Publisher. 1024
KNUDSEN, William S. President, General Motors Corporation; Member, Advisory Commission to Council of National Defense. 834
KOENIG, Sam. Politician. 704
KOMMER, Rudolf K. Theatrical producer. 692
KORMAN, Murray. Photographer. 740
KREISLER, Fritz. Concert violinist. 379
KROYT, Boris. Member, Budapest String Quartet. 140
KUBRICK, Stanley. Motion picture director. 470

LA GUARDIA, Fiorello H. Politician; Mayor of New York City. 514
LACHAISE, Gaston. Sculptor. 450
LACOSTE, Rene. Tennis player. 1107
LAMB, Thomas. Designer of handles. 195
LAMBERT, Gerard B. Yachtsman; President, Lambert Company. 18
LANDOLF, Bluch. Circus clown. 446
LANGER, Susanne K. Philosopher of aesthetics; author. 787
LANGNER, Lawrence. Co-director of Theatre Guild; lawyer; author. 142
LASKY, Jesse L. Motion picture executive. 141
LASSER, Jacob Kay. Author; income tax expert. 975
LASTFOGEL, Abe. Theatrical agent, U.S.O. shows. 857
LATHAM, Natalie Wales. Founder, Bundles for Britain. 8
LAUBACH, Frank Charles. Congregational minister; educator. 1001

LAURENCE, William L. Science reporter, New York Times. 503
LAWES, Lewis E. Warden, New York State Prison. 217
LAWRANCE, Charles Lanier. Inventor of airplane engines. 254
LE CORBUSIER. see Jeanneret, Charles Edouard.
LE GALLIENNE, Eva. Actress; director; translator. 551
LEADER, Edward. Crew coach, Yale University. 422
LEBLANG, Joe. Theatrical ticket agent. 825
LEDOUX, Urbain ("Mr. Zero"). Philanthropist. 929
LEE, Tsung-Dao. Theoretical physicist; Nobel Prize winner. 855
LEFEBVRE, Channing. Choirmaster, organist, Trinity Church. 922
LEHMAN, Herbert Henry. Governor, New York State. 409
LEHMANN, Lotte. Singer, Metropolitan Opera Company. 938
LEIBOWITZ, Samuel S. Lawyer. 570
LEIGH, Douglas. Designer, luminous signs and neon signs. 574
LEIGH, William Colston. Owner, Leigh Bureau of Lectures and Entertainment. 324
LEITZEL, Lillian. Aerialist, Ringling Brothers and Barnum & Bailey Circus. 955
LENGLEN, Suzanne. Tennis player. 977
LESCAZE, William. Architect. 678
LETERMAN, Elmer G. Insurance salesman. 631
LEVINE, Joseph E. Motion picture producer. 1069
LEWIS, Joseph. Publisher. 68
LEWIS, Rosa. Proprietor, Cavendish Hotel. 756
LEWIS, Sinclair. Novelist. 496, 1118
LEWIS, Wilmarth Sheldon. Author; Horace Walpole scholar. 958
LHEVINNE, Rosina. Piano teacher. 566
LIBMAN, Emanuel. Physician; diagnostician. 483
LICHINE, Alexis. Vintner; wine merchant. 279
LIE, Trygve. Secretary-general, United Nations. 490
LILIENTHAL, David Eli. Financier; corporation director; author; Chairman, U.S. Atomic Energy Commission. 910
LILLIE, Beatrice. Comedienne; actress. 136
LINDBERGH, Charles Augustus. Aviator. 1132
LINDSAY, John V. Mayor, New York City. 642
LIPPOLD, Richard. Sculptor. 990
LIPTON, Thomas. Importer; merchant. 129
LITTLE, Lou. Football coach, Columbia University. 280
LITTLETON, Martin J. Orator. 867

LIVERIGHT, Horace B. Publisher. 741
LLOYD, Harold. Motion picture actor. 781
LOGAN, Joshua Lockwood. Playwright; director; producer. 1020
LOMBARDO, Guy. Orchestra leader. 814
LONDON, George. Singer, Metropolitan Opera Company. 1078
LONDOS, Jim. Professional wrestler. 852
LONERGAN, Anna. Head, stevedore union. 548
LONGWORTH, Alice Roosevelt. Socialite. 827
LONGWORTH, Nicholas. Speaker, U.S. House of Representatives. 797
LOOS, Anita. Author; playwright. 173
LORD, Mary Stinson Pillsbury. U.S. representative to U.N. Commission on Human Rights. 745
LOREE, Leonor F. President, Delaware & Hudson Railroad. 697
LORENZ, Konrad Z. Zoologist; authority on aggression; author. 209
LOVETT, Robert A. U.S. Assistant Secretary of War for Air. 993
LUCAS, Diane Wilson. Owner of cooking school. 1108
LUCE, Clare Boothe. see Boothe, Clare
LUCE, Henry Robinson. Publisher. 1008
LUDWIG, Leopold. Concert pianist and conductor. 275
LUKS, George. Painter. 493
LUNT, Alfred. Actor. 374
LYDIG, Rita de Alba de Acosta. Socialite; author. 550
LYONS, Harry. Barge and small boat owner. 877
LYONS, Leonard. Newspaper gossip columnist. 986

MacARTHUR, Charles Gordon. Playwright. 1134
McBRIDE, John. Theatrical ticket agent. 1037
McBRIDE, Mary Margaret. Radio personality (housewives' program). 346
McCARTHY, Stitch. see Rothberg, Sam.
McCLELLAN, George Brinton. Mayor, New York City; historian. 761
McCOOEY, John H. Democratic Leader, Kings County, Brooklyn. 298
MacCORMICK, Austin H. Commissioner of Correction; prison reformer. 351
MACDONALD, James Aloysius. see Stingo, John R.
MacDOUGALL, Alice Foote. Restaurant owner. 880
MACFADDEN, Bernarr. Publisher; physical fitness advocate. 50, 789
McGOLDRICK, Joseph D. Comptroller, New York City; Professor of Government, Columbia University. 835

McGOORTY, John. Tramp. 124
McGOVERN, Artie. Head, McGovern's Gymnasium; prize-fighter. 60
McGRAW, John. Manager, New York Giants. 668
McGUINNESS, Peter J. Democratic leader, Greenpoint, Brooklyn. 95
MACK, Walter S., Jr. Chairman, Pepsi-Cola Company. 681
McKEE, Joseph Vincent. President, New York City Board of Aldermen. 135
McLAUGHLIN, George V. Police Commissioner, New York City. 973
McLEAN, Alice Throckmorton. Founder, American Women's Voluntary Services. 545
MacLEISH, Archibald. Poet. 733
McNAIR, Lesley James. Lieutenant-general, U.S. Army. 288
McNAMEE, Graham. Radio announcer. 218
MacPHAIL, Larry. President, Brooklyn Dodgers. 117
MACY, W. Kingsland. Leader, Republican Party, New York State. 533
MADDEN, Joe. Saloonkeeper. 627
MADISON, Dolly. see Paul, Maury H.B.
MADO, Marie-Louise. see Point, Marie-Louise Mado.
MALLON, Mary (Typhoid Mary). Cook; typhoid carrier. 1043
MALRAUX, André. Novelist; French cabinet minister. 476
MANEY, Richard Sylvester. Broadway press agent. 230
MANN, Thomas. Novelist. 395
MANNING, William T. Bishop, Protestant Episcopal Diocese of New York. 330
MANSHIP, Paul. Sculptor. 206
MARA, Timothy James. Founder, Turf and Gridiron Club (Bookmakers). 1033
MARBURY, Elisabeth. National Democratic Committeewoman, New York. 914
MARDERSTEIG, Giovanni. Publisher; printer; literary scholar. 401
MARIE, Queen of Roumania. 885
MARIN, John. Painter. 569
MARK, Herman F. Scientist; Professor of Organic Chemistry, Polytechnic Institute of Brooklyn. 809
MARKOVA, Alicia. Ballerina. 504
MARKOWITZ, Ernest. see Martin, Ernest H.
MARQUAND, John P. Novelist. 985
MARSHALL, George Catlett. U.S. Secretary of State; Chief of Staff, U.S. Army. 170

MARTIN, Ernest H. Theatrical producer. 452
MARTIN, Glenn L. Airplane manufacturer. 447
MARX, Harpo. Comedian; actor. 813
MARY, Queen of England. 445
MATISSE, Henri. Artist. 537
MATTHAU, Walter. Actor. 800
MATTHEWS, J.B. Consulting expert, Dies Committee, U.S. House of Representatives. 983
MATTIOLI, Raffaele. Publisher; historian; translator; economist. 2
MAUGHAM, William Somerset. Novelist; playwright; short story writer. 1068
MAURY, Reuben. Chief editorial writer, New York Daily News. 286
MAXIM, Hudson. Inventor. 1097
MAXWELL, Elsa. Party giver. 194
MAY, Elaine. Comedienne; actress; playwright. 1007
MAYER, Louis B. Motion picture executive. 1125
MEAD, Margaret. Anthropologist; author. 515
MEDALIE, George Z. U.S. District Attorney. 558
MEEHAN, John Francis (Chick). Football coach, New York University. 626
MEHTA, Zubin. Symphony orchestra conductor. 817
MELLON, Andrew W. Financier; U.S. Secretary of the Treasury. 225
MENDL, Lady (Elsie de Wolfe). Actress; socialite. 433
MENGELBERG, Willem. Director, New York Philharmonic Orchestra. 54
MENJOU, Adolphe. Motion picture actor. 82
MENOTTI, Gian Carlo. Opera composer. 755
MENUHIN, Yehudi. Concert violinist. 833
MEREDITH, Burgess. Actor. 1055
MERTON, Robert K. Professor of Sociology, Columbia University. 472
MEYER, Alfred. Physician. 269
MEYER, Annie Nathan. Founder, Bernard College. 269
MEYER, Arthur Simon. Chairman, New York State Board of Mediation. 1091
MIELZINER, Jo. Theatre set designer. 19
MILBURN, Devereux. Polo player; lawyer. 998
MILLAY, Edna St. Vincent. Poet. 1077
MILLER, Alice Duer. Novelist. 555
MILLER, Gilbert. Playwright. 667
MILLER, Mitchell William. Orchestra leader; oboist. 353
MILLER, Roger. Popular songwriter; singer. 1103
MILLS, Ogden Livingston. Financier; U.S. Undersecretary of the Treasury. 1058

MILLS, William. Fishing tackle store owner. 463
MITROPOULOS, Dimitri. Conductor, New York Philharmonic. 604
MIZNER, Addison. Architect. 766
MIZNER, Wilson. Confidence man; promoter; Broadway personality. 567
MOLDEN, Otto. Founder, European Forum; political visionary. 936
MOLÉ, Paul. Barber. 528
MOLNÁR, Ferenc. Playwright. 801
MOORE, Alexander Pollock. Newspaper publisher; U.S. Ambassador to Peru. 358
MOORE, Archibald Lee (Archie). Prizefighter. 679
MOORE, Henry. Sculptor. 314
MOORE, Marianne Craig. Poet. 480
MORAN, Eugene F. President, Moran Towing & Transport Company. 297
MOREY, Sigmund M. Machine tool manufacturer. 339
MORGAN, Anne. Club woman; philanthropist. 549
MORGAN, Charles, Jr. Lawyer for American Civil Liberties Union. 933
MORGAN, J. Pierpont. Financier. 658
MORGENTHAU, Henry, Jr. U.S. Secretary of the Treasury. 52
MORINO, Louis. Restaurant owner. 158
MORRIS, Newbold. President, New York City Council. 400
MORSE, Walter P. Missionary in China. 434
MOSES, Robert. Chairman, New York State Council of Parks. 847
MOSKOWITZ, Mrs. Henry. Director of publicity, New York State Democratic Committee. 165
MOSTEL, Zero. Actor. 799
MULDOON, William. Owner, Hygenic Institute; Member, New York State Boxing Commission. 944
MULLIGAN, Gerry. Jazz saxophonist; composer. 497
MULROONEY, Edward Pierce. Police Commissioner, New York City. 214
MUNN, Orson D. Publisher, Scientific American; patent attorney. 106
MURPHY, George. President of Mark Cross; prototype of leading character in Fitzgerald's Tender is the Night. 586
MURPHY, Sara. Prototype of leading character in Fitzgerald's Tender is the Night. 586
MURRAY, Arthur. Dance instructor. 1085
MURROW, Edward R. Radio and television news commentator. 1120

NARAYAN, Rasipuram Krishaswami. Novelist. 1022
NAWKINS, Angeline. Captain, Salvation Army. 402
NELSON, Donald M. Industrialist; Chairman, War Production Board. 145
NERVI, Pier Luigi. Architect; engineer. 603
NESSLER, Charles. Inventor, permanent wave machine. 429
NEWSTEAD, Helaine. Professor of English, Hunter College. 386
NICHOLS, Michael (Mike). Comedian; motion picture director. 1007
NICHOLSON, George. Prizefight sparring partner. 943
NICKERBOCKER, Cholly. see Paul, Maury H. B.
NIKANOV, Johnny. Gypsy king. 536
NILSSON, Birgit. Singer, Metropolitan Opera Company. 16
NORRIS, Stanley. Window washer. 625
NORTH, John Ringling. President, Ringling Brothers and Barnum & Bailey Circus. 1025
NORVILLE, Kenneth. see Norvo, Kenneth (Red).
NORVO, Kenneth (Red). Vibraharp player. 686
NUTHALL, Betty. Tennis player. 305
NYSWANDER, Marie. Psychiatrist, psychoanalyst for narcotics addicts. 1023

O'BRIEN, (Philadelphia) Jack (pseud.). Head, health gymnasium. 125
O'BRIEN, John P. Mayor, New York City. 901
OCHS, Adolph Simon. Publisher, New York Times. 588
ODETS, Clifford. Playwright. 873
ODLUM, Floyd B. Director, investment trust. 1030
O'KEEFFE, Georgia. Artist. 3
OKIE, William Bernard, Jr. Window display designer. 605
OLSEN, Ole. Comedian; stager of Hellz-a-Poppin. 708
OLVANY, George Washington. Judge, New York Court of General Sessions. 707
O'NEILL, Eugene. Playwright. 884, 1021
O'NEILL, Rose. Designer of Kewpie Doll. 531
ORNSTEIN, Leo. Concert pianist. 860
O'ROURKE, William. Diplomatic courier, communications officer, U. S. State Department. 430
OTIS, Harry. Life insurance salesman. 51
OTTINGER, Lawrence. President, United States Plywood Corporation. 805

PADEREWSKI, Ignaz. Concert pianist; Premier of Poland. 273
PAGE, Geraldine. Actress. 800

PAGLIARO, Louis. Ping-pong champion. 982
PATE, Maurice. Executive director, United Nations International Children's Emergency Fund. 66
PATERNO, Charles Vincent. Building contractor. 607
PATTERSON, Joseph Medill. Publisher, New York Daily News. 1082
PAUL, Maury H. B. Society column writer. 272
PEABODY, Ernest Henry. President, Peabody Engineering Corporation; anti-noise campaigner. 940
PENNINGTON, Mary Engle. Chief, Food Research Laboratory; refrigeration expert. 486
PERKINS, Anthony. Actor. 800
PERKINS, Frances. U. S. Secretary of Labor; sociologist. 600
PERKINS, Maxwell Evarts. Editor; vice-president, Charles Scribner's Sons. 1053
PERSHING, John J. General, U. S. Army. 714
PERSKY, Daniel. Hebrew scholar; member, Herzliah Institute. 927
PÉTAIN, Henri Philippe. Marshall of France; head, Vichy France government. 543
PETERS, Clinton. Painter; art teacher. 233
PETRUNKEVITCH, Alexander I. Expert on spiders. 56
PETZOLD, Theodore. Boy Scout. 1031
PHELPS, William Lyon. Professor of English, Yale University. 532
PHILIPPE, Claudius Charles. Vice-president, catering, Waldorf-Astoria Hotel. 1071
PICASSO, Pablo Ruiz y. Painter. 746, 965
PICKFORD, Mary. Motion picture actress. 968
PIERCE, John R. Executive Director of Communications Research, Bell Telephone Laboratories. 1114
PILLSBURY, Mary Stinson. see Lord, Mary Stinson Pillsbury.
PITKIN, Walter B. Author; Professor of Journalism, Columbia University. 252
PLATZKER, Joseph. Director, New York City Vacancy Listing Bureau. 166
POINT, Marie-Louise Mado. Manager, Restaurant de la Pyramide. 464
POIRET, Paul. Couturier. 292
POLIZIANO, Angelo. Poet. 46
POLLOCK, Channing. Playwright. 255
POND, James Burton. Owner, lecture agency. 227
PONS, Lily. Singer, Metropolitan Opera Company. 354
"POP" (Bookmaker). 923
POPE, Arthur Upham. Authority on Iran; author; philosophy professor. 1050

PORTER, Cole. Song writer; musical comedy writer. 1117
PORTER, Wilma. see Soss, Wilma Porter.
POST, Emily. Author; authority on etiquette. 547
POST, Marjorie. see Davies, Marjorie Post Close Hutton.
POWERS, Bertram A. President, New York Typographical Union No. 6. 829
PRAJADHIPOK. King of Siam. 583
PRATT, Ruth. Member, New York City Board of Aldermen. 743
PREMINGER, Otto. Motion picture producer and director. 44
PRENDERGAST, Charles. Artist. 390
PRENDIVILLE, Joseph P. Staff-sergeant, U.S. Army. 868
PRINTEMPS, Yvonne. Actress. 308
PUROBAYEV, Pavel Petrovich. Secret agent. 1046
PYLE, C.C. Sports promoter. 153

QUALTINGER, Helmut. Actor; playwright. 302

RABKIN, William. Manufacturer of coin-operated amusement machines. 780
RACHMANINOFF, Sergei Vassilievitch. Composer. 58
RAMEY, John Daniel. American soldier. 134
RAPEE, Erno. Orchestra conductor, Radio City Music Hall. 489
RAUSCHENBERG, Robert. Artist. 684
RAY, Randolph. Rector, Little Church Around the Corner. 276
RAYMOND, Gaston. Croupier at Monte Carlo. 883
REDGRAVE, Michael. Actor. 798
REILLY, Edward J. Lawyer. 342
REISELIN, Walter. Milk delivery man. 886
REISNER, Christian F. Methodist Episcopal minister, Broadway Temple. 529
RENOIR, Jean. Motion picture director. 563
RICH, Buddy. Jazz drummer. 81
RICKARD, George L. (Tex). Director, Madison Square Garden. 875
RICKEY, Branch. President, Brooklyn Dodgers. 1000
RINGLING, Charles. Owner, Ringling Brothers Circus. 1040
RINGLING, John. Owner, Ringling Brothers Circus. 1040
RIPLEY, Robert L. "Believe it or Not" cartoonist; radio personality. 721
RIPLEY, Sidney Dillon, II. Associate Curator of Zoology, Peabody Museum; authority on birds of Far East. 228

RIVERA, Diego. Painter. 303
ROBARDS, Jason. Actor. 800
ROBBINS, William J. Director, New York Botanical Gardens. 953
ROBESON, Paul. Actor; concert singer. 534
ROBINSON, Bill. Dancer; philanthropist. 113
ROBINSON, Frederick B. President, College of the City of New York. 289
ROBINSON-DUFF, Frances. Drama coach. 267
ROCKEFELLER, David. President, Chase Manhattan Bank. 870
ROCKEFELLER, John D. Industrialist. 715
ROCKEFELLER, John D., Jr. Industrialist; philanthropist. 903
ROCKEFELLER, Nelson Aldrich. Governor, New York State; Latin American expert. 91
ROCKWELL, Norman. Artist; illustrator. 1044
RODGERS, Richard. Song writer; musical comedy writer. 1116, 1126
ROGERS, Anne Hone. Professional show dog handler; breeder. 1019
ROGERS, Joe. Midway concessionaire, New York World's Fair. 639
ROISMAN, Joseph. Member, Budapest String Quartet. 140
ROMANOFF, Alexis Lawrence. Professor of Chemical Embryology, Cornell University. 291
ROMANOFF, Michael Alexandrovitch. Impostor; restaurant owner. 287
ROOSEVELT, Eleanor. Author; lecturer; statesman. 710, 1124
ROOSEVELT, Franklin Delano. Governor, New York State; President, United States. 408, 822
ROOT, Elihu. Lawyer; U.S. Senator; U.S. Secretary of State; U.S. Ambassador to Russia. 244
ROPER, William W. Football coach, Princeton University; politician. 882
ROSE, Billy. Stage show producer. 629
ROSEN, Al. Hollywood agent. 413
ROSENBACH, A.S.W. Book dealer. 695
ROSENBERG, Anna. Labor mediator; Regional Director, Social Security Board; Head, New York State National Recovery Administration. 657
ROSENDAHL, Charles E. Aviator, lighter-than-air craft. 706
ROSENFELD, Henry Jonas. Dress manufacturer. 660
ROSENSTEIN, Nettie. Couturière. 1070
ROSENTHAL, Jean. Theatre lighting expert. 802

ROSOFF, Sam. Contractor, Eighth Avenue Subway. 632
ROSS, Rita. Cat-catcher. 552
ROTHAFEL, Samuel L. (Roxy). Theatre builder and manager. 253
ROTHBERG, Sam. Bondsman. 75
ROVENSTINE, Emery Andrew. Director, Department of Anesthesia, Bellevue Hospital. 45
ROYAL, John F. Vice-president, National Broadcasting Company. 1064
ROYCE, William H. Scholar (Balzac); author. 994
RUBIN, Louis. Marriage broker. 79
RUBINSTEIN, Artur. Concert pianist. 654
RUBINSTEIN, Helena. Cosmetics manufacturer. 84
RUDEL, Julius. Conductor, New York City Opera. 319
RUDKIN, Margaret. President, Pepperidge Farms, Inc. (bakery). 961
RUML, Beardsley. Economist; author; government advisor. 696
RUPPERT, Jacob. Brewer; owner, New York Yankees; U.S. Congressman. 85
RUSSELL, Charles Ellsworth (Pee Wee). Jazz clarinetist. 309
RUTH, George Herman (Babe). Baseball player. 74
RYAN, Elizabeth (Bunny). Tennis player. 635
RYAN, George J. Member, New York City Board of Education. 779

SABIN, Pauline Morton. Politician; President, Women's Organization for National Prohibition Reform. 698
SAFFORD, Frank. Trainer and driver of harness horses. 482
SAHL, Mort. Comedian. 367
SAITO, Hirosi. Japanese Ambassador to the United States. 260
SANDBURG, Carl. Poet. 778
SANDE, Earl. Jockey. 919
SANDERS, Harland. Founder, restaurant chain. 530
SANGER, Margaret. Author; birth control advocate. 172, 989
SANTELLI, George (Giorgio). Fencing master. 1013
SARACINI, Guido Chigi. Italian count; music patron. 1018
SARRA, Valentino. Photographer; president of advertising agency. 637
SAUNDERS, Blanche. Dog obedience trainer. 274
SCAMMON, Richard M. Statistician; political scientist. 748
SCHEEPERS, John T. Flower bulb broker. 334
SCHEFF, Fritzi. Opera and light-opera singer. 628

SCHELL, Maria. Actress. 799
SCHENCK, Nicholas M. President, Loew's Incorporated, and Metro-Goldwin-Meyer. 144
SCHER, Louis. Book scout. 115
SCHIAPARELLI, Elsa. Couturière. 199
SCHIFF, Dorothy. Owner and publisher, New York Post. 850
SCHINDLER, Raymond C. Head, private detective agency. 830
SCHLEMMER, William. Head, Hammacher Schlemmer & Co. (hardware). 653
SCHLING, Max. Florist. 337
SCHNABEL, Artur. Concert pianist. 690
SCHNEIDER, Alexander. Member, Budapest String Quartet. 140
SCHNEIDER, Hannes. Inventor of skiing techniques. 1086
SCHNEIDER, Mischa. Member, Budapest String Quartet. 140
SCHULTZ, Sam. Sidewalk grate "fisherman." 917
SCHUMANN-HEINK, Ernestine. Opera singer. 441
SCHUSTER, M. Lincoln. Publisher. 474
SCHWAB, Charles M. President, United States Steel Corporation. 956
SCHWARTZ, A. Charles. Financier. 596
SCHWARTZ, Louis G. Waiter; war bond salesman. 78
SCOTTI, Antonio. Singer, Metropolitan Opera Company. 1076
SCULL, Robert Cooper. Art dealer; owner of taxicab company. 619
SEABURY, Samuel. Politician; judge. 507
SEIDEN, Irving. President, Mercury Service Systems. 1060
SELL, Henry Blackman. Maker of canned meat products. 946
SENDAK, Maurice. Author; illustrator of children's books. 42
SERVICE, Robert W. Poet. 1102
SHAPIRO, Elliott. Elementary school principal. 828
SHATTUCK, Frank G. Owner, Schraffts Restaurants. 1110
SHAW, Artie. Jazz clarinetist; orchestra leader. 656
SHEROVER, Max. President, Linguaphone Institute of America (language teaching). 65
SHERWOOD, Robert Emmet. Playwright. 731
SHIPPEY, Hartwell Stuart. Barge captain. 931
SHOR, Bernard (Toots). Restaurant owner. 1017
SHORT, Bobby. Popular singer; pianist. 479
SHUBERT, J.J. Theatre operator. 132
SHUBERT, Lee. Theatre operator. 132

SIEGEL, Morris. Insurance expert. 673
SIGNORET, Simone. Actress. 800
SIKORSKY, Igor Ivanovitch. Airplane designer, engineer, executive. 1105
SIMENON, Georges. Novelist. 759
SIMON, Richard L. Publisher. 474
SIMPSON, Kenneth F. Chairman, New York County Republican Party. 121
SINATRA, Francis Albert (Frank). Popular singer. 785
SINGH, Sirdar Jagjit. Interpreter; president, India League of America. 747
SIROVICH, William I. U.S. Congressman, Fourteenth District, New York; orator; physician. 128
SLOAN, John. Historical artist. 13
SLOTKIN, Samuel. President, Hygrade Food Products Corporation. 259
SMITH, Alfred E. Governor of New York. 139
SMITH, Bernard E. Stock broker. 522
SMITH, Bruce. Director, Institute of Public Administration. 712
SMITH, Eleanor. Aviatrix. 700
SMITH, Kate. Popular singer. 458
SMITH, Maynard. Staff-sergeant, U.S. Army Air Force. 245
SMITH, Robert Lansing. Executive, Smith Brothers, Inc. 130
SMITH, William W., II. Executive, Smith Brothers, Inc. 130
SNYDER, Daniel. Captain, U.S. Army Air Forces. 1129
SOKOLOF, Vladimir. Actor. 798
SOMERVELL, Brehon Burke. Works Progress Administrator for New York City; Colonel, U.S. Army. 59
SONNEBORN, Dorothy. see Schiff, Dorothy.
SONNENBERG, Benjamin. Public-relations counsellor. 468
SOSS, Wilma Porter. Founder, Federation of Women Shareholders in American Business, Inc. 454
SOULÉ, Henri. Maître d'hôtel. 34
SPENCER, Shirley. Graphologist, New York Daily News; handwriting analyst. 976
SPERRY, Elmer A. Inventor. 368
SPEYER, James. Banker; patron of arts. 76
STANLEY, Kim. Actress. 798
STANTON, Frank. President, Columbia Broadcasting System. 571
STAPLETON, Maurine. Actress. 799
STEFANSSON, Vilhjalmur. Arctic explorer. 540
STEICHEN, Edward. Photographer; Commander, U.S. Navy. 201

STEIGER, Rod. Actor. 799
STEIN, Ben. Wallpaper-hanger. 420
STEPHENS, Olin. Yacht designer and builder. 1056
STEPHENS, Roderick. Yacht builder. 1056
STERN, Isaac. Concert violinist. 590
STEUER, Max D. Lawyer. 691, 970
STEVENS, Harry S. Concessionaire. 865
STEVENS, Roger Lacey. Theatrical producer; real estate tycoon. 187
STIEGLITZ, Alfred. Photographer. 1036
STILLMAN, Lou (Lou Ingber). Owner, Stillman's Gymnasium. 156
STIMSON, Henry L. U.S. Secretary of State. 557
STINGO, John R. (pseud.). Columnist, New York Enquirer. 1123
STOKOWSKI, Leopold. Conductor, Philadelphia Orchestra. 819
STONE, Edward D. Architect. 359
STOUT, Rex. Mystery story writer. 21
STRATON, John Roach. Fundamentalist minister. 652
STRAVINSKY, Igor. Composer; conductor. 892
STRYKER, Lloyd Paul. Lawyer. 541
STUYVESANT, Polly. see Paul, Maury H.B.
SUESS, DR. see Geisel, Theodor Seuss.
SULZBERGER, Arthur Ochs. President and publisher, New York Times. 1075
SUMNER, John S. Censor; Secretary, New York Society for the Suppression of Vice. 211
SUZUKI, Daisetz Teitaro. Authority on Zen Buddhism. 418
SWANSON, Gloria. Motion picture actress. 1045
SWIFT, J. Otis. Nature Editor, New York World-Telegram. 900
SWINBURNE, Algernon Charles. Poet. 67
SWING, Raymond Gram. Radio commentator. 1079
SZELL, George. Conductor, Cleveland Orchestra. 410

TALLEY, Marion. Singer, Metropolitan Opera Company. 694
TAYLOR, Deems. Music critic. 1066
TAYLOR, Marion Sayle. Radio "Voice of Experience." 1080
TEAGUE, Walter Dorwin. Industrial designer. 502
TEAL, John J., Jr. Associate Professor of Geography and Anthropology, University of Vermont; explorer; author. 356
THACKREY, Dorothy. see Schiff, Dorothy.
THOMAS, Norman. Presidential candidate, Socialist Party. 29

THOMPSON, Dorothy. Newspaper columnist. 512
THOMPSON, Ellery Franklin. Captain in dragger fleet. 277
TIBBETT, Lawrence. Singer, Metropolitan Opera Company. 461
TIEBOR, John W., I. Seal trainer. 151
TIEBOR, John W., II. Seal trainer. 151
TIEBOR, Roland. Seal trainer. 151
TILDEN, William Tatem, 2nd. Tennis Player. 487
TILLEY, George Dudley. Operator, ornamental-bird farm. 869
TINGUELY, Jean. Motion sculptor. 93
TOBIN, Ralph C. Colonel, 7th Regiment, New York City; socialite. 190
TODD, John R. Co-manager, Rockefeller Center. 610
TOJO, Hideki. Premier of Japan. 861
TOLSTOY, Alexandra Lvovna. Daughter of Leo Tolstoy; founder of Russian welfare agency. 362
TOMLINSON, Homer A. Bishop, Church of God. 737
TOSCANINI, Arturo. Conductor, New York Philharmonic. 210
TOWNSEND, A.J. Advertising consultant. 560
TOWNSEND, Edward T. Game warden. 442
TOWNSEND, William. Advertising consultant. 560
TREMAINE, Morris Sawyer. Comptroller, New York State. 207
TRESCA, Carlo. Labor organizer; revolutionist. 1027
TRUDEAU, Pierre. Prime Minister, Canada. 824
TRUMAN, Harry S. U.S. President. 669
TUGWELL, Rexford Guy. U.S. Under-Secretary of Agriculture; Professor of Economics, Columbia University. 890
TUNNEY, Gene. Prizefighter. 370
TURNER, Hilary F. Ferryboat captain. 436
TURNESA, William. Golfer. 32
TUTTLE, Charles H. U.S. District Attorney; lawyer. 897
TWYEFFORT, Raymond G. Custom tailor. 191
TWYNAM, Robert. Groundskeeper at Wimbledon. 561
TYPHOID MARY. see Mallon, Mary.
TYSEN, John Colquhoun. President, real estate firm. 992

UNTERMYER, Samuel. Lawyer. 580
URBAN, Joseph. Theatrical stage designer; architect. 149

VALDO, Patrick Francis. Personnel director, Ringling Brothers and Barnum & Bailey Circus. 120
VALENTINE, Lewis J. Police Commissioner, New York City. 501

VAN ANDA, Carr Vatell. Managing editor, New York Times. 47, 1061
VAN DYKE, W. S. Motion picture director. 592
van LOON, Hendrik Willem. Author; historian. 810, 960
VANDERBILT, Alfred Gwynne. Race track operator. 23
VANDERBILT, Cornelius, Jr. Publisher; socialite. 322
VANDERBILT, Harold. Yachtsman; contract bridge authority. 399
VEREKER, Elliot. Author; dilettante. 935
VINCENT, George Robert. Collector, voices of famous persons. 1081
VISHNIAC, Roman. Photographer of microscopic life; zoologist; physician. 1011
von KARAJAN, Herbert. Symphony orchestra conductor. 942
von STERNBERG, Josef. Motion picture director. 22
VOORHIS, John R. New York State Superintendent of Elections. 161

WAGNER, Robert F., Sr. New York State Senator; Supreme Court Justice; Member, U. S. Senate. 519
WAGNER, Robert F., Jr. Mayor, New York City. 641
WAHL, Jean. Philosopher. 786
WALD, Lillian D. Philanthropist; Founder, Henry Street Settlement. 859
WALKER, Edward Patrick (Mickey). Prizefighter; artist. 393
WALKER, Jimmie. Politician; Mayor of New York. 352
WALLACE, DeWitt. Editor, Reader's Digest. 582
WALLACH, Eli. Actor. 798
WALSH, Arthur. Cigar store owner. 616
WALSH, Christy. Ghost writer. 385
WALSH, Patrick. Fire Chief, New York City. 168
WARBURG, Siegmund G. Merchant banker. 826
WARNER, Albert. Motion picture producer. 538
WARNER, Harry. Motion picture producer. 538
WARNER, Jack. Motion picture producer. 538
WARNER, Karl. American soldier. 854
WARNER, Sam. Motion picture producer. 538
WATSON, John Broadus. Professor of Experimental and Comparative Psychology, Johns Hopkins University; author. 11
WATSON, Phil. Professional hockey player. 264
WATTS-DUNTON, Walter Theodore. Poet; novelist; critic. 67
WEAVER, Sylvester L., Jr. (Pat). President, National Broadcasting Company. 203

WEBSTER, Harold Tucker. Comic-strip cartoonist. 1119
WEBSTER, Margaret. Actress; director. 1087
WEIL, Richard, Jr. President, R.H. Macy. 1098
WEINBERG, Sidney James. Investment banker; corporation director. 263
WELLES, Orson. Actor; director; radio personality. 996
WERRENRATH, Reinald. Concert singer. 702
WEST, Mae. Actress; playwright. 257
WESTCOTT, Cynthia. Plant pathologist. 790
WESTLEY, Helen. Actress; director of Theatre Guild. 12
WHALEN, Grover A. Chairman, Mayor's Reception Committee; Police Commissioner, New York City. 338, 387
WHARTON, Edith. Novelist. 247
WHEELER, Elmer. Head, Tested Selling Institute. 925
WHITE, Walter. Sociologist; author. 364
WHITE, William Allen. Newspaper editor. 1004
WHITEMAN, Paul. Orchestra leader. 765
WHITMAN, Lucilla Mara de Vescovi. Owner of men's shop (Countess Mara). 1054
WHITNEY, Cornelius Vanderbilt. Corporation director; polo player; racing stables owner. 620
WHITNEY, Harry Payne. Socialite; polo player. 1057
WHITNEY, John Hay (Jock). Foundation director; philanthropist. 615
WHITNEY, Richard. President, New York Stock Exchange. 424
WIDENER, Joseph E. Horse breeder; owner, Belmont Park. 80
WIDMARK, Richard. Actor. 800
WIESNER, Jerome Bert. Professor of Electrical Engineering, Massachusetts Institute of Technology; President's Special Assistant for Science and Technology. 905
WIGHTMAN, Hazel Hotchkiss. Tennis player; coach; author. 888
WILLEBRANDT, Mabel Walker. Reformer; lawyer; Assistant U.S. Attorney-General. 674
WILLIAM, Maurice. Historian; author; dentist. 618
WILLIAMS, Albert Moran. Patrolman, New York City. 73
WILLIAMS, Mary Lou. Jazz pianist; composer. 758
WILLIS, Charles Fountain, Jr. President, non-scheduled airlines. 954
WILLKIE, Wendell Lewis. U.S. Presidential candidate; business executive; lawyer. 891
WILLS, Helen. Tennis player. 48
WILSON, Edmund. Author; critic. 820
WILSON, Halsey William. Publisher, Readers' Guide to

Periodical Literature. 682
WINCHELL, Walter. Newspaper columnist. 407
WING, Mock Sai. Tong leader. 1015
WINLOCK, Herbert E. Director, Metropolitan Museum; archeologist. 293
WINSTON, Harry. Jewelry dealer. 101
WINTER, Benjamin. Real estate speculator. 323
WISE, Stephen S. Rabbi, Jewish Institute of Religion. 840
WOODS, A. H. Theatrical producer. 894
WOOLEY, Monty. Actor. 516
WOOLLCOTT, Alexander. Critic; author; columnist; radio personality. 97
WOOLTON, Frederick James. British Minister of Reconstruction. 417
WORK, Milton C. Auction bridge authority. 72
WRIGHT, Frank Lloyd. Architect. 832
WRIGHT, John Kirtland. Director, American Geographical Society. 94
WRIGHT, Orville. Airplane inventor, manufacturer. 444
WYLIE, Elinor. Poet. 811

YANG, Chen Ning. Theoretical physicist; Nobel Prize winner. 855
YERESHERSKY, Izzy. Cigar store owner. 138
YOUNG, Art. Political cartoonist. 403

ZANUCK, Darryl Francis. Motion picture producer. 1083
ZECKENDORF, William. Realtor. 98
ZIEGFELD, Florenz. Theatrical producer. 391
ZIMBALIST, Efrem. Concert violinist. 208
ZOLOTOW, Sam. Publisher, *Advance Theatrical Guide.* 724
ZUKOR, Adolph. President, Paramount Famous-Lasky. 769

B. Profiles Not of Individuals

American Kennel Club. 270

The American Museum of Natural History. 38

Amnesty International: Society for freeing political prisoners. 649

Blackwell, B. H., Ltd.: Book store. 856

Brooks Brothers: Clothing store. 921

Budapest String Quartet. 140

Church of St. Matthew and St. Timothy: Episcopal church. 177

Cleveland Orchestra. 753

Coca-Cola Company. 1052

Colony Restaurant. 1038

Common Market, Europe. 202

Cooper Union: Educational institution. 948

Dixie Demo crew: Crew of flying fortress. 266

Feminists. 349

Ford Foundation: Philanthropic organization. 348

General Dynamics Corporation. 282

Hambros Bank Ltd.: Merchant bank. 4

Howe and Hummel: Criminal law office. 294

John-Frederics, Inc.: Milliners. 131

McSorley's: Saloon. 727

The Mafia: Criminal secret society. 462

Metropolitan Museum of Art. 638

New theology and theologians. 699

Pilgrim State Hospital, New York: Mental institution. 793

Reader's Digest. 582

Restaurant Associates: Restaurant chain. 261

Sloppy Louie's: Restaurant. 158

Smith Brothers, Inc.: Cough drop manufacturers. 130

Smithsonian Institution. 307

Theatre Guild: Theatrical company. 428

Time magazine. 1008

West Forty-seventh Street Police Station, New York. 360

William Mills & Son: Fishing tackle store. 463

Worth et Cie.: Couturier. 999

Xerox Corporation. 1121

Geographical locations

Calcutta, India. 182

Cambridge, Massachusetts. 162
Central Park, New York. 163
Chicago, Illinois. 909
Colonsay Island. 511

Florence, Italy. 183

Long Island Sound. 505
Los Angeles, California. 1047

The Netherlands. 585
New York Harbor. 123
Newport, Rhode Island. 40
Northeast Corridor, U.S.A. 1006

Ootacamund, India. 751

Pine Barrens: New Jersey forest land. 794

Stapleton, Nebraska. 776

Texas. 964

Valencia, Spain. 524
Venice, Italy. 872
Vienna, Austria. 184

Ships, airplanes, buildings, etc.

Berlin Wall. 258
Brooklyn Bridge. 27

DC-3: Airplane. 1002

The Great Eastern: Ocean liner. 416

Jollity Building, New York. 521

M.S. Sagafjord: Ocean liner. 1128

S.S. Marquette: Troop transport. 238

U.S.S. New York: Battleship. 701

Animals

Egon: German shepherd dog. 763

Man o' War: Racehorse. 99

Nornay Saddler: Smooth haired fox terrier. 90

Miscellaneous

American elm. 414

Electronic computers. 43

Hurricane Donna. 542

Life at the edge of the sea. 285

The sea. 908

U.S. Income tax. 974

Part III

SUBJECT CATEGORY INDEX

Subject Categories

Acting
Animals: sport, show, game
Architecture
Art: general
Art: painting, sculpture, drawing, illustrating
Athletics
Aviation
Banking and finance
Bohemians
Business, industry, insurance
Dance
Education
Engineering and design
Entertainment: comedy
Entertainment: general
Exploration
Farming
Fashion, cosmetics, hairdressing
Gambling
Geographical locations
Government and politics
History
Hotels and restaurants
Inventions
Journalism
Labor
Law and law enforcement
Lecture, oratory
Literature
Maritime
Medicine
Military
Miscellaneous
Motion pictures
Museums
Music
Philanthrophy
Philosophy
Photography
Publishing: book and magazine
Radio - television
Railroads
Real estate, contracting
Reform
Religion
Retail merchandising, advertising, sales
Science
Society
Theatre
Transportation

SUBJECT CATEGORY INDEX

ACTING

Beery, Wallace. Actor; comedian. 525
Bergman, Ingrid. Actress. 798
Boothe, Clare. Playwright; actress; U.S. Ambassador to Italy. 148
Brando, Marlon. Actor. 281
Brice, Fannie. Comedienne; actress. 328
Brown, Joe E. Comedian; actor. 198
Cantor, Eddie. Comedian; actor. 178
Chaplin, Charlie. Actor; director. 366
Cohan, George M. Playwright; song writer; dancer; actor. 937
Cornell, Katharine. Actress. 9, 799
Coward, Noël. Playwright; composer; actor. 449
Cronyn, Hume. Actor. 798
Damita, Lily. Actress. 584
Davis, Bette. Actress. 216
De Sica, Vittorio. Director; actor. 133
Fields, W. C. Comedian; actor; juggler. 568
Fonda, Henry. Actor. 799
Garbo, Greta. Actress. 39
Gielgud, John. Actor. 800
Hardwicke, Cedric. Actor. 799
Hayes, Helen. Actress. 1065
Holden, William. Actor. 798
Jannings, Emil. Actor. 179
Le Gallienne, Eva. Actress; director; translator. 551
Lillie, Beatrice. Comedienne; actress. 136
Lloyd, Harold. Actor; comedian. 781
Lunt, Alfred. Actor. 374
Marx, Harpo. Comedian; actor. 813
Matthau, Walter. Actor. 800
May, Elaine. Comedienne; actress; playwright. 1007
Mendl, Lady (Elsie de Wolfe). Actress; socialite. 433
Menjou, Adolphe. Actor. 82
Meredith, Burgess. Actor. 1055
Mostel, Zero. Actor. 799
Page, Geraldine. Actress. 800
Perkins, Anthony. Actor. 800
Pickford, Mary. Actress. 968
Printemps, Yvonne. Actress. 308
Qualtinger, Helmut. Actor; playwright. 302
Redgrave, Michael. Actor. 798
Robards, Jason. Actor. 800
Robeson, Paul. Actor; concert singer. 534

Schell, Maria. Actress. 799
Signoret, Simone. Actress. 800
Sokolof, Vladimir. Actor. 798
Stanley, Kim. Actress. 798
Stapleton, Maurine. Actress. 799
Steiger, Rod. Actor. 799
Swanson, Gloria. Actress. 1045
Wallach, Eli. Actor. 798
Webster, Margaret. Actress; director. 1087
Welles, Orson. Actor; director; radio personality. 996
West, Mae. Actress; playwright. 257
Westley, Helen. Actress; director of Theatre Guild. 12
Widmark, Richard. Actor. 800
Wooley, Monty. Actor. 516

ANIMALS: SPORT, SHOW, GAME

American Kennel Club. 270
Arcaro, Eddie. Jockey. 742
Bostwick, Pete. Polo player. 808
Bradley, Edward Riley. Horse breeder; gambling casino owner. 491
Clark, F. Ambrose. Horse breeder; president, United Hunts. 959
Cox, Walter. Horse trainer. 1122
Egon. German shepherd dog. 763
Hertz, Mr. and Mrs. John D. Horse breeders. 221
Hildreth, Samuel. Racehorse trainer. 24
Hitchcock, Louise Eustis. Horsewoman. 369
Hitchcock, Thomas, Sr. Polo player. 369
Hitchcock, Thomas, Jr. Polo player. 369
Jacobs, Hirsch. Racehorse trainer. 792
Man o' War. Racehorse. 99
Milburn, Devereux. Polo player; lawyer. 998
Nornay Saddler. Smooth haired fox terrier. 90
Rogers, Anne Hone. Professional show dog handler; breeder. 1019
Ross, Rita. Cat-catcher. 552
Safford, Frank. Trainer, driver, harness horses. 482
Sande, Earl. Jockey. 919
Saunders, Blanche. Dog obedience trainer. 274
Townsend, Edward T. Game warden. 442
Whitney, Cornelius Vanderbilt. Corporation director; polo player; racing stables owner. 620
Whitney, Harry Payne. Socialite; polo player. 1057
Widener, Joseph E. Horse breeder; owner, Belmont Park. 80

ARCHITECTURE

Bach, Richard F. Architect; Associate in Industrial Arts, Metropolitan Museum of Art. 608
Chanin, Irwin S. Realtor; architectural engineer. 926
Cram, Ralph Adams. Ar-

chitect. 913
Dowling, Robert W. Architect; Head, Advisory Arts Committee for National Cultural Center. 1060
Doxiadis, Constantinos. City planner. 295
Fuller, Richard Buckminster. Architect; designer; inventor; engineer. 498
Gibbs, William Francis. Naval architect. 89
Harrison, Wallace Kirkman. Director of planning, U.N. headquarters. 57
Hood, Raymond. Architect. 609
Jeanneret, Charles Edouard (Le Corbusier). Architect. 361
Lescaze, William. Architect. 678
Mizner, Addison. Architect. 766
Nervi, Pier Luigi. Architect; engineer. 603
Stone, Edward D. Architect. 359
Urban, Joseph. Theatrical stage designer; architect. 149
Wright, Frank Lloyd. Architect. 832

ART: GENERAL

Bach, Richard F. Architect; Associate in Industrial Arts, Metropolitan Museum of Art. 608
Bagby, Albert Morris. Patron of arts; socialite. 688
Barnes, Albert C. Art collector; drug manufacturer. 243
Barr, Alfred H., Jr. Director of Collections, Museum of Modern Art. 7
Calder, Alexander. Maker and seller of mobiles. 310
Clark, Walter L. Curator, Grand Central Gallery of Art. 377
Dale, Chester. President, National Gallery of Art; investment banker. 229
d'Harnoncourt, René. Director, Museum of Modern Art. 495
Dowling, Robert W. Architect; Head, Advisory Arts Committee for National Cultural Center. 1060
Duveen, Joseph. Art dealer. 242, 709
Frick, Helen Clay. Director, Frick Art Reference Library; philanthropist. 240
Gallatin, Albert Eugene. Founder, manager, Museum of Living Art. 651
Gutman, Walter Knowlton. Investment counselor; art critic. 842
Heydenryk, Henry. Picture framer. 306
Hoving, Thomas P. F. Parks Commissioner, New York City; Director, Metropolitan Museum of Art. 881
Janis, Sidney. Art dealer. 1104
Kahn, Otto H. Financier; patron of arts. 499
Metropolitan Museum of Art. 638
Scull, Robert Cooper. Art dealer; owner of taxicab company. 619
Speyer, James. Banker; patron of arts. 76

ART: PAINTING, SCULP-

TURE, DRAWING, ILLUSTRATING

Avinoff, Andrey. Lepidopterist; painter. 109
Barnard, George Grey. Sculptor. 907
Beard, Daniel Carter. National Commissioner, Boy Scouts of America; book and magazine illustrator. 1063
Beerbohm, Henry Maximilian (Max). Caricaturist; author; critic. 212
Biddle, George. Painter. 425
Braque, Georges. Painter. 630
Buffet, Bernard. Painter. 562
Caniff, Milton. Comic-strip cartoonist. 918
Capp, Al. Comic-strip cartoonist. 750
Dali, Salvador. Painter. 278
Davidson, Jo. Sculptor. 906
Duchamp, Marcel. Painter. 713
Eilshemius, Louis Michel. Painter. 606
Fisher, Harry Conway (Bud). Comic-strip cartoonist. 647
Geisel, Theodor Seuss (Dr. Seuss). Author; illustrator of children's books. 174
Grosz, George. Painter. 61
Lachaise, Gaston. Sculptor. 450
Lippold, Richard. Sculptor. 990
Luks, George. Painter. 493
Manship, Paul. Sculptor. 206
Marin, John. Painter. 569
Matisse, Henri. Painter. 537
Moore, Henry. Sculptor. 314
O'Keeffe, Georgia. Painter. 3
Peters, Clinton. Painter; art teacher. 233
Picasso, Pablo Ruiz y. Painter. 746, 965
Prendergast, Charles. Painter. 390
Rauschenberg, Robert. Painter. 684
Rivera, Diego. Painter. 303
Rockwell, Norman. Painter; illustrator. 1044
Sendak, Maurice. Author; illustrator of children's books. 42
Sloan, John. Historical painter. 13
Tinguely, Jean. Motion sculptor. 93
Walker, Edward Patrick (Mickey). Prizefighter; painter. 393
Webster, Harold Tucker. Comic-strip cartoonist. 1119

ATHLETICS

Adams, Charles Francis. Lawyer; politician; Treasurer of Harvard University; yachtsman. 902
Arcaro, Eddie. Jockey. 742
Ashe, Arthur. Tennis player. 573
Atlas, Charles. Musclebuilder. 485
Baer, Max Adalbert. Prizefighter. 831
Bimstein, Morris. Prizefight second. 613
Borotra, Jean. Tennis player. 239
Bostwick, Pete. Polo play-

er. 808
Bradley, Edward Riley. Horse breeder; gambling casino owner. 491
Bradley, William Warren. Basketball player. 912
Brown, Bill. Health farm owner; member New York State Athletic Commission. 317
Brundage, Avery. President, International Olympic Committee. 31
Brunet, Pierre. Senior professional, New York Skating Club. 788
Burgess, W. Starling. Racing yacht designer. 614
Butler, James. Chain-grocery owner; race track owner. 421
Carey, William. Contractor; Director, Madison Square Garden. 952
Clark, F. Ambrose. Horse breeder; President, United Hunts. 959
Cochet, Henri. Tennis player. 594
(Composite portrait). College football coach. 729
Collett, Glenna. Golfer. 951
Cousy, Robert Joseph. Basketball player. 1072
Cox, Walter. Horse trainer. 1122
Curley, Jack. Sports promoter. 157
Dempsey, Jack. Prizefighter. 969
Ederle, Gertrude. Swimmer. 997
Falcaro, Joe. Bowler. 623
Franklin, Sidney. Matador. 296
Gehrig, Louis Henry. Baseball player. 581
Glendon, Richard G., Sr. Crew coach, U.S. Naval Academy. 726
Glendon, Richard G., Jr. Crew Coach, Columbia University. 726
Graebner, Clark. Tennis player. 573
Grange, Harold E. (Red). Football player. 25
Green, Cecil. Fishing guide, Florida Keys. 542
Grenet, Augustine J. Horse racing bookmaker. 578
Hagen, Walter. Golfer. 812
Henrich, Thomas David. Baseball player. 732
Hertz, Mr. and Mrs. John D. Horse breeders. 221
Hewitt, Edward Ringwood. Director, International Motor Company; fisherman; inventor. 204
Hildreth, Samuel. Racehorse trainer. 24
Hitchcock, Louise Eustis. Horsewoman. 369
Hitchcock, Thomas, Sr. Polo player. 369
Hitchcock, Thomas, Jr. Polo player. 369
Hood, Frederick E. Sailmaker. 893
Hoppe, William Frederick. Professional billiard player. 815
Huggins, Miller. Manager, New York Yankees. 928
Humphreys, Joseph E. Prizefight announcer. 957
Jacobs, Hirsch. Racehorse trainer. 792
Johnston, James Jay. Boxing promoter; Assistant to President, Madison Square Garden. 205
Jones, Robert Trent. Golf course architect. 579

Jones, Robert Tyre (Bobby), Jr. Golfer. 397
Kilpatrick, John Reed. President, Madison Square Garden. 340
King, Charles Brady. Automobile designer, builder, racer. 1012
Klem, Bill. Baseball umpire. 612
Lacoste, Rene. Tennis player. 1107
Lambert, Gerard B. Yachtsman; President Lambert Company. 18
Leader, Edward. Crew coach, Yale University. 422
Lenglen, Suzanne. Tennis player. 977
Little, Lou. Football coach, Columbia University. 280
Londos, Jim. Professional wrestler. 852
Macfadden, Bernarr. Publisher; physical fitness advocate. 50, 789
McGovern, Artie. Head, McGovern's Gymnasium; prizefighter. 60
McGraw, John. Manager, New York Giants. 668
MacPhail, Larry. President, Brooklyn Dodgers. 117
Mara, Timothy James. Founder, Turf and Gridiron Club (Bookmakers). 1033
Meehan, John Francis (Chick). Football coach, New York University. 626
Milburn, Devereux. Polo player; lawyer. 998
Moore, Archibald Lee (Archie). Prizefighter. 679
Muldoon, William. Owner, Hygenic Institute; Member, New York State Boxing Commission. 944
Nicholson, George. Prizefight sparring partner. 943
Nuthall, Betty. Tennis player. 305
O'Brien, (Philadelphia) Jack (pseud.). Head, health gymnasium. 125
Pagliaro, Louis. Ping-pong champion. 982
Pyle, C. C. Sports promoter. 153
Rickard, George L. (Tex). Director, Madison Square Garden. 875
Rickey, Branch. President, Brooklyn Dodgers. 1000
Roper, William W. Football coach, Princeton University; politician. 882
Ruppert, Jacob. Brewer; owner, New York Yankees; U. S. Congressman. 85
Ruth, George Herman (Babe). Baseball player. 74
Ryan, Elizabeth (Bunny). Tennis player. 635
Safford, Frank. Trainer and driver of harness horses. 482
Sande, Earl. Jockey. 919
Santelli, George (Giorgio). Fencing master. 1013
Schneider, Hannes. Inventor of skiing techniques. 1086
Stillman, Lou (Lou Ingber). Owner, Stillman's Gymnasium. 156
Tilden, William Tatem, 2nd. Tennis player. 487
Tunney, Gene. Prizefighter. 370
Turnesa, William. Golfer. 32
Twynam, Robert. Groundskeeper at Wimbledon. 561
Vanderbilt, Alfred Gwynne.

Race track operator. 23
Vanderbilt, Harold. Yachtsman; contract bridge authority. 399
Walker, Edward Patrick (Mickey). Prizefighter; artist. 393
Watson, Phil. Professional hockey player. 264
Whitney, Cornelius Vanderbilt. Corporation director; polo player; racing stables owner. 620
Whitney, Harry Payne. Socialite; polo player. 1057
Widener, Joseph E. Horse breeder; owner, Belmont Park. 80
Wightman, Hazel Hotchkiss. Tennis player; coach; author. 883
William Mills & Son. Fishing tackle store. 463
Wills, Helen. Tennis player. 48

AVIATION

Bellanca, Giuseppe Mario. Airplane designer, manufacturer. 1106
Blackburn, Harold Frederic. Pilot, Trans World Airlines. 576, 1127
Cochran, Philip. Major, U.S. Army Air Forces. 427
Crane, Joe. National champion parachute jumper. 768
DC-3. Airplane. 1002
Dixie Demo crew. Crew of flying fortress. 266
Fairchild, Sherman Mills. Airplane manufacturer; authority on aerial photography. 20
Finucane, Brendan. Flight Lieutenant, Royal Air Force. 764
Fokker, Anthony Herman Gerard. Airplane designer; manufacturer. 335
Hallock, Joseph Theodore. 1st Lieutenant, U.S. Army Air Forces. 1130
Istel, Jacques André. Parachutist. 705
Julian, Hubert. Aviator; parachute jumper; Minister of Air, Abyssinia. 107
Lindbergh, Charles Augustus. Aviator. 1132
Martin, Glenn L. Airplane manufacturer. 447
Rosendahl, Charles E. Aviator, lighter-than-air craft. 706
Sikorsky, Igor Ivanovitch. Airplane designer, engineer, executive. 1105
Smith, Eleanor. Aviatrix. 700
Smith, Maynard. Staff-sergeant, U.S. Army Air Forces. 245
Snyder, Daniel. Captain, U.S. Army Air Forces. 1129
Willis, Charles Fountain, Jr. President, non-scheduled airlines. 954
Wright, Orville. Airplane inventor, manufacturer. 444

BANKING AND FINANCE

Adams, Charles Francis. Lawyer; politician; Treasurer of Harvard University; yachtsman. 902
Astor, William Vincent.

Real estate owner and manager; investment-manager. 396
Babson, Roger W. Economist; Director, Babson Park. 841
Baruch, Bernard Mannes. Financier; speculator; government advisor. 728, 1048
Bob, Charles V. Promoter; financier. 941
Bullock, Hugh. Investment-manager. 435
Common Market, Europe. 202
Content, Harry. Stock broker. 325
Dale, Chester. President, National Gallery of Art; investment banker. 229
Dillon, Clarence. Banker. 103
Fraser, Leon. President, First National Bank. 439
Gilbert, Lewis Dusenbery. Minority stockholder. 972
Gutman, Walter Knowlton. Investment-counselor; art critic. 842
Hambros Bank Ltd. 4
Jackson, David Sidney. Specialist, New York Stock Exchange. 1028
Johnson, James William. Collector, Internal Revenue Service. 357
Kahn, Otto H. Financier; patron of arts. 499
Lasser, Jacob Kay. Author; income tax expert. 975
Lilienthal, David Eli. Financier; corporation director; author; Chairman, U.S. Atomic Energy Commission. 910
McGoldrick, Joseph D. Comptroller, New York City; Professor of Government, Columbia University. 835
Mattioli, Raffaele. Publisher; historian; translator; economist. 2
Mellon, Andrew. Financier; U.S. Secretary of the Treasury. 225
Mills, Ogden Livingston. Financier; U.S. Undersecretary of the Treasury. 1058
Morgan, J. Pierpont. Financier. 658
Morgenthau, Henry, Jr. U.S. Secretary of the Treasury. 52
Odlum, Floyd B. Director, investment trust. 1030
Rockefeller, David. President, Chase Manhattan Bank. 870
Ruml, Beardsley. Economist; author; government advisor. 696
Schwartz, A. Charles. Financier. 596
Smith, Bernard E. Stock broker. 522
Soss, Wilma Porter. Founder, Federation of Women Shareholders in American Business, Inc. 454
Speyer, James. Banker; patron of arts. 76
Tremaine, Morris Sawyer. Comptroller, New York State. 207
Tugwell, Rexford Guy. U.S. Under-secretary of Agriculture; Professor of Economics, Columbia University. 890
U.S. Income tax. 974
Warburg, Siegmund G. Merchant banker. 826
Weinberg, Sidney James. Investment banker; corpo-

ration director. 263
Whitney, Richard. President, New York Stock Exchange. 424

BOHEMIANS

Dutch, Commodore (pseud.) Confidence man; Broadway character. 1016
Franklin, Marty (pseud.). Confidence man. 137
Gould, Joseph Ferdinand. Bohemian; author of unpublished book. 520, 837
McGoorty, John. Tramp. 124
Mizner, Wilson. Confidence man; promoter; Broadway personality. 567
Nikanov, Johnny. Gypsy king. 536
Schultz, Sam. Sidewalk grate "fisherman." 917
Vereker, Elliott. Author; dilettante. 935

BUSINESS, INDUSTRY, INSURANCE

Amsden, Sherman C. Head, Telephone Answering Service. 617
Arnold, Paul Dean. Owner of bakery. 871
Barnes, Albert C. Art collector; drug manufacturer. 243
Bellanca, Giuseppe Mario. Airplane designer, manufacturer. 1106
Bogdanov, Peter Alexyevitch. Chairman, Amtorg Corporation. 114
Cherne, Leo M. Executive Secretary, Research Institute of America. 154
Chrysler, Walter P. Automobile manufacturer. 1042
Coca-Cola Company. 1052
Cook, Emory. Sound expert; president, phonograph record company. 283
Cowen, Joshua Lionel. Chairman, "Lionel Lines," toy electric trains. 451
Cravath, Paul Drennan. Lawyer; corporation director. 845
Cullman, Howard J. Theatrical investor; President, Beekman Hospital; Partner, Cullman Brothers (tobacco). 1014
Deskey, Donald. Furniture manufacturer. 591
Eastman, George. Inventor; industrialist. 147
Fairchild, Sherman Mills. Airplane manufacturer; authority on aerial photography. 20
Fuller, Alfred Carl. President, Fuller Brush Company. 640
Ganger, I. Arthur. Head, bar equipment business. 911
General Dynamics Corporation. 282
Gifford, Walter Sherman. President, American Telephone & Telegraph Company. 171
Gilbert, Alfred Carlton. Founder, A. C. Gilbert Co. 35
Haft, Louis. Owner, Haft Glass Company. 775
Heckscher, August. Industrialist; philanthropist. 1093.

Johnson, Robert J. (pseud.). Insurance salesman. 509
Kapp, Jack. President, Decca Records. 853
Kayshus, Effie. Shoe manufacturer. 1062
Kellems, Vivien. Manufacturer of electrical parts. 423
Kenny, William Frank. Industrialist. 488
King, Charles Brady. Automobile designer, manufacturer, racer. 1012
Klein, S. Clothing manufacturer, distributor. 736
Knudsen, William S. President, General Motors Corporation; Member, Advisory Commission to Council of National Defense. 834
Lambert, Gerard B. Yachtsman; President, Lambert Company. 18
Leterman, Elmer G. Insurance salesman. 631
Lilienthal, David Eli. Financier; corporation director; author; Chairman, U.S. Atomic Energy Commission. 910
Mack, Walter S., Jr. Chairman, Pepsi-Cola Company. 681
Martin, Glenn L. Airplane manufacturer. 447
Morey, Sigmund M. Machine tool manufacturer. 339
Nelson, Donald M. Industrialist; Chairman, War Production Board. 145
Otis, Harry. Life insurance salesman. 51
Ottinger, Lawrence. President, United States Plywood Corporation. 805
Pierce, John R. Executive Director of Communications Research, Bell Telephone Laboratories. 1114
Rockefeller, John D. Industrialist. 715
Rockefeller, John D., Jr. Industrialist; philanthropist. 903
Rudkin, Margaret. President, Pepperidge Farms, Inc. 961
Ruppert, Jacob. Brewer; owner, New York Yankees; U.S. Congressman. 85
Schwab, Charles M. President, United States Steel Corporation. 956
Seiden, Irving. President, Mercury Service Systems. 1060
Sell, Henry Blackman. Maker of canned meat products. 946
Siegel, Morris. Insurance expert. 673
Sikorsky, Igor Ivanovitch. Airplane designer, engineer, executive. 1105
Slotkin, Samuel. President, Hygrade Food Products Corporation. 259
Smith, Robert Lansing. Cough drop manufacturer. 130
Smith, William W., II. Cough drop manufacturer. 130
Todd, John R. Co-manager, Rockefeller Center. 610
Weinberg, Sidney James. Investment banker; corporation director. 263
Whitney, Cornelius Vanderbilt. Corporation director; polo player; racing stables owner. 620
Whitney, John Hay (Jock). Foundation director; phi-

lanthropist. 615
Willkie, Wendell Lewis. U.S. Presidential candidate; business executive; lawyer. 891
Xerox Corporation. Manufacturer of photocopying machinery. 1121
Keeler, Elisha. Square-dance caller. 346
Markova, Alicia. Ballerina. 504
Murray, Arthur. Dance instructor. 1085
Robinson, Bill. Dancer; philanthropist. 113

DANCE

Allers, Franz. Conductor: ballet, opera, symphony, musical comedy. 350
Balanchine, George. Chief choreographer, New York City Ballet. 176
Barstow, Richard. Director and choreographer, Ringling Brothers and Barnum & Bailey Circus. 312
Brecker, Louis. Owner, Roseland Dance Hall. 459
Cohan, George M. Playwright; song writer; dancer; actor. 937
Cunningham, Merce. Choreographer. 55
deMille, Agnes. Theatrical choreographer. 175
DeMarco, Renée. Dancer. 234
DeMarco, Tony. Dancer. 234
de Valois, Ninette. Director, Sadler's Wells Ballet. 599
Draper, Paul. Tap-dancer. 235
Duncan, Isadora. Dancer. 510
Gadd, May. Authority on folk dancing. 577
Graham, Martha. Dancer. 1
Grayce (no last name given). Chorus girl. 723
Josephs, Louis (Frisco). Jazz dancer. 1131

EDUCATION

Auer, Leopold. Concert violinist; music teacher. 636
Boyden, Frank Learoyd. Headmaster, Deerfield Academy. 443
Butler, Nicholas Murray. President, Columbia University; author. 215
Conant, James Bryant. President, Harvard University. 670
Condon, John F. Public school teacher. 406
Cooper Union. Educational institution. 948
Copeland, Charles Townsend. Professor of Rhetoric and Oratory, Harvard University. 772
Cosgrave, Jessica Garretson. Educator; founder of Finch Junior College. 863
Delehanty, Michael Joseph. President, Civil Service school. 823
Dewey, John. Philosopher; educator; author. 621
Erskine, John. Professor of English, Columbia University; author. 838
Flexner, Abraham. Educator; philanthropist; Secretary, Rockefeller Foundation General Education Board. 878

Frick, Helen Clay. Director, Frick Art Reference Library; philanthropist. 240
Gould, Samuel B. Chancellor, State University of New York. 164
Hoopingarner, Newman Leander. Professor of Business Psychology, New York University. 226
Illich, Ivan. Roman Catholic priest; educator; author. 887
Laubach, Frank Charles. Congregational minister; educator. 1001
McGoldrick, Joseph D. Comptroller, New York City; Professor of Government, Columbia University. 835
Mardersteig, Giovanni. Publisher; printer; literary scholar. 401
Mark, Herman F. Scientist; Professor of Organic Chemistry, Polytechnic Institute of Brooklyn. 809
Merton, Robert K. Professor of Sociology, Columbia University. 472
Meyer, Annie Nathan. Founder of Bernard College. 269
Newstead, Helaine. Professor of English, Hunter College. 386
Phelps, William Lyon. Professor of English, Yale University. 532
Pitkin, Walter B. Author; Professor of Journalism, Columbia University. 252
Robinson, Frederick B. President, College of the City of New York. 289
Romanoff, Alexis Lawrence. Professor of Chemical Embryology, Cornell University. 291
Royce, William H. Scholar (Balzac); author. 994
Ryan, George J. Member, New York City Board of Education. 779
Shapiro, Elliott. Elementary school principal. 828
Sherover, Max. President, Linguaphone Institute of America (language teaching). 65
Teal, John J., Jr. Associate Professor of Geography and Anthropology, University of Vermont; explorer; author. 356
Tugwell, Rexford Guy. U.S. Under-Secretary of Agriculture; Professor of Economics, Columbia University. 890
Watson, John Broadus. Professor of Experimental and Comparitive Psychology, Johns Hopkins University; author. 11
Wiesner, Jerome Bert. Professor of Electrical Engineering, Massachusetts Institute of Technology; President's Special Assistant for Science and Technology. 905

ENGINEERING AND DESIGN

Abrams, Charles. City planner. 593
Ammann, Othmar Hermann. Chief Engineer, Port of New York Authority. 806
Brooklyn Bridge. 27
Burgess, W. Starling. Racing yacht designer. 614
Chanin, Irwin S. Realtor; architectural engineer. 926

de Florez, Luis. Captain, U.S. Naval Reserve; mechanical engineer; inventor of synthetic training devices. 150
Feder, Abe H. Lighting designer. 876
Fuller, Richard Buckminster. Architect; designer; inventor; engineer. 498
Geddes, Norman Bel. Stage and industrial designer. 251
Gibbs, William Francis. Naval architect. 89
Jones, Bassett. Chairman, Committee on Display, New York World's Fair; Elevator designer; Electrical engineer. 241
Ketcham, Howard. Color, design and illumination engineer. 300
King, Charles Brady. Automobile designer, manufacturer, racer. 1012
Lamb, Thomas. Designer of handles. 195
Leigh, Douglas. Designer, luminous signs and neon signs. 574
Nervi, Pier Luigi. Architect; engineer. 603
Peabody, Ernest Henry. President, Peabody Engineering Corporation; anti-noise campaigner. 940
Rosoff, Sam. Contractor, Eighth Avenue Subway. 632
Sikorsky, Igor Ivanovitch. Airplane designer, engineer, executive. 1105
Stephens, Olin. Yacht designer and builder. 1056
Stephens, Roderick. Yacht designer and builder. 1056
Teague, Walter Dorwin. Industrial designer. 502
Wiesner, Jerome Bart. Professor of Electrical Engineering, Massachusetts Institute of Technology; President's Special Assistant for Science and Technology. 905

ENTERTAINMENT: COMEDY

Borge, Victor. Comedian; pianist; poultry breeder. 104
Brice, Fannie. Comedienne; actress. 328
Brown, Joe E. Comedian; actor. 198
Burrows, Abe. Comedian; playwright; director. 284
Butterworth, Charles. Comedian; motion picture actor. 598
Cantor, Eddie. Comedian; actor. 178
Clark, Bobby. Comedian. 197
Fields, W. C. Comedian; actor; juggler. 568
Harrigan, Edward Green. Musical comedy team member. 770
Johnson, Chic. Comedian; Stager of Hellz-a-Poppin. 708
Lillie, Beatrice. Comedienne; actress. 136
Marx, Harpo. Comedian; actor. 813
May, Elaine. Comedienne; actress; playwright. 1007
Olsen, Ole. Comedian; Stager of Hellz-a-Poppin. 708
Sahl, Mort. Comedian. 367

ENTERTAINMENT: GENERAL

Barnell, Jane. Bearded lady in circus sideshow. 554
Barstow, Richard. Director and choreographer, Ringling Brothers and Barnum & Bailey Circus. 312
Brecker, Louis. Owner, Roseland dance hall. 459
Butler, Roland. Publicity director, Ringling Brothers and Barnum & Bailey Circus. 321
Concello, Antoinette. Aerial trapeze artist. 315
Concello, Arthur. Aerial trapeze artist. 315
Cook, Joe. Vaudeville performer. 126
Delacour, Jean. Aviculturist; operator, Bronx Zoo. 412
Ditmars, Raymond. Supervisor, Bronx Zoo Snake House. 945
Dunnenger, Joseph. Magician. 718
Eagle, Nate. Sideshow manager, Ringling Brothers and Barnum & Bailey Circus. 971
Evans, Merle. Band leader, Ringling Brothers and Barnum & Bailey Circus. 739
Furst, Bruno. Mnemonist; hypnotist; handwriting expert. 675
Dufour, Lew. Midway concessionaire, New York World's Fair. 639
Grayce (no last name given). Chorus girl. 723
Hamid, George A. President, amusement park booking agency. 15
Gumpertz, Samuel W. Director, Ringling Brothers and Barnum & Bailey Circus. 119
Jones, Bassett. Chairman, Committee on Display, New York World's Fair; Elevator designer; Electrical engineer. 241
Katz, Hymie (pseud.). Nightclub owner. 1032
Landolf, Bluch. Circus clown. 446
Leigh, William Colston. Owner, Leigh Bureau of Lectures and Entertainment. 324
Leitzel, Lillian. Aerialist, Ringling Brothers and Barnum & Bailey Circus. 955
Madden, Joe. Saloonkeeper. 627
North, John Ringling. President, Ringling Brothers and Barnum & Bailey Circus. 1025
Rabkin, William. Manufacturer of coin-operated amusement machines. 780
Raymond, Gaston. Croupier at Monte Carlo. 883
Ringling, Charles. Owner, Ringling Brothers Circus. 1040
Ringling, John. Owner, Ringling Brothers Circus. 1040
Rogers, Joe. Midway concessionaire, New York World's Fair. 639
Tiebor, John W., I. Seal trainer. 151
Tiebor, John W., II. Seal trainer. 151
Tiebor, Roland. Seal trainer. 151
Valdo, Patrick Francis. Personnel director, Ring-

ling Brothers and Barnum & Bailey Circus. 120

EXPLORATION

Andrews, Roy Chapman. Explorer; author. 481
Stefansson, Vilhjalmur. Arctic explorer. 540
Teal, John J., Jr. Associate Professor of Geography and Anthropology, University of Vermont; explorer; author. 356

FARMING

Borge, Victor. Comedian; pianist; poultry breeder. 104
Chavez, Cesar. Farm labor organizer. 754
Dillon, John J. Publisher, Rural New-Yorker. 890
Tilley, George Dudley. Operator, ornamental-bird farm. 869
Tugwell, Rexford Guy. U.S. Under-secretary of Agriculture; Professor of Economics, Columbia University. 890

FASHION, COSMETICS, HAIR DRESSING

Arden, Elizabeth. Owner, beauty salon and company. 389
Avedon, Richard. Fashion photographer. 1112
Bocher, Main. Couturier. 795
Carnegie, Hattie. Couturière. 597
Chanel, Gabrielle. Couturière. 995
Cierplikowski, Antoine. Coiffeur. 189
Coty, François. Perfume maker; journalist; politician. 783
Daché, Lilly. Milliner. 440
DeZembler, Charles. Barber shop owner. 77
Dengel, Veronica. Beautician. 744
Gheen, Celeste. Model. 818
Harburger, John. Milliner. 131
Hurst, Frederic. Milliner. 131
Jaeckel, Richard. Furrier. 666
John-Frederics, Inc. Millinary store. 131
Molé, Paul. Barber. 528
Nessler, Charles. Inventor, permanent wave machine. 429
Poiret, Paul. Couturier. 292
Rosenfeld, Henry Jonas. Couturier. 660
Rosenstein, Nettie. Couturière. 1070
Rubinstein, Helena. Cosmetics manufacturer. 84
Schiaparelli, Elsa. Couturière. 199
Worth et Cie. Couturier. 999

GAMBLING

Bradley, Edward Riley. Horse breeder; gambling casino owner. 491
Diamond, Jack (Legs). Gambler; racketeer. 100

Dutch, Commodore (pseud.). Confidence man; Broadway character. 1016
Grenet, Augustine J. Horse racing bookmaker. 578
Mara, Timothy James. Founder, Turf and Gridiron Club (bookmakers). 1033
"Pop" (pseud.). Bookmaker. 923

GEOGRAPHICAL LOCATIONS

Calcutta, India. 182
Cambridge, Massachusetts. 162
Central Park, New York City. 163
Chicago, Illinois. 909
Colonsay Island. 511
Florence, Italy. 183
Long Island Sound. 505
Los Angeles, California. 1047
The Netherlands. 585
New York Harbor. 123
Newport, Rhode Island. 40
Northeast Corridor, U.S.A. 1006
Ootacamund, India. 751
Pine Barrens. New Jersey forest land. 794
Stapleton, Nebraska. 776
Texas. 964
Valencia, Spain. 524
Venice, Italy. 872
Vienna, Austria. 184

GOVERNMENT AND POLITICS

Acheson, Dean Gooderham. U.S. Secretary of State. 672
Adams, Charles Francis. Lawyer; politician; Treasurer of Harvard University; yachtsman. 902
Arnstein, Daniel. U.S. Ambassador to China; Burma Road expert. 475
Baldwin, Joseph Clark, III. U.S. Congressman, New York County. 320
Baruch, Bernard Mannes. Financier; speculator; government advisor. 728, 1048
Berle, Adolf Augustus, Jr. U.S. Assistant Secretary of State. 69
Biddle, Anthony J. Drexel, Jr. U.S. Ambassador to Polish, Belgian, Netherlands and Norwegian governments in London. 734
Birkhead, Leon Milton. National director, Friends of Democracy, Inc. 250
Bloom, Sol. U.S. Congressman, New York State. 484
Boothe, Clare. Playwright; actress; U.S. Ambassador to Italy. 148
Brophy, Thomas Patrick. Chief Fire Marshall, New York City. 329
Browder, Earl. General Secretary, U.S. Communist Party. 771
Bryan, William Jennings. Politician. 920
Bullitt, William Christian. U.S. Ambassador to France. 663
Cabot, John Moore. U.S. Ambassador to Brazil. 33
Clay, Lucius Du Bignon. General, U.S. Army; Head, Office of Defense Mobilization. 932
Coolidge, Grace. Wife, President Calvin Coolidge. 331

Copeland, Royal S. Member, U. S. Senate. 663
Corsi, Edward. Director, Emergency Home Relief Bureau; Commissioner of Immigration. 432
Coty, François. Perfume maker; journalist; French politician. 783
Cripps, Stafford. British statesman. 719
Cuda, Tony. Mayor of Futani, Italy. 643
Curran, Henry Hastings. Lawyer; politician; President, American Association Against the Prohibition Amendment. 1088
Curry, John Francis. Leader, New York County Democratic Party. 587
Darlington, Thomas. Physician; Commissioner of Health, New York City; author; lecturer; Grand Sachem, Society of Tammany. 411
Davies, Marjorie Post Close Hutton. Wife, U. S. Ambassador to Russia; socialite. 546
Dewey, Thomas Edmund. District attorney, New York City; Governor, New York State; Presidential candidate. 895
Duke, Angier Biddle. U. S. Chief of Protocol. 404
Eden, Robert Anthony. British foreign minister, prime minister. 345
Edge, Rosalie Barrow. Chairman, Emergency Conservation Committee. 725
Edward, Prince of Wales. 290
Farley, James A. Politician; U. S. Postmaster General. 96
Fish, Hamilton, Jr. U. S. Congressman. 380
Flynn, Edward Joseph. Lawyer; Chairman, Democratic National Committee. 717
Foster, William Zebulon. Presidential candidate, U. S. Communist Party. 757
Goldberg, Arthur Joseph. Lawyer; U. S. Secretary of Labor; United Nations representative; Justice, U. S. Supreme Court. 777
Hague, Frank. Mayor, Jersey City, New Jersey. 311
Harriman, William Averell. U. S. statesman; governor, New York State. 803
Harvey, George Upton. Borough President, New York City. 738
Hayes, James Edward. Liaison officer, Democratic Party, New York City. 419
Herrick, Myron T. U. S. Ambassador to France. 634
Hines, James J. Leader, Eleventh Assembly District, New York City. 265
Hitler, Adolf. Führer, Third Reich. 365
Hoover, Herbert. U. S. President. 821
Hoover, John Edgar. Director, U. S. Federal Bureau of Investigation. 262
Hopkins, Harry L. Special advisor and assistant to U. S. President. 467
Hoving, Thomas P. F. Parks Commissioner, New York City; Director, Metropolitan Museum of Art. 881

Hughes, Charles Evans. U.S. Supreme Court Chief Justice. 169
Isaacs, Stanley M. New York City Council member. 844
Javits, Jacob K. Member, U.S. House of Representatives, U.S. Senate. 378
Johnson, Hugh Samuel. Director, National Recovery Administration; General, U.S. Army. 371
Johnson, James William. Collector, Internal Revenue Service. 357
Julian, Hubert. Aviator; parachute jumper; Minister of Air, Abyssinia. 107
Kenlon, John. Chief, New York City Fire Department. 188
Kiely, John J. Postmaster, New York City. 398
Knudsen, William S. President, General Motors Corporation; Member, Advisory Commission to Council of National Defense. 834
Koenig, Sam. Politician. 704
La Guardia, Fiorello H. Mayor, New York City. 514
Lehman, Herbert Henry. Governor, New York State. 409
Lie, Trygve. Secretary-general, United Nations. 490
Lilienthal, David Eli. Financier; corporation director; author; Chairman, U.S. Atomic Energy Commission. 910
Lindsay, John V. Mayor, New York City. 642
Longworth, Nicholas. Speaker, U.S. House of Representatives. 797
Lord, Mary Stinson Pillsbury. U.S. representative to U.N. Commission on Human Rights. 745
Lovett, Robert A. U.S. Assistant Secretary of War for Air. 993
McClellan, George Brinton. Mayor, New York City; historian. 761
McCooey, John H. Democratic Leader, Kings County, Brooklyn. 298
McGoldrick, Joseph D. Comptroller, New York City; Professor of Government, Columbia University. 835
McGuinness, Peter J. Democratic leader, Greenpoint, Brooklyn. 95
McKee, Joseph Vincent. President, New York City Board of Aldermen. 135
Macy, W. Kingsland. Leader, Republican Party, New York State. 533
Malraux, André. Novelist; French cabinet minister. 476
Marbury, Elisabeth. National Democratic Committeewoman, New York. 914
Marie, Queen of Roumania. 885
Marshall, George Catlett. U.S. Secretary of State; Chief of Staff, U.S. Army. 170
Mary, Queen of England. 445
Matthews, J.B. Consulting expert, Dies Committee, U.S. House of Representatives. 983
Mellon, Andrew W. Financier; U.S. Secretary of the Treasury. 225
Mills, Ogden Livingston.

Financier; U.S. Undersecretary of the Treasury. 1058
Molden, Otto. Founder, European Forum; political visionary. 936
Moore, Alexander Pollock. Newspaper publisher; U.S. Ambassador to Peru. 358
Morgenthau, Henry, Jr. U.S. Secretary of the Treasury. 52
Morris, Newbold. President, New York City Council. 400
Moses, Robert. Chairman, New York State Council of Parks. 847
Moskowitz, Mrs. Henry. Director of publicity, New York State Democratic Committee. 165
Nelson, Donald M. Industrialist; Chairman, War Production Board. 145
O'Brien, John P. Mayor, New York City. 901
O'Rourke, William. Diplomatic courier, communications officer, U.S. State Department. 430
Paderewski, Ignaz. Concert pianist; Premier of Poland. 273
Pate, Maurice. Executive director, United Nations International Children's Emergency Fund. 66
Perkins, Frances. U.S. Secretary of Labor; sociologist. 600
Pétain, Henri Philippe. Marshall of France; head, Vichy France government. 543
Platzker, Joseph. Director, New York City Vacancy Listing Bureau. 166
Prajadhipok, King of Siam. 583
Pratt, Ruth. Member, New York City Board of Aldermen. 743
Purobayev, Pavel Petrovich. Secret agent. 1046
Rockefeller, Nelson Aldrich. Governor, New York State; Latin American expert. 91
Roosevelt, Eleanor. Author; lecturer; statesman. 710, 1124
Roosevelt, Franklin Delano. Governor, New York State; President, United States. 408, 822
Root, Elihu. Lawyer; U.S. Senator; U.S. Secretary of State; U.S. Ambassador to Russia. 244
Roper, William W. Football coach, Princeton University; politician. 882
Rosenberg, Anna. Labor mediator; Regional Director, Social Security Board; Head, New York State National Recovery Administration. 657
Ruml, Beardsley. Economist; author; government advisor. 696
Ruppert, Jacob. Brewer; owner, New York Yankees; U.S. Congressman. 85
Sabin, Pauline Morton. Politician; President, Women's Organization for National Prohibition Reform. 698
Saito, Hirosi. Japanese Ambassador to the United States. 260
Scammon, Richard M. Stat-

istician; political scientist. 748
Seabury, Samuel. Politician; judge. 507
Simpson, Kenneth F. Chairman, New York County Republican Party. 121
Singh, Sirdar Jagjit. Interpreter; president, India League of America. 747
Sirovich, William I. U.S. Congressman, Fourteenth District, New York; orator; physician. 128
Smith, Alfred E. Governor of New York. 139
Somervell, Brehon Burke. Works Progress Administrator for New York City; Colonel, U.S. Army. 59
Stimson, Henry L. U.S. Secretary of State. 557
Thomas, Norman. Presidential candidate, Socialist Party. 29
Tojo, Hideki. Premier of Japan. 861
Tremaine, Morris Sawyer. Comptroller, New York State. 207
Tresca, Carlo. Labor organizer; revolutionist. 1027
Trudeau, Pierre. Prime Minister, Canada. 824
Truman, Harry S. U.S. President. 669
Tugwell, Rexford Guy. U.S. Under-Secretary of Agriculture; Professor of Economics, Columbia University. 890
U.S. Income Tax. 974
Voorhis, John R. New York State Superintendent of Elections. 161
Wagner, Robert F., Sr. Member, U.S. Senate, New York State Senate, Supreme Court. 519
Wagner, Robert F., Jr. Mayor, New York City. 641
Walker, Jimmie. Politician, Mayor of New York. 352
Walsh, Patrick. Fire Chief, New York City. 168
Whalen, Grover. Chairman, Mayor's Reception Committee; Police Commissioner, New York City. 338, 387
Wiesner, Jerome Bert. Professor of Electrical Engineering, Massachusetts Institute of Technology; President's Special Assistant for Science and Technology. 905
Willkie, Wendell Lewis. U.S. Presidential candidate; business executive; lawyer. 891
Wing, Mock Sai. Tong leader. 1015
Woolton, Frederick James. British Minister of Reconstruction. 417

HISTORY

Hannon, Bryan. Historian; author; streetcar driver. 879
McClellan, George Brinton. Mayor, New York City; historian. 761
Mattioli, Raffaele. Publisher; historian; translator; economist. 2
van Loon, Hendrik Willem. Author; historian. 810, 960
William, Maurice. Historian; author; dentist. 618

HOTELS AND RESTAURANTS

Bates, B. L. M. Owner and manager, Murray Hill Hotel. 804
Baum, Joseph. Originator of restaurant Chain. 261
Boomer, Lucius. President, hotel and restaurant chain. 363
Bowman, John McEntee. Director, Bowman Biltmore Hotels Corporation. 41
Cavallero, Gene. Waiter, Colony Restaurant. 1038
Cerutti, Ernest. Waiter, Colony Restaurant. 1038
Childs, William. Owner, Childs' Restaurants. 431
Colony Restaurant. 1038
Donon, Joseph. Private chef. 92
Dumaine, Alexandre. Chef. 978
Ellis, Abraham. Hat check concessionaire. 28
Frey, Fritz. Swiss hotel owner. 494
Hartman, Alfred. Chef, Colony Restaurant. 1038
Lewis, Rosa. Proprietor, Cavendish Hotel. 756
Lucas, Diane Wilson. Owner of cooking school. 1108
MacDougall, Alice Foote. Restaurant owner. 880
McSorley's. Saloon. 727
Mallon, Mary (Typhoid Mary). Cook; typhoid carrier. 1043
Morino, Louis. Restaurant owner. 158
Philippe, Claudius Charles. Vice-president, catering, Waldorf-Astoria Hotel. 1071
Point, Marie-Louise Mado. Manager, Restaurant de la Pyramide. 464
Restaurant Associates. Restaurant chain. 261
Romanoff, Michael Alexandrovitch. Imposter; restaurant owner. 287
Sanders, Harland. Founder, restaurant chain. 530
Schwartz, Louis G. Waiter; war bond salesman. 78
Shattuck, Frank G. Owner, Schraffts Restaurants. 1110
Shor, Bernard (Toots). Restaurant owner. 1017
Sloppy Louie's. Restaurant. 158
Soulé, Henri. Maître d'hôtel. 34

INVENTIONS

Achelis, Elisabeth. Advocate of permanent calendar. 556
de Florez, Luis. Captain, U. S. Naval Reserve; mechanical engineer; inventor of synthetic training devices. 150
DuMont, Allen Balcom. Inventor; pioneer in television industry. 843
Eastman, George. Inventor; industrialist. 147
Edison, Thomas Alva. Inventor. 1111
Fuller, Richard Buckminster. Architect; designer; inventor; engineer. 498
Garand, John C. Inventor, semi-automatic rifle. 611
Godowsky, Leopold. Co-inventor, Kodachrome process; concert violist. 1096
Hammond, John Hays, Jr. Inventor. 438

Hewitt, Edward Ringwood. Director, International Motor Company; fisherman; inventor. 204
Lawrance, Charles Lanier. Inventor of airplane engines. 254
Maxim, Hudson. Inventor. 1097
Nessler, Charles. Inventor, permanent wave machine. 429
Sperry, Elmer A. Inventor. 368
Wright, Orville. Airplane inventor, manufacturer. 444

JOURNALISM

Allen, Kelcey. Drama critic, Women's Wear Daily. 473
Beebe, Lucius Morris. Newspaper society columnist. 256
Broun, Heywood. Newspaper columnist. 858
Caniff, Milton. Comic-strip cartoonist. 918
Capp, Al. Comic-strip cartoonist. 750
Coty, François. Perfume maker; journalist; politician. 783
Eliot, George Fielding. Military analyst; author. 143
Fisher, Harry Conway (Bud). Comic-strip cartoonist. 647
Hearst, William Randolph. Newspaper publisher. 716
Henderson, William James. Music critic. 752
Howard, Roy Wilson. Publisher, Scripps-Howard Newspapers. 851
Ingersoll, Ralph. Editor of PM. 1067
James, Edwin L. European correspondent, New York Times. 622
Kenny, Nick. Columnist, New York Daily Mirror. 966
Laurence, William L. Science reporter, New York Times. 503
Lyons, Leonard. Newspaper gossip columnist. 986
Maney, Richard Sylvester. Broadway press agent. 230
Maury, Reuben. Chief editorial writer, New York Daily News. 286
Moore, Alexander Pollock. Newspaper publisher; U.S. Ambassador to Peru. 358
Ochs, Adolph Simon. Publisher, New York Times. 588
Patterson, Joseph Medill. Publisher, New York Daily News. 1082
Paul, Maury H.B. Society column writer. 272
Pitkin, Walter B. Author; Professor of Journalism, Columbia University. 252
Ripley, Robert L. "Believe it or Not" cartoonist; radio personality. 721
Schiff, Dorothy. Owner and publisher, New York Post. 850
Spencer, Shirley. Graphologist, New York Daily News. 976
Stingo, John R. (pseud.). Columnist, New York Enquirer. 1123
Sulzberger, Arthur Ochs. President and publisher, New York Times. 1075
Swift, J. Otis. Nature Ed-

itor, New York World-Telegram. 900
Taylor, Deems. Music critic. 1066
Thompson, Dorothy. Newspaper columnist. 512
Van Anda, Carr Vatell. Managing editor, New York Times. 47, 1061
Walsh, Christy. Ghost writer (esp. sports). 385
Webster, Harold Tucker. Comic-strip cartoonist. 1119
White, William Allen. Newspaper editor. 1004
Winchell, Walter. Newspaper columnist. 407
Woollcott, Alexander. Critic; author; columnist; radio personality. 97
Young, Art. Political cartoonist. 403

LABOR

Chavez, Cesar. Farm labor organizer. 754
Curran, Joseph. President, National Maritime Union. 1051
Day, Dorothy. Author; founder, Catholic Worker movement. 336
Goldberg, Arthur Joseph. Lawyer; U.S. Secretary of Labor; United Nations representative; Justice, U.S. Supreme Court. 777
Kheel, Theodore. Lawyer; labor mediator. 650
Lonergan, Anna. Head, stevedore union. 548
Meyer, Arthur Simon. Chairman, New York State Board of Mediation. 1091
Powers, Bertram A. President, New York Typographical Union No. 6. 829
Rosenberg, Anna. Labor mediator; Regional Director, Social Security Board; Head, New York State National Recovery Administration. 657
Tresca, Carlo. Labor organizer; revolutionist. 1027

LAW AND LAW ENFORCEMENT

Adams, Charles Francis. Lawyer; politician; Treasurer of Harvard University; yachtsman. 902
Baldwin, Roger. Founder, American Civil Liberties Union. 249
Battle, George Gordon. Lawyer; philanthropist; money raiser. 664
Broderick, John J. Detective, New York City Police. 1089
Buckner, Emery R. Lawyer. 219
Campion, Daniel J. Detective, New York City Police. 83
Cardozo, Benjamin Nathan. Chief Justice, New York Supreme Court. 186
Cashin, William E. Pastor, St. Andrew's Roman Catholic Church; Chaplain, New York State Prison. 318
Cordes, John. Detective, New York City Police. 1109
Corrigan, Joseph E. Judge, New York City Criminal

Courts. 405
Coughlin, John D. Inspector, New York City Police. 213
Cravath, Paul Drennan. Lawyer; corporation director. 845
Curran, Henry Hastings. Lawyer; politician; President, American Association Against the Prohibition Amendment. 1088
Dewey, Thomas Edmund. District attorney, New York City; Governor, New York State; Presidential candidate. 895
Feldman, Sam. Lawyer. 304
Flynn, Edward Joseph. Lawyer; Chairman, Democratic National Committee. 717
Frankfurter, Felix. Justice, U.S. Supreme Court. 526
Goldberg, Arthur Joseph. Lawyer; U.S. Secretary of Labor; United Nations representative; Justice, U.S. Supreme Court. 777
Greenspan, Benjamin E. Magistrate, New York City. 478
Grossman, Harry. Process-server. 796
Holtzmann, Fanny. Lawyer for theatrical profession. 661
Hoover, John Edgar. Director, U.S. Federal Bureau of Investigation. 262
Howe and Hummel, Criminal law office. 294
Howe, William F. Criminal Lawyer. 294
Hughes, Charles Evans. Chief Justice, U.S. Supreme Court. 169
Hummel, Abraham. Criminal Lawyer. 294
Jerome, William Travers. Reformer; District Attorney, Manhattan. 896
Kheel, Theodore. Lawyer; labor mediator. 650
Langner, Lawrence. Co-director of Theatre Guild; lawyer; author. 142
Lawes, Lewis E. Warden, New York State Prison. 217
Leibowitz, Samuel S. Lawyer. 570
MacCormick, Austin H. Commissioner of Correction; prison reformer. 351
McLaughlin, George V. Police Commissioner, New York City. 973
Medalie, George Z. U.S. District Attorney. 558
Milburn, Devereux. Polo player; lawyer. 998
Morgan, Charles, Jr. Lawyer for American Civil Liberties Union. 933
Mulrooney, Edward Pierce. Police Commissioner, New York City. 214
Munn, Orson D. Publisher, Scientific American; patent attorney. 106
Olvany, George Washington. Judge, New York Court of General Sessions. 707
Reilly, Edward J. Lawyer. 342
Root, Elihu. Lawyer; U.S. Senator; U.S. Secretary of State; U.S. Ambassador to Russia. 244
Rothberg, Sam. Bondsman. 75
Seabury, Samuel. Politician; judge. 507
Schindler, Raymond C. Head, private detective agency. 830
Smith, Bruce. Director, In-

stitute of Public Administration. 712
Steuer, Max D. Lawyer. 691, 970
Stryker, Lloyd Paul. Lawyer. 541
Tuttle, Charles H. U.S. District Attorney; lawyer. 897
Untermyer, Samuel. Lawyer. 580
Valentine, Lewis J. Police Commissioner, New York City. 501
West Forty-seventh Street Police Station. 360
Whalen, Grover. Chairman, Mayor's Reception Committee; Police Commissioner, New York City. 338, 387
Willebrandt, Mabel Walker. Reformer; lawyer; Assistant U.S. Attorney-General. 674
Williams, Albert Moran. Patrolman, New York City Police. 73
Willkie, Wendell Lewis. U.S. presidential candidate; business executive; lawyer. 891

LECTURE, ORATORY

Brown, John Mason. Drama critic; editor; author; lecturer. 180
Copeland, Charles Townsend. Professor of Rhetoric and Oratory, Harvard University. 772
Darlington, Thomas. Physician; Commissioner of Health, New York City; author; lecturer; Grand Sachem, Society of Tammany. 411
Keller, Helen. Author; lecturer. 10
Leigh, William Colston. Owner, Leigh Bureau of Lectures and Entertainment. 324
Littleton, Martin J. Orator. 867
Pond, James Burton. Owner, lecture agency. 227
Roosevelt, Eleanor. Author; lecturer; statesman. 710, 1124
Sirovich, William I. U.S. Congressman, Fourteenth District, New York; orator; physician. 128

LITERATURE

Andrews, Roy Chapman. Explorer; author. 481
Bartlett, Frederic Huntington. Pediatrician; author. 299
Barton, Bruce. Author; advertising executive. 513
Beerbohm, Henry Maximilian (Max). Caricaturist; author; critic. 212
Berrigan, Daniel. Roman Catholic priest; militant pacifist leader; author. 10
Berrigan, Philip. Roman Catholic priest; militant pacifist leader; author. 10
Betjeman, John. Poet. 963
Borges, Jorge Luis. Novelist; poet; short story writer. 71
Brown, John Mason. Drama critic; editor; author; lecturer. 180
Butler, Nicholas Murray. President, Columbia Uni-

versity; author. 215
Carr, John Dickson. Mystery writer. 1035
Cather, Willa. Novelist. 36
Clarke, Arthur C. Science fiction author. 760
Darlington, Thomas. Physician; Commissioner of Health, New York City; author; lecturer; Grand Sachem, Society of Tammany. 411
Day, Dorothy. Author; founder, Catholic Worker movement. 336
Dewey, John. Philosopher; educator; author. 621
Dilley, Arthur Urbane. Oriental rug dealer; author. 720
Dreiser, Theodore. Novelist. 193
Eliot, George Fielding. Military analyst; author. 143
Erskine, John. Professor of English, Columbia University; author. 838
Fielding, Temple Hornaday. Author of guidebooks. 979
Fitzgerald, F. Scott. Novelist. 984
Forster, Edward Morgan. Novelist. 539
Fosdick, Harry Emerson. Protestant minister; author. 1034
Frost, Robert. Poet. 711
Geisel, Theodor Seuss (Dr. Seuss). Author; illustrator of children's books. 174
Gibbons, Euell Theophilus. Author of books on wild food. 343
Gilbert, Eugene. Advertising researcher for teen culture; author. 155
Ginsberg, Allen. Poet. 773
Gould, Joseph Ferdinand. Bohemian; author of unpublished book. 520, 837
Gunther, John. Author; geographer. 508
Hannon, Bryan. Historian; author; streetcar driver. 879
Hemingway, Ernest. Novelist; short story writer. 64, 471
Hoffer, Eric. Philosopher; author; longshoreman. 223
Illich, Ivan. Roman Catholic priest; educator; author. 887
Johnson, James Weldon. Author; Executive Secretary, NAACP. 237
Kazan, Avraam Elia (Joe). Author; rug merchant. 864
Keller, Helen. Author; lecturer. 110
Kemp, Harry. Poet. 807
Langer, Susanne K. Philosopher of aesthetics; author. 787
Langner, Lawrence. Co-director of Theatre Guild; lawyer; author. 142
Lasser, Jacob Kay. Author; income tax expert. 975
Le Gallienne, Eva. Actress; director; translator. 551
Lewis, Sinclair. Novelist. 496, 1118
Lewis, Wilmarth Sheldon. Author; Horace Walpole scholar. 958
Lilienthal, David Eli. Financier; corporation director; author; Chairman, U.S. Atomic Energy Commission. 910
Loos, Anita. Author; playwright. 173
Lorenz, Konrad Z. Zoolo-

gist; authority on aggression; author. 209
Lydig, Rita de Alba de Acosta. Socialite; author. 550
MacLeish, Archibald. Poet. 733
Malraux, André. Novelist; French cabinet minister. 476
Mann, Thomas. Novelist. 395
Marquand, John P. Novelist. 985
Maugham, William Somerset. Novelist; playwright; short story writer. 1068
Mead, Margaret. Anthropologist; author. 515
Millay, Edna St. Vincent. Poet. 1077
Miller, Alice Duer. Novelist. 555
Moore, Marianne Craig. Poet. 480
Murphy, George. President, Mark Cross; prototype of leading character in Fitzgerald's <u>Tender is the Night</u>. 586
Murphy, Sara. Prototype of leading character in Fitzgerald's <u>Tender is the Night</u>. 586
Narayan, Rasipuram Krishaswami. Novelist. 1022
Pitkin, Walter B. Author; Professor of Journalism, Columbia University. 252
Poliziano, Angelo. Poet. 46
Pope, Arthur Upham. Authority on Iran; author; philosophy professor. 1050
Post, Emily. Author; authority on etiquette. 547
Roosevelt, Eleanor. Author; lecturer; statesman. 710, 1124
Royce, William H. Scholar (Balzac); author. 994
Ruml, Beardsley. Economist; author; government advisor. 696
Sandburg, Carl. Poet. 778
Sanger, Margaret. Author; birth control advocate. 172, 989
Scher, Louis. Book scout. 115
Sendak, Maurice. Author; illustrator of children's books. 42
Service, Robert W. Poet. 1102
Simenon, Georges. Novelist. 759
Stout, Rex. Mystery story writer. 21
Sumner, John S. Censor; Secretary, New York Society for the Suppression of Vice. 211
Swinburne, Algernon Charles. Poet. 67
Teal, John J., Jr. Associate Professor of Geography and Anthropology, University of Vermont; explorer; author. 356
Tolstoy, Alexandra Lvovna. Daughter of Leo Tolstoy; founder of Russian Welfare agency. 362
van Loon, Hendrik Willem. Author; historian. 810, 960
Vereker, Elliot. Author; dilettante. 935
Watson, John Broadus. Professor of Experimental and Comparative Psychology, Johns Hopkins University; author. 11
Watts - Dunton, Walter. Poet; novelist; critic. 67
Wharton, Edith. Novelist. 247

White, Walter. Sociologist; author. 364
Wightman, Hazel Hotchkiss. Tennis player; coach; author. 888
William, Maurice. Historian; author; dentist. 618
Wilson, Edmund. Author; critic. 820
Woollcott, Alexander. Critic; author; columnist; radio personality. 97
Wylie, Elinor. Poet. 811

MARITIME

Adams, Charles Francis. Lawyer; politician; Treasurer of Harvard University; yachtsman. 902
Ammann, Othmar Hermann. Chief Engineer, Port of New York Authority. 806
Bellet, Robert. Chief Purser, S.S. Liberté. 222
Burgess, W. Starling. Racing yacht designer. 614
Carlsen, Henrik Kurt. Merchant ship captain. 816
Curran, Joseph. President, National Maritime Union. 1051
de Florez, Luis. Captain, U.S. Naval Reserve; mechanical engineer; inventor of synthetic training devices. 150
Edwards, Everett Joshua. Shore whaler. 915
Gibbs, William Francis. Naval architect. 89
Green, Cecil. Fishing guide, Florida Keys. 542
Hodge, Paul. Chief Petty Officer, U.S. Navy. 146
Hoffer, Eric. Philosopher; longshoreman. 223
Hood, Frederick E. Sailmaker. 893
Johnson, Frederick. Captain, S.S. Josiah Crabtree. 589
Lambert, Gerard B. Yachtsman; President, Lambert Company. 18
Lonergan, Anna. Head, longshoremen's union. 548
Lyons, Harry. Barge and small boat owner. 877
M.S. Sagafjord. Ocean liner. 1128
Moran, Eugene F. President, Moran Towing and Transport Company. 297
New York Harbor. 123
S.S. Great Eastern. Ocean liner. 416
S.S. Marquette. Troop transport. 238
Shippey, Hartwell Stuart. Barge captain. 931
Steichen, Edward. Photographer; Commander, U.S. Navy. 201
Stephens, Olin. Yacht designer and builder. 1056
Stephens, Roderick. Yacht designer and builder. 1056
Thompson, Ellery Franklin. Captain in dragger fleet. 277
Turner, Hilary F. Ferryboat captain. 436
U.S.S. New York. Battleship. 701
Vanderbilt, Harold. Yachtsman; contract bridge authority. 399

MEDICINE

Adler, Alfred. Psycholo-

gist. 1074
Bartlett, Frederic Huntington. Pediatrician; author. 299
Blair, Bruce. Veterinarian. 271
Brill, Abraham Arden. Psychiatrist. 523
Couney, Martin A. Physician; specialist in premature births. 774
Crumbine, Samuel J. Physician; public health worker. 967
Cullman, Howard J. Theatrical investor; President, Beekman Hospital; partner, Cullman Brothers. 1014
Darlington, Thomas. Physician; Commissioner of Health, New York City; author; lecturer; Grand Sachem, Society of Tammany. 411
Erdmann, John Frederick. Surgeon. 767
Erikson, Erik H. Psychoanalyst. 648
Gumpert, Martin. Physician, geriatrics. 384
Libman, Emanuel. Physician; diagnostician. 483
Mallon, Mary (Typhoid Mary). Cook; typhoid carrier. 1043
Meyer, Alfred. Physician. 269
Nyswander, Marie. Psychiatrist; psychoanalyst for narcotics addicts. 1023
Pilgrim State Hospital, New York. Mental institution. 793
Rovenstine, Emery Andrew. Director, Department of Anesthesia, Bellevue Hospital. 45
Sirovich, William I. U. S. Congressman, Fourteenth District, New York; orator; physician. 128
Vishniac, Roman. Photographer of microscopic life; zoologist; physician. 1011
William, Maurice. Historian; author; dentist. 618

MILITARY

Allen, Terry de la Mesa. Major-general, U. S. Army. 327
Bradley, Omar Nelson. General, U. S. Army; Chairman, Joint Chiefs of Staff. 333
Clay, Lucius Du Bignon. General, U. S. Army; Head, Office of Defense Mobilization. 932
Cochran, Philip. Major, U. S. Army Air Forces. 427
Craige, John H. Captain, U. S. Marine Corps. 382
de Florez, Luis. Captain, U. S. Naval Reserve; mechanical engineer; inventor of synthetic training devices. 150
Dixie Demo crew. Crew of flying fortress. 266
Drebin, Sam. Soldier of fortune. 899
Eliot, George Fielding. Military analyst; author. 143
Finucane, Brendan. Flight Lieutenant, Royal Air Force. 764
Gamelin, Maurice-Gustave. Generalissimo, Allied Armies in France. 375
Garand, John C. Inventor, semi-automatic rifle. 611

Hallock, Joseph Theodore. 1st Lieutenant, U.S. Army Air Forces. 1130

Harding, Edwin Forrest. Major-general, U.S. Army. 1041

Hodge, Paul. Chief Petty Officer, U.S. Navy. 146

Hollins, Albert. Worker in bomb factory. 947

Johnson, Hugh Samuel. Director, National Recovery Administration; General, U.S. Army. 371

McNair, Lesley James. Lieutenant-general, U.S. Army. 288

Marshall, George Catlett. U.S. Secretary of State; Chief of Staff, U.S. Army. 170

Pershing, John J. General, U.S. Army. 714

Prendiville, Joseph P. Staff-sergeant, U.S. Army. 868

Ramey, John Daniel. American soldier. 134

Smith, Maynard. Staff sergeant, U.S. Army Air Forces. 245

Snyder, Daniel. Captain, U.S. Army Air Forces. 1129

Somervell, Brehon Burke. Works Progress Administrator for New York City; Colonel, U.S. Army. 59

Steichen, Edward. Photographer; Commander, U.S. Navy. 201

Tobin, Ralph C. Colonel, 7th Regiment, New York City socialite. 190

U.S.S. New York. Battleship. 701

Warner, Karl. American soldier. 854

MISCELLANEOUS

Adams, Gridley. Chairman, National Flag Code Committee. 1003

American elm. 414

Benjamin, Mary A. Autograph dealer. 1090

Berlin Wall. 258

Campbell, Frank E. Mortician. 196

Cosey, Joseph (pseud.). Forger. 1135

Creel, George. Chairman, Committee of Public Information. 500

Gallup, George Horace. Public opinion poll taker. 105

Hagstrom, Andrew Gunnar. Cartographer. 916

Hammer, Armand. Jewelry collector. 506

Hurricane Donna. 542

Kelly, Alvin (Shipwreck). Flagpole sitter. 1059

Life at the edge of the sea. 285

The Mafia. Criminal secret society. 462

O'Neill, Rose. Designer of Kewpie Doll. 531

Rubin, Louis. Marriage broker. 79

The sea. 908

Singh, Sirdar Jagjit. Interpreter; president, India League of America. 747

Stein, Ben. Wallpaper-hanger. 420

Vincent, George Robert. Collector, voices of famous persons. 1081

Work, Milton C. Auction bridge authority. 72

MOTION PICTURES

Beery, Wallace. Motion picture actor; comedian. 525
Bergman, Ingrid. Stage, motion picture actress. 798
Brando, Marlon. Stage, motion picture actor. 281
Brown, Joe E. Comedian; stage, motion picture actor. 198
Butterworth, Charles. Comedian; motion picture actor. 598
Cantor, Eddie. Comedian; stage, motion picture actor. 178
Capra, Frank. Motion picture director. 991
Chaplin, Charlie. Motion picture actor. 366
Cooper, Merian. Motion picture photographer. 624
Cronyn, Hume. Stage, motion picture actor. 798
Damita, Lily. Motion picture actress. 584
Davis, Bette. Motion picture actress. 216
De Sica, Vittorio. Motion picture director; actor. 133
DeMille, Cecil B. Motion picture director. 456
Disney, Walt. Motion picture cartoonist. 655
Fellini, Federico. Motion picture director. 980
Fields, W. C. Comedian; stage, motion picture actor. 568
Flaherty, Robert J. Documentary film producer. 683
Fonda, Henry. Stage, motion picture actor. 799
Garbo, Greta. Motion picture actress. 39
Gielgud, John. Stage, motion picture actor. 800
Goldwin, Samuel. Motion picture producer. 160
Hardwicke, Cedric. Stage, motion picture actor. 799
Hayes, Helen. Stage, motion picture actress. 1065
Hays, Will H. Director, Motion Picture Producers and Distributors' Association of America; censor. 231, 268
Hitchcock, Alfred. Motion picture director. 1092
Holden, William. Stage, motion picture actor. 798
Jannings, Emil. Motion picture actor. 179
Kubrick, Stanley. Motion picture director. 470
Lasky, Jesse L. Motion picture executive. 141
Levine, Joseph E. Motion picture producer. 1069
Lillie, Beatrice. Comedienne; stage and motion picture actress. 136
Lloyd, Harold. Motion picture actor. 781
Lunt, Alfred. Stage, motion picture actor. 374
Marx, Harpo. Comedian; stage, motion picture actor. 813
Matthau, Walter. Stage, motion picture actor. 800
May, Elaine. Comedienne; stage, motion picture actress; playwright. 1007
Mayer, Louis B. Motion picture executive. 1125
Menjou, Adolphe. Motion picture actor. 82

Meredith, Burgess. Stage, motion picture actor. 1055
Mostel, Zero. Stage, motion picture actor. 799
Nichols, Michael (Mike). Comedian; motion picture director. 1007
Page, Geraldine. Stage, motion picture actress. 800
Perkins, Anthony. Stage, motion picture actor. 800
Pickford, Mary. Motion picture actress. 968
Preminger, Otto. Motion picture producer and director. 44
Redgrave, Michael. Stage, motion picture actor. 798
Renoir, Jean. Motion picture director. 563
Robards, Jason. Stage, motion picture actor. 800
Robeson, Paul. Actor; concert singer. 534
Rosen, Al. Hollywood agent. 413
Schell, Maria. Stage, motion picture actress. 799
Schenck, Nicholas M. President, Loew's Incorporated, and Metro-Goldwin-Meyer. 144
Signoret, Simone. Stage, motion picture actress. 800
Sokolof, Vladimir. Actor. 798
Stanley, Kim. Stage, motion picture actress. 798
Stapleton, Maurine. Stage, motion picture actress. 799
Steiger, Rod. Stage, motion picture actor. 799
Swanson, Gloria. Motion picture actress. 1045
Van Dyke, W. S. Motion picture director. 592
von Sternberg, Josef. Motion picture director. 22
Wallach, Eli. Stage, motion picture actor. 798
Warner, Albert. Motion picture producer. 538
Warner, Harry. Motion picture producer. 538
Warner, Jack. Motion picture producer. 538
Warner, Sam. Motion picture producer. 538
Welles, Orson. Stage, motion picture actor; director; radio personality. 996
West, Mae. Stage, motion picture actress; playwright. 257
Widmark, Richard. Stage, motion picture actor. 800
Wooley, Monty. Stage, motion picture actor. 516
Zanuck, Darryl Francis. Motion picture producer. 1083
Zukor, Adolph. President, Paramount Famous-Lasky. 769

MUSEUMS

The American Museum of Natural History. 38
Metropolitan Museum of Art. 638
Smithsonian Institution. 307

MUSIC

Adler, Larry. Harmonica player. 102
Allen, Henry (Red). Jazz trumpet player. 111
Allers, Franz. Conductor: ballet, opera, symphony,

musical comedy. 350
Auer, Leopold. Concert violinist; music teacher. 636
Bennett, Robert Russell. Orchestrator for musical comedies. 49
Bernstein, Leonard. Conductor, New York Philharomic; composer. 784
Bing, Rudolf. General manager, Metropolitan Opera Company. 373
Bloch, Ernest. Composer. 601
Bodanzky, Artur. Conductor, Metropolitan Opera Company. 30
Borge, Victor. Comedian; pianist; poultry breeder. 104
Brubeck, David. Jazz pianist; orchestra leader. 185
Buchter, Jacob. Chief electrician, Metropolitan Opera Company. 1101
Buck, Gene. Songwriter; President of American Society of Composers, Authors and Publishers; theatrical producer. 232
Budapest String Quartet. 140
Cage, John M., Jr. Composer. 326
Casals, Pablo. Concert cellist. 159
Chaliapin, Feodor C. Singer, Metropolitan Opera Company. 63
Charles, Ray. Popular singer; pianist; composer; music publisher. 517
Cleveland Orchestra. 753
Cohan, George M. Playwright; song writer; dancer; actor. 937
Coleman, Emil. Popular orchestra leader. 687
Condon, Albert Edwin (Eddie). Jazz guitarist. 950
Coward, Noël. Playwright; composer; actor. 449
Crawford, Cheryl. Musical comedy producer. 1113
Damrosch, Walter. Conductor, New York Symphony. 394
Davis, Meyer. Popular orchestra leader. 646
Dilling, Mildred. Concert harpist. 437
Dreyfus, Max. Music publisher. 6
Dylan, Bob. Popular music composer; singer. 220
Ellington, Edward Kennedy (Duke). Popular orchestra leader; composer. 465
Evans, Merle. Band leader, Ringling Brothers and Barnum & Bailey Circus. 739
Farrell, Eileen. Concert singer. 460
Finn, William J. Roman Catholic priest; leader of Paulist choristers. 924
Fishberg, Isaac. Flutist. 332
Garden, Mary. Opera singer. 898
Gatti-Casazza, Giulio. Impresario, Metropolitan Opera Company. 602
Gershwin, George. Composer. 1026
Gillespie, John Birks (Dizzy). Popular orchestra leader; trumpet player. 116
Glow, Bernie. Trumpet player. 564
Godowsky, Leopold. Co-inventor, Kodachrome process; concert violist. 1096
Goodman, Benny. Popular orchestra leader; clari-

netist. 26
Gould, Glenn. Concert pianist. 53
Grainger, Percy. Composer; concert pianist. 689
Hammerstein, Oscar, II. Song writer; musical comedy writer. 782
Hammond, John Henry, Jr. Popular music critic; Director, Columbia Recording Corporation. 1133
Harbach, Otto. Author, musical comedies. 565
Hart, Lorenz. Song writer; musical comedy writer. 1115
Hart, Tony (pseud.). Variety-show, musical comedy performer. 770
Heifetz, Jascha. Concert violinist. 376
Henderson, William James. Music critic. 752
Herrmann, Emil. Violin dealer. 1029
Hines, Earl (Father). Jazz pianist; orchestra leader. 874
Hupfer, William. Piano tone regulator. 791
Janssen, Werner. Conductor, New York Philharmonic Orchestra. 37
Jeritza, Maria. Singer, Metropolitan Opera Company. 1073
Johnson, Edward. General Director, Metropolitan Opera Company; opera singer. 372
Jones, Elvin. Jazz drummer. 1084
Kapp, Jack. President, Decca Records. 853
Kern, Jerome. Song writer; musical comedy writer. 1116
Kreisler, Fritz. Concert violinist. 379
Kroyt, Boris. Member, Budapest String Quartet. 140
Lefebvre, Channing. Choirmaster, organist, Trinity Church. 922
Lehmann, Lotte. Singer, Metropolitan Opera Company. 938
Lhevinne, Rosina. Piano teacher. 566
Lombardo, Guy. Popular orchestra leader. 814
London, George. Singer, Metropolitan Opera Company. 1078
Ludwig, Leopold. Concert pianist and conductor. 275
Mehta, Zubin. Symphony orchestra conductor. 817
Mengelberg, Willem. Director, New York Philharmonic Orchestra. 54
Menotti, Gian Carlo. Opera composer. 755
Menuhin, Yehudi. Concert violinist. 833
Miller, Mitchell William. Popular orchestra leader; oboist. 353
Miller, Roger. Popular songwriter; singer. 1103
Mitropoulos, Dimitri. Conductor, New York Philharmonic Orchestra. 604
Mulligan, Gerry. Jazz saxophonist; composer. 497
Nilsson, Birgit. Singer, Metropolitan Opera Company. 16
Norvo, Kenneth (Red). Vibraharp player. 686
Ornstein, Leo. Concert pianist. 860
Paderewski, Ignaz. Concert pianist; Premier of Po-

land. 273
Pons, Lily. Singer, Metropolitan Opera Company. 354
Porter, Cole. Songwriter; musical comedy writer. 1117
Rachmaninoff, Sergei Vassilievitch. Composer. 58
Rapee, Erno. Orchestra conductor, Radio City Music Hall. 489
Rich, Buddy. Jazz drummer. 81
Robeson, Paul. Actor; concert singer. 534
Rodgers, Richard. Song writer; musical comedy writer. 1116, 1126
Roisman, Joseph. Member, Budapest String Quartet. 140
Rubinstein, Artur. Concert pianist. 654
Rudel, Julius. Conductor, New York City Opera. 319
Russell, Charles Ellsworth (Pee Wee). Jazz clarinetist. 309
Saracini, Guido Chigi. Italian count; music patron. 1018
Scheff, Fritzi. Opera and light-opera singer. 628
Schnabel, Artur. Concert pianist. 690
Schneider, Alexander. Member, Budapest String Quartet. 140
Schneider, Mischa. Member, Budapest String Quartet. 140
Schumann-Heink, Ernestine. Opera singer. 441
Scotti, Antonio. Singer, Metropolitan Opera Company. 1076
Shaw, Artie. Popular orchestra leader, clarinetist. 656
Short, Bobby. Popular singer; pianist. 479
Sinatra, Francis Albert (Frank). Popular singer. 785
Smith, Kate. Popular singer. 458
Stern, Isaac. Concert violinist. 590
Stokowski, Leopold. Conductor, Philadelphia Orchestra. 819
Stravinsky, Igor. Composer; conductor. 892
Szell, George. Conductor, Cleveland Orchestra. 410
Talley, Marion. Singer, Metropolitan Opera Company. 694
Taylor, Deems. Music critic. 1066
Tibbett, Lawrence. Singer, Metropolitan Opera Company. 461
Toscanini, Arturo. Conductor, New York Philharmonic Orchestra. 210
von Karajan, Herbert. Symphony orchestra conductor. 942
Werrenrath, Reinald. Concert singer. 702
Whiteman, Paul. Popular orchestra leader. 765
Williams, Mary Lou. Jazz pianist; composer. 758
Zimbalist, Efrem. Concert violinist. 208

PHILANTHROPY

Amnesty International. Society for freeing political prisoners. 649
Battle, George Gordon. Lawyer; philanthropist; money raiser. 664

Beard, Daniel Carter. National Commissioner, Boy Scouts of America; book and magazine illustrator. 1063
Booth, Evangeline. Commander, Salvation Army. 200
Flexner, Abraham. Educator; philanthropist; Secretary, Rockefeller Foundation General Education Board. 878
Ford Foundation. Philanthropic organization. 348
Frick, Helen Clay. Director, Frick Art Reference Library; philanthropist. 240
Geer, Alpheus. Philanthropist; reformer; Director of Marshall Stillman Movement. 685
Gmeiner, Hermann. Organizer, SOS Children's Villages. 466
Heckscher, August. Industrialist; philanthropist. 1093
Humphrey, Elliott (Jack). Head, Seeing eye dog school. 469
Johnson, Hugh K. Anthropologist; social worker. 1100
Latham, Natalie Wales. Founder, Bundles for Britain. 8
Ledoux, Urbain ("Mr. Zero"). Philanthropist. 929
McLean, Alice Throckmorton. Founder, American Women's Voluntary Services. 545
Morgan, Anne. Club woman; philanthropist. 549
Nawkins, Angeline. Captain, Salvation Army. 402
Pate, Maurice. Executive director, United Nations International Children's Emergency Fund. 66
Petzold, Theodore. Boy Scout. 1031
Robinson, Bill. Dancer; philanthropist. 113
Rockefeller, John D., Jr. Industrialist; philanthropist. 903
Tolstoy, Alexandra Lvovna. Daughter of Leo Tolstoy; founder of Russian welfare agency. 362
Wald, Lillian D. Philanthropist; Founder, Henry Street Settlement. 859
Whitney, John Hay (Jock). Foundation director; philanthropist. 615

PHILOSOPHY

Dewey, John. Philosopher; educator. author. 621
Hoffer, Eric. Philosopher; author; longshoreman. 223
Langer, Susanne K. Philosopher of aesthetics; author. 787
Pope, Arthur Upham. Authority on Iran; author; philosophy professor. 1050
Wahl, Jean. Philosopher. 786

PHOTOGRAPHY

Avedon, Richard. Fashion photographer. 1112
Cooper, Merian. Motion picture photographer. 624
Fairchild, Sherman Mills. Airplane manufacturer; authority on aerial photography. 20

Flaherty, Robert J. Documentary film producer. 683
Funt, Allen. Radio, television personality; cameraman. 962
Jackson, Edward N. Photographer, New York Daily News. 703
Korman, Murray. Photographer. 740
Sarra, Valentino. Photographer; president of advertising agency. 637
Steichen, Edward. Photographer; Commander, U.S. Navy. 201
Stieglitz, Alfred. Photographer. 1036
Vishniac, Roman. Photographer of microscopic life; zoologist; physician. 1011
Xerox Corporation. Manufacturers of photocopying machinery. 1121

PUBLISHING: BOOK AND MAGAZINE

Cerf, Bennett A. President, Random House; radio and television personality. 849
Crowninshield, Frank. Editor, Vanity Fair. 559
Dillon, John J. Publisher, Rural New-Yorker. 890
Doubleday, Nelson. Publisher. 426
Giegengack, Augustus E. Head, U.S. Government Printing Office. 671
Goudy, Frederic William. Type designer. 392
Grosvenor, Gilbert H. Editor, National Geographic Magazine. 383
Haldeman-Julius, E. Publisher. 14
Knopf, Alfred A. Publisher. 849, 1024
Knopf, Blanche. Publisher. 1024
Knopf, Samuel. Publisher. 1024
Lewis, Joseph. Publisher. 68
Liveright, Horace B. Publisher. 741
Luce, Henry Robinson. Publisher. 1008
Macfadden, Bernarr. Publisher; physical fitness advocate. 50, 789
Mardersteig, Giovanni. Publisher; printer; literary scholar. 401
Mattioli, Raffaele. Publisher; historian; translator; economist. 2
Munn, Orson D. Publisher, Scientific American; patent attorney. 106
Perkins, Maxwell Evarts. Editor; vice-president, Charles Scribner's Sons. 1053
Reader's Digest. 582
Schuster, M. Lincoln. Publisher. 474
Simon, Richard L. Publisher. 474
Time Magazine. 1008
Vanderbilt, Cornelius, Jr. Publisher; socialite. 322
Wallace, DeWitt. Editor, Reader's Digest. 582
Wilson, Halsey William. Publisher, Readers' Guide to Periodical Literature. 682
Zolotow, Sam. Publisher, Advance Theatrical Guide. 724

RADIO-TELEVISION

Block, Martin. Radio "disc jockey." 930
Brinkley, David. Television news commentator. 5
Carney, Don. Radio broadcaster for children. 1049
Cerf, Bennett A. President, Random House; radio and television personality. 849
Corwin, Norman. Radio script writer and director. 722
DuMont, Allen Balcom. Inventor; pioneer in television industry. 843
Friendly, Fred W. Television producer. 749
Funt, Allen. Radio, television personality; cameraman. 962
Garroway, David. Television personality. 1009
Heatter, Gabriel. Radio commentator. 224
Huntley, Chet. Television news commentator. 5
McBride, Mary Margaret. Radio personality (housewives' program). 346
McNamee, Graham. Radio announcer. 218
Murrow, Edward R. Radio and television news commentator. 1120
Ripley, Robert L. "Believe it or Not" cartoonist; radio personality. 721
Royal, John F. Vice-president, National Broadcasting Company. 1064
Stanton, Frank. President, Columbia Broadcasting System. 571
Swing, Raymond Gram. Radio commentator. 1079
Taylor, Marion Sayle. Radio "Voice of Experience." 1080
Weaver, Sylvester L., Jr. (Pat). President, National Broadcasting Company. 203
Welles, Orson. Actor; director; radio personality. 996
Woollcott, Alexander. Critic; author; columnist; radio personality. 97

RAILROADS

Cesoli, Leo. European train conductor. 693
Loree, Leonor F. President, Delaware & Hudson Railroad. 697

REAL ESTATE, CONTRACTING

Astor, William Vincent. Real estate owner and manager; investment manager. 396
Blumenthal, Alfred Cleveland. Real estate, theatrical promoter. 112
Carey, William. Contractor; Director, Madison Square Garden. 952
Chanin, Irwin S. Realtor; architectural engineer. 926
Davies, J. Clarence. Real estate developer. 535
Day, Joseph P. Real estate auctioneer. 839
Flood, Hugh G. Housewrecking contractor. 644
Fraad, Daniel, Jr. President, Allied Maintenance Corporation. 457

French, Fred F. Realtor; building contractor. 862
Hart, Richard Olney. Head, window-washing crew, Empire State Building. 518
Jollity Building, New York. 521
Jones, Bassett. Chairman, Committee on Display, New York World's Fair; Elevator designer; Electrical engineer. 241
Norris, Stanley. Window washer. 625
Paterno, Charles Vincent. Building contractor. 607
Stevens, Roger Lacey. Theatrical producer; real estate tycoon. 187
Tysen, John Colquhoun. President, real estate firm. 992
Winter, Benjamin. Real estate speculator. 323
Zeckendorf, William. Realtor. 98

REFORM

Berrigan, Daniel. Roman Catholic priest; militant pacifist leader; author. 10
Berrigan, Philip. Roman Catholic priest; militant pacifist leader; author. 10
Bishop, Howard Berkey. Crusader against tobacco habit. 735
Curran, Henry Hastings. Lawyer; politician; President, American Association Against the Prohibition Amendment. 1088
Feminists. 349
Geer, Alpheus. Philanthropist; reformer; Director of Marshall Stillman Movement. 685
Hallett, George Hervey, Jr. Executive Secretary, Citizens Union; reformer. 181
Jerome, William Travers. Reformer; District Attorney, Manhattan. 896
Johnson, James Weldon. Author; Executive Secretary, NAACP. 237
Lord, Mary Stinson Pillsbury. U.S. representative to U.N. Commission on Human Rights. 745
MacCormick, Austin H. Commissioner of Correction; prison reformer. 351
Molden, Otto. Founder, European Forum; political visionary. 936
Peabody, Ernest Henry. President, Peabody Engineering Corporation; antinoise campaigner. 940
Sabin, Pauline Morton. Politician; President, Women's Organization for National Prohibition Reform. 698
Sanger, Margaret. Author; birth control advocate. 172, 989
Sumner, John S. Censor; Secretary, New York Society for the Suppression of Vice. 211
Tresca, Carlo. Labor organizer; revolutionist. 1027
Willebrandt, Mabel Walker. Reformer; lawyer; Assistant U.S. Attorney-General. 674

RELIGION

Baker, George (Father Divine). Leader, religious cult. 1099
Berrigan, Daniel. Roman Catholic priest; militant pacifist leader; author. 10
Berrigan, Philip. Roman Catholic priest; militant pacifist leader; author. 10
Bowie, Walter Russell. Pastor, Grace Episcopal Church. 381
Bowlby, Harry Laity. Protestant minister; General Secretary, Lord's Day Alliance. 866
Brown, William Montgomery. Bishop of Arkansas. 88
Buchman, Frank. Evangelistic minister. 939
Cashin, William E. Pastor, St. Andrew's Roman Catholic Church; Chaplain, New York State Prison. 318
Church of St. Matthew and St. Timothy. Episcopal church. 177
Finn, William J. Roman Catholic priest; leader of Paulist choristers. 924
Fosdick, Harry Emerson. Protestant minister; author. 1034
Gusweller, James. Episcopal minister. 177
Guthrie, William Norman. Rector, St. Mark's-in-the-Bouwerie. 575
Hall, James Jefferson Davis. Street preacher. 949
Hayes, Patrick Joseph. Cardinal, Archdiocese of New York. 152
Hunter, George H. Chairman, Board of Trustees, African Methodist Church. 665
Illich, Ivan. Roman Catholic priest; educator; author. 887
Laubach, Frank Charles. Congregational minister; educator. 1001
Lefebvre, Channing. Choirmaster; organist, Trinity Church. 922
Manning, William T. Bishop, Protestant Episcopal Diocese of New York. 330
Morse, Walter P. Missionary in China. 434
New theology and theologians. 699
Persky, Daniel. Hebrew scholar; member, Herzliah Institute. 927
Ray, Randolph. Rector, Little Church Around the Corner. 276
Reisner, Christian F. Methodist Episcopal minister, Broadway Temple. 529
Straton, John Roach. Fundamentalist minister. 652
Suzuki, Daisetz Teitaro. Authority on Zen Buddhism. 418
Tomlinson, Homer A. Bishop, Church of God. 737
Wise, Stephen S. Rabbi, Jewish Institute of Religion. 840

RETAIL MERCHANDISING, ADVERTISING, SALES

Arnold, Stanley N. Marketing and sales-management consultant. 987
Barton, Bruce. Author; advertising executive. 513
Birdwell, Russell. Press agent, publicity man. 846
Blackwell, Basil. Owner

of bookstore. 856
Brooks Brothers. Clothing store. 921
Butler, James. Chain-grocery owner; race track owner. 421
D'Agostino, Pasquale. Grocer. 492
Denison, Frank Emerson. Tea grader and blender. 167
Dilley, Arthur Urbane. Oriental rug dealer; author. 720
Duff, Peter (pseud.). Auctioneer. 70
Elliott, James W. Sales promoter. 192
Gabler, Milton. Owner, Commodore Music Shop. 341
Gilbert, Eugene. Advertising researcher for teen culture; author. 155
Goodman, Edwin. Owner, Bergdorf Goodman. 118
Herrmann, Emil. Violin dealer. 1029
Jeffers, Henry William. Milk distributor. 659
Kauffman, Bernie. Owner, Kauffman Saddlery Company. 1005
Kauffman, Ike. Owner, Kauffman Saddlery Company. 1005
Kauffman, Jake. Owner, Kauffman Saddlery Company. 1005
Kazan, Avraam Elia (Joe). Author; rug merchant. 864
Klein, S. Clothing manufacturer, distributor. 736
Lichine, Alexis. Vintner; wine merchant. 279
Lipton, Thomas. Importer; merchant. 129
Mills, William. Fishing tackle store owner. 463
Murphy, George. President Mark Cross; prototype of leading character in Fitzgerald's Tender is the Night. 586
Okie, William Bernard, Jr. Window display designer. 605
Reiselin, Walter. Milk delivery man. 886
Rosenbach, A. S. W. Book dealer. 695
Sarra, Valentino. Photographer; president of advertising agency. 637
Scheepers, John T. Flower bulb broker. 334
Schlemmer, William. Head, Hammacher Schlemmer & Co. (hardware). 653
Schling, Max. Florist. 337
Sonnenberg, Benjamin. Public-relations counsellor. 468
Stevens, Harry S. Concessionaire. 865
Townsend, A. J. Advertising consultant. 560
Townsend, William. Advertising consultant. 560
Twyeffort, Raymond G. Custom tailor. 191
Walsh, Arthur. Cigar store owner. 616
Weil, Richard, Jr. President, R. H. Macy. 1098
Wheeler, Elmer. Head, Tested Selling Institute. 925
Whitman, Lucilla Mara de Vescovi. Owner of men's shop (Countess Mara). 1054
William Mills & Son. Fishing tackle store. 463
Winston, Harry. Jewelry dealer. 101
Yereshersky, Izzy. Cigar

store owner. 138

SCIENCE

Adams, Evangeline. Astrologer. 553
Avinoff, Andrey. Lepidopterist; painter. 109
Breder, Charles M., Jr. Director, New York Aquarium. 86
Chapman, Frank M. Curator of Ornithology, American Museum of Natural History. 127
Cook, Emory. Sound expert; President, phonograph record company. 283
Craig, John C. Consultant on pyrotechnics to Board of Display, New York World's Fair. 477
Delacour, Jean. Aviculturist; operator, Bronx Zoo. 412
Dewey, Edward Russell. Director, Foundation for the Study of Cycles. 934
Ditmars, Raymond. Supervisor, Bronx Zoo Snake House. 945
Dublin, Louis I. Statistician. 355
Einstein, Albert. Mathemetician; scientist. 904
Electronic computers. 43
Fisher, Clyde. Curator-in-Chief, Hayden Planetarium. 680
Goudsmit, Samuel A. Chairman, Physics Department, Brookhaven National Laboratory. 316
Green, E.R.H. Owner, Round Hill Experimental Laboratories. 448
Johnson, Hugh K. Anthropologist; social worker. 1100
Kimball, James H. Meteorologist, U.S. Weather Bureau. 344
Laurence, William L. Science reporter, New York Times. 503
Lee, Tsung-Dao. Theoretical physicist; Nobel Prize winner. 855
Lorenz, Konrad Z. Zoologist; authority on aggression; author. 209
Mark, Herman F. Scientist; Professor of Organic Chemistry, Polytechnic Institute of Brooklyn. 809
Mead, Margaret. Anthropologist; author. 515
Pennington, Mary Engle. Chief, Food Research Laboratory; refrigeration expert. 486
Petrunkevitch, Alexander I. Expert on spiders. 56
Pierce, John R. Executive Director of Communications Research, Bell Telephone Laboratories. 1114
Ripley, Sidney Dillon, II Associate Curator of Zoology, Peabody Museum; authority on birds of Far East. 228
Robbins, William J. Director, New York Botanical Gardens. 953
Romanoff, Alexis Lawrence. Professor of Chemical Embryology, Cornell University. 291
Scammon, Richard M. Statistician. 748
Vishniac, Roman. Photographer of microscopic life; zoologist; physician. 1011
Westcott, Cynthia. Plant

pathologist. 790
Winlock, Herbert E. Director, Metropolitan Museum; archeologist. 293
Wright, John Kirtland. Director, American Geographical Society. 94
Yang, Chen Ning. Theoretical physicist; Nobel Prize winner. 855

SOCIETY

Bagby, Albert Morris. Patron of arts; socialite. 688
Beebe, Lucius Morris. Newspaper society columnist. 256
Burke, Randolph Forrest. Socialite. 388
Davies, Marjorie Post Close Hutton. Wife, U.S. Ambassador to Russia; socialite. 546
Duke, Angier Biddle. U.S. Chief of Protocol. 404
Frazier, Brenda Diana Duff. Socialite; débutante. 527
Longworth, Alice Roosevelt. Socialite. 827
Lydig, Rita de Alba de Acosta. Socialite; author. 550
Lyons, Leonard. Newspaper gossip columnist. 986
Maxwell, Elsa. Party giver. 194
Mendl, Lady (Elsie de Wolfe). Actress; socialite. 433
Morgan, Anne. Club woman; philanthropist. 549
Paul, Maury H.B. Society column writer. 272
Post, Emily. Author; authority on etiquette. 547
Tobin, Ralph C. Colonel, 7th Regiment, New York City; socialite. 190
Vanderbilt, Cornelius, Jr. Publisher; socialite. 322
Whitney, Harry Payne. Socialite; polo player. 1057
Winchell, Walter. Newspaper gossip columnist. 407

THEATRE

Aldrich, Richard Stoddard. Summer-theatre producer. 572
Allen, Kelcey. Drama critic, Women's Wear Daily. 473
Allers, Franz. Conductor: ballet, opera, symphony, musical comedy. 350
Ames, Winthrop. Theatrical producer. 122
Belasco, David. Theatrical producer. 415
Bennett, Robert Russell. Orchestrator for musical comedies. 49
Bergman, Ingrid. Stage, motion picture actress. 798
Bernstein, Leonard. Conductor, New York Philharmonic; composer, classical and musical comedy. 784
Blumenthal, Alfred Cleveland. Real estate, theatrical promoter. 112
Boothe, Clare. Playwright; actress; U.S. Ambassador to Italy. 148
Brecht, Bertolt. Playwright. 1094
Brown, Joe E. Comedian; stage, motion picture actor. 198
Brown, John Mason. Drama critic; editor; author; lec-

turer. 180
Buck, Gene. Songwriter; President of American Society of Composers, Authors and Publishers; theatrical producer. 232
Burrows, Abe. Comedian; playwright; director. 284
Cantor, Eddie. Comedian; stage, motion picture actor. 178
Cohan, George M. Playwright; song writer; dancer; actor. 937
Connelly, Marcus Cook (Marc). Playwright. 1039
Coward, Noël. Playwright; composer; actor. 449
Crawford, Cheryl. Musical comedy producer. 1113
Cronyn, Hume. Stage, motion picture actor. 798
Cullman, Howard J. Theatrical investor; President, Beekman Hospital; partner, Cullman Brothers (tobacco). 1014
Davis, Bette. Stage, motion picture actress. 216
deMille, Agnes. Theatrical choreographer. 175
Dreyfuss, Henry. Theatrical designer. 6
Feuer, Cy. Theatrical producer. 452
Fields, W. C. Comedian; stage, motion picture actor. 568
Fischer, Clifford C. Producer of revues. 544
Fonda, Henry. Stage, motion picture actor. 799
Frohman, Daniel. Theatrical producer. 246
Geddes, Norman Bel. Stage and industrial designer. 251
Gershwin, George. Composer, classical and musical comedy. 1026
Gest, Morris. Theatrical producer. 108
Gielgud, John. Stage, motion picture actor. 800
Gordon, Max. Theatrical producer. 730
Gordon, Mazie P. Ticket seller, Venice Theatre on Bowery. 645
Guitry, Sacha. Playwright. 308
Hammerstein, Oscar, II. Song writer; musical comedy writer. 782
Harbach, Otto. Author, musical comedies. 565
Hardwicke, Cedric. Stage, motion picture actor. 799
Harrigan, Edward Green. Musical comedy performer. 770
Hart, Lorenz. Composer; musical comedy writer. 1126
Hart, Moss. Playwright; producer. 453
Hart, Tony (pseud.). Musical comedy performer. 770
Hayes, Helen. Stage, motion picture actress. 1065
Hayward, Leland. Theatrical agent. 455
Helburn, Theresa. Director, The Theatre Guild. 87
Hellman, Lillian. Playwright. 662
Holden, William. Stage, motion picture actor. 798
Holtzmann, Fanny. Lawyer for theatrical profession. 661
Hopkins, Arthur. Theatri-

cal producer. 1010
Johnson, Chic. Comedian; Stager of Hellz-a-Poppin. 708
Jones, Robert Edmond. Stage designer. 301
Kaufman, Beatrice (Mrs. George S.). Wife of playwright. 236
Kaufman, George S. Playwright. 248
Kern, Jerome. Composer; musical comedy writer. 1116
Kommer, Rudolf K. Theatrical producer. 692
Langner, Lawrence. Co-director of Theatre Guild; lawyer; author. 142
Lastfogel, Abe. Theatrical agent, U.S.O. shows. 857
Le Gallienne, Eva. Actress; director; translator. 551
Leblang, Joe. Theatrical ticket agent. 825
Lillie, Beatrice. Comedienne; stage and motion picture actress. 136
Logan, Joshua Lockwood. Playwright; director; producer. 1020
Loos, Anita. Author; playwright. 173
Lunt, Alfred. Stage, motion picture actor. 374
MacArthur, Charles Gordon. Playwright. 1134
McBride, John. Theatrical ticket agent. 1037
Maney, Richard Sylvester. Broadway press agent. 230
Martin, Ernest H. Theatrical producer. 452
Marx, Harpo. Comedian; stage, motion picture actor. 813
Matthau, Walter. Stage, motion picture actor. 800
Maugham, William Somerset. Novelist; short story writer; playwright. 1068
May, Elaine. Comedienne; actress; playwright. 1007
Mendl, Lady (Elsie de Wolfe). Actress, socialite. 433
Meredith, Burgess. Stage, motion picture actor. 1055
Mielziner, Jo. Theatre set designer. 19
Miller, Gilbert. Playwright. 667
Molnár, Ferenc. Playwright. 801
Mostel, Zero. Stage, motion picture actor. 799
Odets, Clifford. Playwright. 873
Olsen, Ole. Comedian; stager of Hellz-a-Poppin. 708
O'Neill, Eugene. Playwright. 884, 1021
Page, Geraldine. Stage, motion picture actress. 800
Perkins, Anthony. Stage, motion picture actor. 800
Pollock, Channing. Playwright. 255
Porter, Cole. Songwriter; musical comedy writer. 1117
Printemps, Yvonne. Actress. 308
Qualtinger, Helmut. Actor; playwright. 302
Redgrave, Michael. Stage, motion picture actor. 798
Robards, Jason. Stage, motion picture actor. 800
Robeson, Paul. Actor; concert singer. 534
Robinson-Duff, Frances. Drama coach. 267

Rodgers, Richard. Composer; musical comedy writer. 1126
Rose, Billy. Stage show producer. 629
Rosenthal, Jean. Theatre lighting expert. 802
Rothafel, Samuel L. (Roxy). Theatre builder and manager. 253
Schell, Maria. Stage, motion picture actress. 799
Sherwood, Robert Emmet. Playwright. 731
Shubert, J.J. Theatre Operator. 132
Shubert, Lee. Theatre operator. 132
Signoret, Simone. Stage, motion picture actress. 800
Stanley, Kim. Stage, motion picture actress. 798
Stapleton, Maurine. Stage, motion picture actress. 799
Steiger, Rod. Stage, motion picture actor. 799
Stevens, Roger Lacey. Theatrical producer; real estate tycoon. 187
Theatre Guild. 428
Urban, Joseph. Theatrical stage designer; architect. 149
Wallach, Eli. Stage, motion picture actor. 798
Webster, Margaret. Actress; director. 1087
West, Mae. Actress; playwright. 257
Westley, Helen. Actress; director of Theatre Guild. 12
Widmark, Richard. Stage, motion picture actor. 800
Woods, A.H. Theatrical producer. 894
Wooley, Monty. Stage, motion picture actor. 516
Ziegfeld, Florenz. Theatrical producer. 391

TRANSPORTATION

Bellanca, Giuseppe Mario. Airplane designer, manufacturer. 1106
Bellet, Robert. Chief purser, S.S. Liberté. 222
Blackburn, Harold Frederic. Pilot, Trans World Airlines. 576, 1127
Bush, Irving T. Originator, director, Bush Terminal. 762
Carlsen, Henrik Kurt. Merchant ship captain. 816
Casey, James E. President, United Parcel Service. 17
Cesoli, Leo. European train conductor. 693
Chrysler, Walter P. Automobile manufacturer. 1042
Fairchild, Sherman Mills. Airplane manufacturer; authority on aerial photography. 20
Ferrari, Enzo. Automobile designer, manufacturer. 981
Fokker, Anthony Herman Gerard. Airplane designer, manufacturer. 335
Ford, Henry. Automobile manufacturer. 676
Gillhaus, John. Motorman, Sixth Avenue trolley line. 313
Hannon, Bryan. Historian; author; streetcar driver. 879

Hedley, Frank. President, Interborough Rapid Transit Company. 1095
Hewitt, Edward Ringwood. Director, International Motor Company; fisherman; inventor. 204
Johnson, Frederick. Captain, S. S. Josiah Crabtree. 589
King, Charles Brady. Automobile designer, builder, racer. 1012
Knudsen, William S. President, General Motors Corporation; Member, Advisory Commission to Council of National Defense. 834
Loree, Leonor F. President, Delaware & Hudson Railroad. 697
Lyons, Harry. Barge and small boat owner. 877
Martin, Glenn L. Airplane manufacturer. 447
Moran, Eugene F. President, Moran Towing & Transport Company. 297
Rosendahl, Charles E. Aviator, lighter-than-air craft. 706
Scull, Robert Cooper. Art dealer; owner of taxicab company. 619
Shippey, Hartwell Stuart. Barge captain. 931
Sikorsky, Igor Ivanovitch. Airplane designer, engineer, executive. 1105
Turner, Hilary F. Ferryboat captain. 436
Willis, Charles Fountain, Jr. President, non-scheduled airlines. 954
Wright, Orville. Airplane inventor, manufacturer. 444

Part IV

AUTHOR INDEX

AUTHOR INDEX

Adams, Franklin P. 1115
Alexander, Jack. 18, 171, 260, 262, 265, 396, 501, 617, 1082
Allen, Robert S. 484, 1058
Alsop, Joseph. 209
Angly, Edward. 207
Arendt, Hannah. 1094
Armstrong, Elizabeth. 694

Bailey, Anthony. 585, 893, 1006
Bainbridge, John. 35, 65, 130, 143, 258, 286, 475, 576, 582, 640, 861, 895, 918, 961, 964, 972, 1016, 1127
Balliett, Whitney. 81, 111, 309, 479, 517, 686, 758, 874, 1084
Barnes, Djuna. 551
Barry, Griffin. 1077
Bartlett, Arthur. 99, 350, 546, 889, 1122
Basso, Hamilton. 390, 786, 1021, 1068, 1119
Behrman, S.N. 6, 178, 212, 242, 267, 483, 666, 731, 801, 864, 1026
Berger, Meyer. 75, 79, 137, 360, 548, 808, 917, 957
Bernstein, Jeremy. 43, 470, 760, 855
Betjeman, John. 963
Blassingame, Lurton. 997, 1024, 1034, 1042
Bliven, Bruce, Jr. 791
Boal, Sam. 245
Bodenheim, Maxwell. 884
Bogan, Louise. 36
Borges, Jorge Luis. 71
Boyer, Richard O. 61, 77, 116, 128, 191, 238, 280, 334, 381, 402, 465, 482, 507, 529, 604, 646, 657, 720, 732, 960, 1051, 1079
Breuer, Bessie. 189
Brandt, Carl. 160, 1057
Brooks, John. 202, 282, 306, 435, 842, 910, 934, 974, 1028, 1104, 1121
Broun, Heywood. 772, 858
Brown, Carlton. 70
Bryan, Joseph, III. 756
Burns, Paul A. 331
Busch, Niven, Jr. 24, 122, 213, 276, 298, 323, 328, 363, 415, 581, 612, 676, 762, 765, 767, 769, 812, 865, 919, 923, 926, 929, 951, 952
Busch, Noel F. 32, 121

Campbell, David B. 491
Capote, Truman. 281
Carples, Esther. 58
Carson, Rachel L. 285, 908
Chotzinoff, Samuel. 210, 819, 878
Coates, Robert M. 3, 13, 60, 110, 436, 535, 678, 862, 886
Coles, Robert. 648
Connelly, Marc. 126
Coombs, Kelly. 370, 647
Cowley, Malcolm. 1053

Crouse, Russel. 125, 625

Davenport, Marcia. 208, 938
Davis, Elmer. 588
Deutsch, Babette. 186, 907, 1093
di Giovanni, Norman Thomas. 71
Dodge, Homer Joseph. 225
Dugan, James. 416
Dunbar, L.D. 59

Eastman, Max. 403, 1027

Ferber, Edna. 1002
Fischer, John. 1046
Flagler, J.M. 844, 962
Flanner, Janet. 194, 199, 216, 247, 292, 354, 365, 395, 433, 445, 476, 510, 537, 543, 545, 562, 630, 663, 746, 783, 795, 891, 892, 965, 995, 999, 1113
Frank, Waldo. 12, 193, 366, 496, 499, 523, 532, 601, 621, 741, 778, 810, 860, 1036
Frankforter, Alice. 628
Freeman, Andrew A. 583

Gabriel, Gilbert W. 108, 602
Gallico, Paul. 831
Garland, George White. 1076
Garrett, Oliver H.P. 50, 165, 351, 704, 743, 973, 1110
Gibbs, Angelica. 1, 175, 274, 577, 744, 863, 976, 1108
Gibbs, Anthony. 129, 290
Gibbs, Wolcott. 97, 230, 256, 473, 552, 895, 1008, 1055, 1067
Gill, Brendan. 299, 339, 759, 931, 1012, 1130
Gilliatt, Penelope. 563
Gilman, Mildred. 534
Gollomb, Joseph. 355, 804
Gray, A. Barr. 213
Gray, Francine du Plessix. 10, 887

Hale, R. 172, 1010
Hall, Donald. 314
Hamburger, Philip. 17, 78, 166, 224, 490, 641, 672, 722, 782, 930, 985
Hammond, Percy. 255, 894
Hansuld, J. 493
Hardin, Nancy. 597
Harriman, Margaret Case. 102, 131, 148, 234, 272, 278, 337, 389, 440, 453, 455, 512, 661, 662, 667, 730, 959, 968, 993, 1038, 1049, 1065, 1070, 1080, 1116, 1117
Heggie, Barbara. 324, 352, 486, 489, 504, 1081, 1087
Hellman, Geoffrey T. 8, 20, 38, 52, 76, 91, 92, 104, 106, 109, 127, 204, 218, 228, 229, 241, 251, 261, 271, 289, 293, 300, 303, 307, 310, 320, 338, 361, 380, 383, 412, 424, 429, 467, 468, 474, 477, 495, 506, 556, 559, 575, 610, 620, 631, 638, 651, 664, 671, 721, 768, 829, 839, 840, 848, 849, 850, 900, 948, 953, 958, 987, 991, 1014, 1030, 1054, 1071, 1075, 1102, 1105
Hentoff, Nat. 42, 220, 497, 642, 828, 1023
Hersey, John. 134, 434, 669, 728
Hodgins, Eric. 444
Holden, Raymond. 711
Hoover, Hubbard. 51
Hunt, Morton M. 386, 472, 505, 793, 809, 1056, 1090

Hyman, Stanley Edgar. 27, 115

Iglauer, Edith. 824
Ish-Kishor, Salamith. 63

James, Marquis. 382, 714, 827
Jarman, Rufus. 1044
Johnston, Alva. 19, 21, 37, 47, 68, 85, 96, 112, 119, 141, 153, 156, 157, 161, 192, 198, 211, 215, 219, 231, 232, 246, 287, 330, 385, 387, 413, 447, 525, 533, 538, 553, 558, 567, 568, 570, 580, 592, 598, 629, 633, 685, 691, 697, 703, 707, 709, 757, 766, 805, 830, 846, 867, 897, 901, 904, 939, 941, 970, 994, 1064, 1083, 1111
Josephson, Matthew. 201, 325, 371, 425, 439, 522, 526, 569, 834, 983

Kahn, E.J., Jr. 90, 94, 98, 174, 187, 195, 250, 263, 270, 284, 288, 340, 357, 364, 378, 388, 404, 437, 452, 463, 527, 574, 615, 649, 680, 681, 718, 750, 770, 785, 803, 814, 818, 857, 870, 932, 975, 992, 1000, 1001, 1020, 1041, 1052, 1091, 1124, 1133
Kelley, Robert F. 726
King, Alexander. 531
Kinkead, Eugene. 56, 163, 291, 442, 552, 605, 790, 1011
Kirkpatrick, John. 146, 618, 1129
Knox, William Boardman. 322
Kobler, John. 459, 1101, 1135
Kramer, Jane. 348, 619, 773
Krock, Arthur. 139, 268, 596, 1048

Lang, Daniel. 283, 316, 384, 905, 1060
Lardner, John. 643
Lardner, Ring. 236
Leech, Margaret K. 549, 550, 880, 914
Leighton, George R. 154, 673
Levy, Newman. 304, 1066
Lewis, Norman. 462, 1062
Liebling, A.J. 15, 86, 124, 132, 138, 151, 170, 266, 327, 333, 375, 427, 430, 446, 521, 544, 565, 578, 613, 639, 708, 734, 742, 764, 774, 851, 854, 909, 943, 1032, 1033, 1099, 1123
Logan, Andy. 332, 423, 454, 637, 735
Long, Lois. 597
Lord, Russell. 226, 600, 659, 890

MacArthur, Charles. 196
McCarten, John. 69, 240, 311, 589, 611, 771, 873, 966, 1003
McCarthy, Mary. 183, 872
McCormick, Elsie. 179
Macdonald, Dwight. 7, 155, 181, 249, 336, 347, 653, 696, 927, 1098
McGeehan, W.O. 875
Macgowan, Kenneth. 11, 149, 253, 1037
McGuiness, James Kevin. 969
McGuire, William. 701
MacKaye, Milton. 214, 227, 252, 342, 392, 399, 405, 408, 432, 606, 698, 736, 761, 806, 835, 845, 847, 896, 1085
McKelway, St. Clair. 73,

113, 145, 329, 406, 407, 478, 509, 796, 947, 1015, 1031, 1099
McNulty, John. 925
McNutt, William Slavens. 668, 899
McPhee, John. 343, 443, 511, 561, 573, 794, 881, 912, 979
Maloney, Russell. 163, 235, 516, 560, 605, 921, 983, 986, 996, 1092
Mannes, Marya. 87
Markey, Morris. 107, 1132
Martin, John S. 674
Matthiessen, Peter. 754
Mehta, Ved. 182, 699, 856, 1022
Millstein, Gilbert. 341
Mitchell, Joseph. 83, 123, 158, 277, 458, 520, 536, 554, 627, 644, 645, 665, 727, 836, 837, 877, 911, 949, 1017
Moorehead, Alan. 46
Mosher, John Chapin. 984
Murphy, Jack. 679
Murphy, Mark. 45, 492, 518, 701, 869

Noble, Hollister. 30, 335, 752

O'Hara, John. 723
O'Higgins, Harvey. 500, 555
O'Malley, J.J. 105, 324
Owen, Russell. 632

Panter-Downes, Mollie. 67, 345, 417, 539, 599, 719, 751
Paramore, Edward E., Jr. 173
Parker, Dorothy. 64
Peeler, Clare. 702
Peet, Creighton. 682
Pemberton, Brock. 431, 825
Pemberton, Murdock. 233, 377, 608, 807
Powell, Hickman. 409
Powledge, Fred. 933
Pringle, Henry F. 22, 29, 135, 136, 144, 169, 188, 244, 318, 368, 514, 519, 557, 584, 587, 670, 706, 821, 822, 841, 866, 928, 1088, 1095, 1125

Ramsaye, Terry. 147
Rand, Christopher. 162, 295, 1047
Reed, Herbert. 369, 397, 422, 882, 998
Rice, Robert. 142, 177, 185, 353, 362, 367, 745, 780, 784, 843, 916, 1004, 1005, 1007, 1019, 1072, 1100
Rigg, H.K. 614
Robbins, Charles. 1059
Robbins, James. 902
Robinson, Arthur. 74
Roddy, Joseph. 53
Rogers, Cameron. 206, 945
Ross, Lillian. 28, 44, 101, 296, 471, 660, 798, 799, 800, 954, 980, 1128
Ross, Malcolm. 488
Ross, Virgilia Peterson. 39, 200
Roueché, Berton. 167, 414, 775, 776, 915
Rovere, Richard H. 95, 294, 400, 508, 675, 717, 946
Ryall, G.F.T. 23, 80, 792

Saerchinger, César. 690
Sanborn, Pitts. 1073
Sargeant, Winthrop. 16, 89, 133, 319, 359, 401, 418, 460, 480, 515, 566, 603, 755, 787, 802, 817, 833, 942, 981, 1018, 1112, 1126
Sayre, Joel. 100, 205,

626, 852, 1063, 1089, 1109
Scarry, Joseph T. 1097
Seldes, Gilbert. 9, 62, 301, 391, 438, 450, 502, 591, 624, 655, 687, 937
Shapiro, Fred C. 650
Shaplen, Robert. 31, 33, 712, 747, 777, 1060
Sherwood, Robert E. 456, 781
Shaw, A. H. 243
Shuman, Ik. 313
Simon, Robert A. 54, 372, 461, 922
Simpson, Lola Jean. 1074
Simpson, Robert. 503
Smedley, Doree. 335
Smith, Helena Huntington. 48, 72, 82, 118, 217, 221, 273, 376, 379, 441, 481, 547, 636, 700, 710, 779, 838, 859, 913, 924, 989, 1040, 1045
Sparling, Earl. 317
Stafford, Jean. 40
Steig, Henry Anton. 26, 420
Strakosch, Avery. 695
Sugrue, Thomas. 152
Swerling, Jo. 84, 1131

Talmey, Allene. 609
Taper, Bernard. 159, 176, 593
Taylor, Deems. 394
Taylor, Robert Lewis. 117, 120, 150, 168, 197, 259, 264, 269, 297, 312, 315, 321, 346, 356, 393, 451, 485, 489, 540, 542, 571, 572, 623, 656, 683, 689, 705, 725, 739, 740, 788, 789, 815, 823, 871, 879, 940, 955, 967, 971, 982, 1003, 1013, 1025, 1035, 1050
Thayer, Mary Van Rensselaer. 688
Thompson, Charles Willis. 920
Thurber, James. 634, 935
Tomkins, Calvin. 55, 93, 164, 223, 326, 498, 586, 684, 713, 990, 1069, 1114
Tunis, John R. 25, 239, 305, 594, 635, 729, 1107
Tuohy, Ferdinand. 308, 906, 977
Tynan, Kenneth. 524

Vanderbilt, Sanderson. 616

Walker, C. Lester. 1086
Walker, Stanley. 419, 421, 652, 944, 1043
Walker, Strother Holland. 673
Ware, Foster. 254, 344, 398, 426, 431, 607
Warfield, Frances. 411
Warner, Richard F. 513, 738
Wechsberg, Joseph. 2, 4, 34, 66, 140, 184, 222, 275, 279, 302, 349, 373, 410, 464, 466, 494, 590, 654, 693, 753, 826, 876, 883, 936, 978, 1029, 1078, 1096
Weimar, William. 41, 1106
Wertenbaker, Charles. 1120
Weybright, Victor. 190
Whitaker, Rogers E. M. 950
White, William C. 114
Whiteside, Thomas. 203, 457, 749, 816, 1009
Whitman, Howard. 853
Whitworth, William. 5, 528, 530, 564, 737, 748, 1103
Wilson, Edmund. 733, 820
Wind, Herbert Warren. 49, 57, 180, 579, 888
Winkler, John K. 103, 358, 448, 487, 658, 715, 716, 797, 885, 898, 903, 956

Winslow, Thyra Samter. 257
Wohlforth, Robert. 237
Wood, Charles W. 88
Woodward, George. 868
Woodward, W.E. 1118
Woollcott, Alexander. 14, 248, 374, 449, 469, 541, 622, 692, 724, 763, 813, 832, 1039, 1061, 1134
Wright, Cuthbert. 428
Wylie, Elinor. 811